REACHING OUT
without
DUMBING DOWN

REACHING OUT
without
DUMBING DOWN

A Theology of Worship for the
Turn-of-the-Century Culture

Marva J. Dawn

WILLIAM B. EERDMANS PUBLISHING COMPANY
GRAND RAPIDS, MICHIGAN

© 1995 Wm. B. Eerdmans Publishing Co.
255 Jefferson Ave. S.E., Grand Rapids, Michigan 49503
All rights reserved

Printed in the United States of America

00 99 98 97 96   7 6 5 4 3

Library of Congress Cataloging-in-Publication Data

ISBN 0-8028-4102-3

This book is dedicated to

worship leaders trying to be faithful against the tides of the times,

teachers who understand the need for new wine and new wineskins,

pastors who seek to invite the world into our sanctuaries,

worship participants wanting more than excitement,

congregations who struggle to survive,

children who love to take part in worship,

teenagers who search for meaning in the Church,

parents who want to nurture their families in the faith,

musicians who sing and play instruments well to the glory of God,

*composers laboring to create new forms consistent
with substantive content,*

preachers discovering both new and old treasures in the Word,

and thinkers recognizing the dying of our present culture —

*and, most of all, to Myron, my worship partner,
beside whom it is a Joy to sing our lives.*

Contents

Foreword *by Martin E. Marty*   ix

PART I
Our Culture *and* the Church's Worship

1. Why This Book Is Critically Needed   3

PART II
The Culture *Surrounding* Our Worship

2. *Inside* the Technological, Boomer, Postmodern Culture   17

3. *Outside* the Idolatries of Contemporary Culture   41

4. *Upside-Down:* Worship as a Subversive Act   57

PART III
The Culture *of* Worship

5. God as the Center of Worship: Who Is Worship For?   75

6. The Character of the Believer: Having Content
   or Being Content?   105

CONTENTS

7. The Character of the Church as Christian
   Community: What Is at Stake?   129

PART IV

The Culture *in* Our Worship

8. Throwing the Baby Out with the Bath Water
   or Putting the Baby in Fresh Clothes: Music   165

9. Worship Ought to Kill Us: The Word   205

10. Discovering Our Place in the Story:
    Ritual and Liturgy and Art   241

PART V

Worship *for the Sake of* the Culture

11. Reaching Out without Dumbing Down   279

12. The Church as Its Own Worst Enemy:
    Is It Happening Again?   297

Appendix: Sample Children's Sermons   305

Works Cited   308

Foreword

Why do "we," the leaders of Christian worship, lead so poorly? Having been a part of too many casual, inept, and routine services of worship, author Annie Dillard has asked a question that must have crossed many minds:

> Since "we" have been doing this for 2,000 years, why can we not do it as well as a high school drama club cast can do after six weeks of rehearsing a play? Not that worship is nothing but rehearsable performance and not that a high school play is worship — though drama and liturgy do have some common ancient roots. But people who attend services of prayer and praise, song and action, preaching and the sacraments, often have to endure mumbling and stumbling of offputting sorts. This is not how God is to be praised, and this is not what worshippers will put up with for indefinite periods to come.

Marva Dawn knows this and has written a kind of manual of worship to help worshipers understand what has gone wrong and to help leaders do better. A manual of worship: that description has a dull ring to it. *Reaching Out without Dumbing Down,* beginning with its very title, reaches out and bids for attention. Dawn's literary style, well recognized by those who know her seven earlier books, does not fail her here, and she has ways to hold readers that far outlast the catchiness of some of her chapter titles. But I have stressed the practical "manual" aspect, since so many other books in this genre fail readers at the point of the "how to."

In many respects this is a "why to" book. These days no one can write on the improvement of worship without being aware that down the block from the undumbed down but often not uplifting worshiping community there is likely to be a competing alternative. Dawn shows her awareness and offers vivid descriptions of this alternative. It is the product of market analysis and sets out to produce or reproduce for late modern folk the sight and sound and smell, the intentions and ambience and aura, of the mall and the market place, the showplace and the entertainment center. Not a few of those who advocate this form of worship make a strong point of the fact that the worshiper is essentially *homo ludens,* the human at play, but at play not in the active sense but in the passive "entertain me" mode. Something is wrong with the attractive and often attracting approach, but saying so without showing why is futile and time-wasting.

That such forms of worship may be appropriate for some of those alienated from, frightened by, or bored because of inept routine worship is not to be denied. The church catholic contains all sorts of believers and behavers, and worship in that sprawling communion of saints has to have room for experiment with the market. Those who are wholly given to the style called "contemporary" often can point to fuller parking lots and busier fingers on the ticker that is used to count people in pews. They can point to the almost empty sanctuaries in grand European cathedrals or the emptying ones in many Roman Catholic, mainstream Protestant, and, though this is often overlooked, thousands of evangelical congregations. The boasting and gloating of those who match the market tastes have to serve as a wake up call, and Dawn knows it and shows it.

The author does believe, however, that the basic assumptions in such worship services about who God is, what worship means, and how humans at worship are to be regarded are wrong, and she shows why. In a series of chapters that I have to call brilliant and pointed, she talks about character: of God, of the believer, of the Church. Whoever disagrees with her depiction of these will be pressed to produce biblical evidence to counter it or will have to do some second-thinking about "alternative worship."

At the same time, those who with Dawn (and in the words of a church advertisement of a friend of mine) are pursuing "the alternative to alternative worship" have to be more sure of their ground than they often have been. She provides such ground in each chapter, for her critiques are always accompanied by constructive alternatives. Whoever writes about *Dumbing Down* could easily amuse the already convinced; it takes little for an esthete to show why so much of the contemporary market style is banal, trivial, ephemeral, dumbing, and numbing. But if Dawn were only producing downers about "down," we would be tempted to say: you are preaching to the congregation. Or: write a smart column about dumbing, but don't waste our time with a whole book of that sort.

No, this is a book of *Reaching Out* about *Reaching Out*. The author does not begin with the assumption that readers are pre-convinced and now need to be confirmed in their snobbery. She does not say that those who promote contemporary-alternative worship are necessarily ill-intending and have nothing to offer. She shows why it is urgent for worshipers to be evangelists, why those who would make the services of worship inviting have to do some inviting, have to make newcomers, strangers, and shoppers at home. But once she gets them home to the house of God, she does not want them to be merely entertained or soothed: "Worship Ought to Kill Us." It ought to go against the "character" of a culture that makes commodities of God and worship, that deals with God and humans in terms of chumminess and folksiness, but never with awe — and thus seldom with power to liberate worshipers from the bonds of a binding and dulling culture.

Readers will note that this is not a book with two parts: first, what's wrong with everyone else and, second, how "we" might right everything. No, the two themes are interwebbed at all points. In each chapter there are analyses and proposed solutions, diagnoses and possible therapies, descriptions and prescriptions. It is not a book but worship itself that "ought to 'kill' us"; this is not a killing book. Its author intends to help heal a warring Christian community, correct a mumbling one, and guide a stumbling one to the place where God meets humans, in words and sounds and sights that connote judgment as a necessary reality before grace comes. As it will. ·

MARTIN E. MARTY

PART I

Our Culture *and* the Church's Worship

I. Why This Book Is Critically Needed

> God of grace and God of glory,
> On your people pour your power;
> Crown your ancient Church's story;
> Bring its bud to glorious flow'r.
> Grant us wisdom, grant us courage
> For the facing of this hour,
> For the facing of this hour.
>
> Harry Emerson Fosdick, 1878-1969

I am worried about the Church. The "worship wars" that rage in so many congregations are preventing us from truly being the Church. Can we find some way to prevent discussions about worship styles from becoming fierce and bitter battles waged between two entrenched camps? Can we instead find common criteria by which to assess what we are doing in worship so that we can bring together opposing sides of various arguments, so that we can truly be the Church as we talk together about our worship practices?

I am writing in this book especially for members of liturgical churches in the United States, because some "worship wars" rage most nastily in those church bodies, although what I say has great applicability to every denomination in this and many other countries, for all of us are

3

more influenced by the world civilization than we acknowledge. I call them "worship wars" because discussions about how to conduct our primary services usually split into two fiercely polarized sides on such issues as "traditional" versus "contemporary" forms of worship. Congregations split into competing camps — for example, members of the boomer generation vs. their elders, returnees vs. loyalists, clergy vs. musicians, clergy vs. laypersons, organists vs. guitarists, or supporters of classical or liturgical styles vs. those who favor folk or evangelistic styles. The very fact that congregations so quickly split into opposing sides on so many questions reveals our modern inability to nuance. A computer chip is either on or off, so in this data-bit world we often phrase our arguments in either/or choices. Can we think together along the lines of both/and?

Moreover, in this image age in which "feeling is believing," rather than "thinking is believing" or "being convinced by logical argument is believing," we often don't ask enough questions or the right kind of questions about the foundations of what we are doing. Just as scientists sometimes begin to perform medical procedures before anyone has raised the necessary moral objections, so it seems that many congregations today are switching worship practices without investigating what worship means and how our worship relates to contemporary culture.

The Scriptures, the history of the Church, and my own faith, experience, and training convince me that the vitality and faithfulness of our personal and corporate Christian lives and the effectiveness of our outreach to the world around us depend on the character that is formed in us. What concerns me is whether our local parishes and denominations have thought thoroughly enough about worship and culture to function effectively in contemporary society. How can we best reach out to this society without "dumbing down" that essential character formation?

My major concern for the Church has to do with worship, because its character-forming potential is so subtle and barely noticed, and yet worship creates a great impact on the hearts and minds and lives of a congregation's members. Indeed, how we worship both reveals and forms our identity as persons and communities.

Christian worship at the turn of the century is being affected adversely by aspects of our culture that "dumb down" everything. Consequently, we must be careful lest our character as individual Christians and the character of our communities lack sufficient substance to reach out to the world around us and to influence the culture. My intentions in this book are to understand both our culture and worship more thoroughly, to name the criteria by which we can judge various influences, and to offer practical suggestions for choosing the best tools and forms to deepen our worship lives, nurture faith development, and increase believers' outreach throughout the universal Church and to the world.

Church members often stand in the middle of the worship wars waged by their leaders and long for better questions and clearer thinking on the basis of the resources inherent in faith. After the controversial 1993 women's conference "Re-Imagining," David Heim of *The Christian Century* concluded that

> many if not most church members don't align themselves with either of [two opposing] camps. They are ready to listen and learn . . . to test what they hear against the witness of scripture, tradition, and Christian experience. This approach will not appeal to those who would banish imagination from theological thought, or who think tradition is fixed and settled. . . . Nor will it attract those who regard the tradition as so corrupt that it must be entirely re-imagined, or so bankrupt that continuity with it is not prized. This approach does promise to treat Christian witness with critical faithfulness and wise openness. . . . Honest and charitable debate and criticism are necessary if Christians are to understand, judge and act on matters that demand the church's attention.[1]

It is with that combination of critical faithfulness and wise openness that I pray we can pursue together the questions of this book. Be patient with the process that it will require, for we have to lay several thorough foundations — an analysis of society and a consideration of the tasks of the Church — before we can look at specific aspects of worship itself. We must enter into these sociological and philosophical and theological underpinnings carefully so that we can understand why the subtle problems I am trying to address are so critically important. The rest of this chapter will introduce the themes of these underpinnings, which will be elaborated in the next two parts of the book. Then the final two parts of the book can build on this cultural and theological groundwork with practical suggestions.

1. David Heim, "Sophia's Choice," *The Christian Century* 111, no. 11 (6 April 1994): 339-40.

5

The State of U.S. Society: "Endangered Minds"

My concern for the Church to reach out without "dumbing down" faith had its origins in Jane Healy's weighty book, *Endangered Minds*.[2] A trainer of educators, Healy wondered why teachers kept asking if they were less capable or if kids were actually dumber than they had been in the past. Their question led to her massive research, which uncovered several shocking facts — the most notable of which is that children who watch a lot of television actually have smaller brains (pp. 47-55, 195-234). Considering multiple factors in home and society, she cites overwhelming evidence to convince us that, indeed, many children in contemporary society actually are less intelligent and less capable of learning than their forebears. As Healy calls for schools to counteract the lack of learning in homes with this summary of our society's crisis, let us think about the Church's situation:

> If we wish to remain a literate culture, someone is going to have to take the responsibility for teaching children at all socioeconomic levels how to talk, listen, and think . . . before the neural foundations for verbal expression, sustained attention, and analytic thought end up as piles of shavings under the workbench of plasticity.
>
> . . . Students [or worship participants] from all walks of life now come with brains poorly adapted for the mental habits that teachers [churches] have traditionally assumed. In the past, deep wells of language and mental persistence had already been filled for most children by experiences at home. . . . Now teachers must fill the gaps before attempting to draw "skills" from brains that lack the underlying cognitive and linguistic base [churches must fill gaps in foundational faith and its language].
>
> We care deeply about the "smartness" of our children, but our culture [churches] lacks patience with the slow, time-consuming handwork by which intellects [faiths] are woven. The quiet spaces of childhood [and worship?] have been disrupted by media assault and instant sensory gratification. Children [worshipers] have been yoked to hectic adult schedules, and assailed by societal anxieties. (pp. 277-78)

2. Jane M. Healy, *Endangered Minds: Why Our Children Don't Think* (New York: Simon and Schuster, 1990). Page references to this book in the following paragraphs are given parenthetically in the text.

Why haven't we noticed? Why hasn't our society taken radical action to correct this situation? Not one of us wants our children to be less bright. Part of the reason for our failure to address the crisis is that the problem's immensity has been hidden by schools and agencies "dumbing down" the tests. Healy demonstrates this by showing the astounding difference between a fourth grade reading test from 1964 and one from 1982. She also prints part of an "advanced" reading achievement test for ninth grade from 1988 (pp. 27-36). The "advanced" ninth grade test is shockingly easier than the 1964 fourth grade test![3]

We don't notice that children's brains are smaller, that they are less able to think and cannot verbalize as well as their predecessors, because the educational system has simply "dumbed down" the tests. Actually, the process hasn't been simple. Teachers *know* that they are dumbing things down, but they are under immense pressures from societal expectations of pupils' achievements. If the children aren't capable of doing the work, they have to find some way to help them have success at school. If students can't handle the test that was used in previous years, the teachers and writers of tests have to make them easier.

Endangered Minds argues persuasively that myriads of forces in contemporary U.S. society lead to deficiencies in people's abilities to think, talk, and listen — dysfunctional homes, media assaults, lack of creative play time, and many more factors than we need to enumerate for this book's purposes. What we must realize is that the dumbing down of our society forces the Church to ask critical questions about its life and worship, its ministries to people in such a world, its ability to survive in post-Christian times. In what ways do we, too, lack the patience necessary for forming the intellect and faith? How has faith formation been disrupted by instant sensory gratification? What resources does Christian faith provide for renewing and sustaining churches in such a culture and for reaching beyond ourselves to persons of that culture?

3. See a similar analysis of lower test results as well as reasons and needs for changes in Christopher Lasch, "Schooling and the New Illiteracy," *The Culture of Narcissism: American Life in an Age of Diminishing Expectations* (New York: W. W. Norton, 1979), pp. 125-53.

The Task of the Church: To Praise God and to Nurture Character

Knowing that Christians are saved totally by God's grace and not by any efforts on our part, the Church throughout the ages has understood that its task as an institution is to provide opportunities for the worship and praise of God and the educating and forming of its people for a life of caring for others in response to that grace. We might compare these two tasks to the two great commandments — to love God with all our heart, soul, mind, and strength and to become the kind of people who will love our neighbors as ourselves.

These tasks were more easily accomplished in the past when many elements in the structure of Western civilization contributed to the Church's goals. We can easily sketch some of the principal elements of that contribution (though, of course, there are many exceptions) in order to get a broad and general idea of the basic social fabric. We must see the vast difference between the present society, which works against the formation of Christian character, and previous societies in which Protestant denominations first began to flourish, the Roman Catholic Church itself went through great reformation, and these religious bodies became planted in the New World.

In the Reformation era, much of the best music and art was inspired by the Christian faith and used for its worship. Homes were undergirded by Christian principles. Whole communities helped to raise children to understand and participate in Christian practices. Furthermore, the Church was a leader in educating people for common life. The clergy were respected as among the highest professionals in society. The Church's schools, monasteries, and priories excelled educationally. Moreover, the Christian ethos permeated society and helped to form citizens' character. Luther instructed princes and nobles, merchants and peasants, to use their vocations to honor God; Calvin created a city founded on Christian principles.

In the early years of U.S. society, the Judeo-Christian ethos was vital. David Wells chronicles this thoroughly as he describes the village of Wenham, Massachusetts, in the first section of his massive study *No Place for Truth*, so I need not elaborate it here.[4] Rather, it will suffice to use a few

---

4. See David F. Wells, *No Place for Truth; or, Whatever Happened to Evangelical Theology?* (Grand Rapids: William B. Eerdmans, 1993), pp. 17-52. Page references to this book in the following paragraphs are given parenthetically in the text.

excerpts from his work to notice the profound changes that have shaken the Church as our culture has moved away from those religious foundations.

Wells protests against viewing culture as "neutral and harmless," as "a partner amenable to being co-opted in the cause of celebrating Christian truth." He considers that naivete dangerous, for culture bears many values

> which work to rearrange the substance of faith, even when they are mediated to us through the benefits that the modern world also bestows upon us. Technology is a case in point. While it has greatly enhanced many of our capabilities and spread its largess across the entirety of our life, it also brings with it an almost inevitable naturalism and an ethic that equates what is efficient with what is good. Technology per se does not assault the gospel, but a technological society will find the gospel irrelevant. What can be said of technology can also be said of many other facets of culture that are similarly laden with values. (p. 11)

The inroads of these values from the culture into the faith, according to Wells, cause historic orthodoxy to be blocked by a worldliness that many fail to recognize as worldliness "because of the cultural innocence with which it presents itself." Wells acknowledges that orthodoxy certainly has "blemishes and foibles" (p. 11), but losing faith's theological core has led to "less biblical fidelity, less interest in truth, less seriousness, less depth, and less capacity to speak the Word of God to our own generation in a way that offers an alternative to what it already thinks" (p. 12). Modern people, including some of faith, who have been "emptied of their metaphysical substance" (p. 51) are "attuned to experience and to appearances, not to thought and character" (p. 52).

Can the Church counteract our culture's loss of family nurturing and training to moor children to the wisdom and values inherent in the faith? It is urgent that Christians understand more clearly their position in this present culture as a minority, an alternative society. Like the earliest Christians, we want to be a people formed not by the ethos of the world around us but by the narratives of the Scriptures and by the community of believers. Because of the nature of our society and its effects on people's abilities to talk, listen, and learn, however, an unusual clash sometimes develops that did not afflict the early Church. Now, if we are not careful, our own worship experiences can militate against the formation of Christian character (in ways this book will spell out). Instead of worship and character formation working dialectically to deepen each other, the latter is sometimes sacrificed in the attempt to preserve worship or to make it "appealing" to the mass culture.

We must therefore consider not only the factors from the outside culture but also the voices from within that influence how the Church understands itself. In this book we must ask new questions about the meaning and means of worshiping and living in the family of faith and of welcoming our children and strangers to live there, too.

Endangered Minds and Character in the Church: The Work of the Powers

We dare not be reductionistic — it is not that the world's culture is terrible and the ancient culture of the Church is good. Jesus set up the dialectical tension for us when he prayed that his followers, whom he was sending into the world, might not be of it (John 17:14-18). We make use of cultural forms, new and old, but we dare never let up in the struggle to make sure they are consistent with the ultimate eternal world to which we belong.

One key aspect of the dialectical tension of being in but not of the world has not been adequately recognized, and that is the influence on us and on the world of the evil forces the New Testament calls "principalities and powers." My research on this subject revealed many confusions about how that biblical concept can be understood in the framework of our modern experience. The subject is critically important for this book because such elements as battles waged in denominations and congregations, divisions between advocates of "contemporary" worship and "traditionalists" that lead to animosities and fractured relationships, the loss of the gospel that sometimes ensues, the weakening of Christian character and the consequent lack of substantive truth or genuine love in our outreach to the world are all certainly the work of evil powers to tear apart the Church. Chapter 3 will look carefully at ways in which these powers function so that we can "stand" against them (see Eph. 6:10-18).

The Task of This Book

Truly, all of us who serve the Church want to be faithful and not to be dumbing down the Church. The question is whether we know when or if we might be doing it. Teachers in schools know that they are dumbing down the work and tests, and many educators are trying to counteract the societal forces that necessitate it. Do pastors, musicians, worship participants, and parish leaders know when we are dumbing down the Church? Do we sometimes know that we are dumbing down worship, but think that we must do so in order to appeal to persons in our culture? On the other hand, do our attempts to avoid such dumbing down cause our worship to be too esoteric to be accessible to the world around us? Do we realize what kinds of options are available to us as we plan worship and teach parishioners? What dialectical tensions would help us balance more effectively the equal demands of being in the world but not of it?

This book's content has been gathered not only from sociological data but also from experiences in specific churches, though their identities are purposely hidden. Certain points might not be true in your denomination or parish, but I am focusing on general problems noticed frequently in almost twenty years of freelance work throughout the U.S. and in other countries, in many kinds of churches and various denominations. I am primarily concerned about what is happening to the Church spiritually, so I plead with you for careful theological reflection concerning the meaning and practice of worship. Please forgive me and correct me if I err, but let my comments challenge us all to think more deeply about the issues at stake for the worship and life of the Church.

This book is written with these four goals: to reflect upon the culture for which we want to proclaim the gospel; to expose the subtle powers that beckon us into idolatries and that upset the necessary dialectical balances in the Church's life and worship; to stimulate better questions about if, why, and how we might be dumbing faith down in the ways we structure, plan, and participate in worship education and in worship itself; and to offer better means for reaching out to people outside the Church. It is my claim that we ought not to, and do not need to, conform to our culture's patterns, but that the Christian community must intentionally sustain its unique character and just as intentionally care about the culture around it in order to be able to introduce people genuinely to Christ and to nurture individuals to live faithfully.

It is impossible for me to write about the subject of worship dispassionately, for I am deeply involved in the issues not only theologically but also practically. School teachers often complain about educational

11

specialists who write articles but don't spend extended time in the class-room. I didn't want this book to be such a mockery, so I continually test my convictions in the congregations for which I work. In my home parish I have given a series of children's sermons on liturgy, served as a table parent for a midweek educational program, taught a four-month course in community life for the adult education program, and directed the adult choir. In these and in preaching and teaching experiences in my freelance work around the country, I have discovered that most children and adults are eager to learn more about the Church's worship. I use experiences in this book not to elevate myself — you will certainly see my weaknesses and failures — but merely to offer ideas, to stimulate your own creativity, to motivate your own better efforts. Feel free to discard my ideas when they don't work in your situations; discuss them with your peers, your denominational leaders, your worship committees; pass them on if they are helpful. Most of all, let us all together always be asking this basic question: Do our efforts in worship lead to genuine praise of God and the growth of character in the members and the whole body of this Christian community?

Evelyn Waugh once remarked that the West is dying of sloth, not wrath. For the most part institutions are lost, not because they are stormed by hostile outsiders, but because their custodians, overcome by apathy, diffidence, and intellectual fecklessness, simply give them away. Will we give away the Church and its gospel power by dumbing it down or by failing to reach out?

Even more impelling than the dichotomy of sloth and wrath is Neil Postman's comparison of two ways

by which the spirit of a culture may be shriveled. In the first — the Orwellian [as in *1984*] — culture becomes a prison. In the second — the Huxleyan [as in *Brave New World*] — culture becomes a burlesque.

What Huxley teaches is that in the age of advanced technology, spiritual devastation is more likely to come from an enemy with a smiling face than from one whose countenance exudes suspicion and hate. In the Huxleyan prophecy, Big Brother does not watch us, by his choice. We watch him, by ours. There is no need for wardens or gates or Ministries of Truth. When a population becomes distracted by trivia, when cultural life is redefined as a perpetual round of entertainments, when serious public conversation becomes a form of baby-talk, when, in short, a people become an audience and their public business a vaudeville act, then a nation finds itself at risk; culture-death is a clear possibility.[5]

In light of the dumbing down that happens in worship in some places, we might change those last phrases to read "when the congregation becomes an audience and its worship a vaudeville act, then the Church finds itself at risk; the death of faith and Christian character is a clear possibility."

This book is written because for most churches it is not too late to ask better questions as we seek to make worship meaningful for persons in our present culture. Will you ask those questions with me? In a time when we all are always too busy, will we exert more effort for what is truly important? Instead of the culture-death of our television society, can the Church be a place of meaningful talking, attentive listening, and profound thinking? In short, can we develop a theology of worship for the Church to flourish and grow in a turn-of-the-century culture?

5. Neil Postman, *Amusing Ourselves to Death: Public Discourse in the Age of Show Business* (New York: Viking Penguin, 1985), pp. 155-56.

PART II

The Culture *Surrounding* Our Worship

2. Inside *the Technological, Boomer, Postmodern Culture*

At MTV we don't shoot for the 14-year-olds, we own them.

MTV Chairman Bob Pittman, quoted in *Dancing in the Dark: Youth, Popular Culture and the Electronic Media*

Inside, outside, upside-down!

Believers in Jesus are called to live *in* the world. We do not escape it to avoid its contaminations and problems, but from the *inside* we seek to understand it so that we can minister to its needs. Simultaneously, we struggle to be not *of* the world; we reject its values and stay *outside* its temptations and idolatries. To maintain this dialectical tension of being *in* but not *of,* the Church's worship must be *upside-down* (at least in the world's eyes) — turning the culture's perspective on its head (thinking from God's revelation rather than human knowledge), teaching an opposite set of values (loving God and others instead of self), enabling believers to make authentic differences in the world. Looking carefully at this inside, outside, upside-down Church, Part II's three chapters sketch a broad view of the culture that surrounds it.

Let us first clarify how the word *culture* is used in this book. Just as the biblical word *world* pejoratively signifies values that are contrary to the gospel and also means in its global sense the universal sphere that God loves totally, so the word *culture* can be used negatively or positively. The term negatively refers to an elitist exclusivism exhibited by high-art snobs. In its general, global sense, however, *culture* connotes every aspect of life that is produced by human beings (as opposed to what is given in creation). In a broad definition hinting at the term's use here, Wade Clark Roof explains that

> Culture has to do with making sense out of life and formulating strategies for action; and the ideas and symbols that people draw on in these fundamental undertakings are, implicitly if not explicitly, saturated with religious meaning. Religion is itself a set of cultural symbols.[1]

In this book I purposely use the word *culture* in several ways. In Part I it is meant ambiguously to invite you into deeper exploration of the relation of the worship of the Church to various aspects and kinds of culture. In this second unit of the book, I intend the word to signify aspects of U.S. society at the turn of the century, attributes of our world that cause people in this time and space to make sense out of life in certain ways. Part III speaks specifically of the "culture of worship," the unique purposes for which God's people congregate and the meaning of the faith that worship symbols convey. Since that meaning is expressed in a mixture of forms that make use of the language, music, and art of the Church and the world around it, the word *culture* in Part IV conveys the peculiarity of the resources used when Christians gather together to listen to God and to respond. In the final portion of the book, the word *culture* signifies both the people not yet part of believers' assemblies and also aspects of society that will be changed as God's people are empowered by their worship to make genuine differences in the world.

All of these nuances of meaning will be apparent to you as you read. I list them now intentionally to move us away from the habits perpetrated by television, which forces its watchers to fix on picture images that are designed to stimulate certain feelings. A word, in contrast, has multiple meanings, which can cause us to reflect in diverse and extensive ways. Just as the worship wars are aggravated by a reductionism that simplifies things

---

1. Wade Clark Roof, *A Generation of Seekers: The Spiritual Journeys of the Baby Boom Generation* (San Francisco: Harper, 1993), p. 5.

into two opposing camps, so our understanding of the relation of worship to culture is minimized if we do not ruminate on several ways in which that relationship unfolds.[2]

The Television Age

Certainly the most obvious aspect of the society in which we presently live in the United States is the ubiquity of television and its excessive power. The first chapter of this book has already referred to studies showing that children who watch excessive amounts of television develop smaller brains, but now we must look more closely at the far-reaching and deleterious effects of this preponderant influence in our culture. Even though I have thought and spoken negatively about television for years and have never owned one, I was not prepared for the horrifying exposé of television in Neil Postman's *Amusing Ourselves to Death: Public Discourse in the Age of Show Business*.[3]

Postman shows that U.S. society has not degenerated according to George Orwell's *1984,* though Orwell's prophetic visions have been fulfilled in some modern totalitarian states. Rather, television has taken over in the way presaged by Aldous Huxley's *Brave New World.* As Postman summarizes Huxley's vision, "no Big Brother is required to deprive people of their autonomy, maturity and history. As he saw it, people will come to love their oppression, to adore the technologies that undo their capacities to think" (p. vii).

Many of the scholars on whom I have drawn in developing this book comment on the destructive nature of television, which amounts, as Wade Clark Roof writes, "to a major transformation in mode of communication," which has "had a powerful effect on how Americans ever since have

---

2. The aspects of culture sketched in this chapter are several that most profoundly affect the Church's worship. For a superb discussion of cultural aspects to be considered in attempts to communicate the gospel specifically to nonbelievers, see William A. Dyrness, *How Does America Hear the Gospel?* (Grand Rapids: William B. Eerdmans, 1989). He focuses particularly on Americans' materialist bias, temperamental optimism, and individualism.

3. Neil Postman, *Amusing Ourselves to Death* (New York: Viking Penguin, 1985). Page references to this book in this section of the chapter are given parenthetically in the text.

defined truth and knowledge, and even reality itself."[4] Few, however, have seen this so astutely and thoroughly as Postman, whose book is

> an inquiry into and a lamentation about the most significant American cultural fact of the second half of the twentieth century: the decline of the Age of Typography and the ascendancy of the Age of Television. This change-over has dramatically and irreversibly shifted the content and meaning of public discourse, since two media so vastly different cannot accommodate the same ideas. As the influence of print wanes, the content of politics, religion, education, and anything else that comprises public business must change and be recast in terms that are most suitable to television. (p. 8)

His recognition that even religion has to be recast in television terms forces us to ask in this book if and how we can do that without dumbing down the substance of the faith. As Part IV will show, I am not convinced that worship must cater to television-age crowds craving entertainment, but our efforts to be faithful, deep, and truthful and yet accessible to society will be improved if we painstakingly analyze precisely how television affects us.

Primarily we must comprehend that television has changed the way our culture perceives reality. Postman demonstrates that the technological process culminating in the television age began when telegraphy robbed from us relevance, power, and coherence. First it conducted us to irrelevance because it

> gave a form of legitimacy to the idea of context-free information; that is, to the idea that the value of information need not be tied to any function it might serve in social and political decision-making and action, but may attach merely to its novelty, interest, and curiosity. The telegraph made information into a commodity, a "thing" that could be bought and sold irrespective of its uses or meaning. . . . [It] made relevance irrelevant. The abundant flow of information had very little or nothing to do with those to whom it was addressed; that is, with any social or intellectual context in which their lives were embedded. . . . The telegraph may have made the country into "one neighborhood," but it was a peculiar one, populated by strangers who knew nothing but the most superficial facts about each other. (pp. 65, 67)

4. Roof, *Seekers*, p. 54.

Certainly this irrelevance is grotesquely amplified by the multitude of "news" and "facts" television now conveys. Consequently, people are inured to knowing only trivial details about each other. The effect of this on prayer and Christian community is easily surmised. Another more subtly dangerous result, to be explored later, is a quest for relevance that becomes misguided.

Loss of relevance led intrinsically to impotence. As Postman says, "most of our daily news is inert, consisting of information that gives us something to talk about but cannot lead to any meaningful action." Because we cannot do anything about the abundance of irrelevant information that we receive, television has dramatically altered the "information-action ratio" (p. 68).

Postman's explanations made me painfully aware of part of the reason why a four-month class I taught on Christian community was so woefully ineffective. Participants in the class told me frequently how much they enjoyed it, how much they were learning — but I wondered why not much was changing in our congregation. In my naivete I believed that most people put truth into practice, that we all seek coherence between what we know and how we live, that knowledge leads to integrity of character and life. Now it seems indisputable to me that television has habituated its watchers to a low information-action ratio, that people are accustomed to "learning" good ideas (even from sermons) and then doing nothing about them. Without doubt a television age requires that we reflect more deeply on how we teach and what we are really learning, on whether what we now "know" has any effect on who we are and what we do.

Irrelevancy and impotence were aggravated and complemented by the incoherence the telegraph caused. Postman explains that now we were "sent information which answered no question we had asked, and which, in any case, did not permit the right of reply." Moreover, telegraphy "brought into being a world of broken time and broken attention," as Lewis Mumford names it (p. 69).

> The receiver of the news had to provide a meaning if he could. . . . And because of all this, the world as depicted by the telegraph began to appear unmanageable, even undecipherable. . . . "Knowing" the facts took on a new meaning, for it did not imply that one understood implications, background, or connections. Telegraphic discourse per-

21

mitted no time for historical perspectives and gave no priority to the qualitative. (p. 70)

Thus, besides being irrelevant and rendering us impotent, "news" became increasingly fragmentary, taken out of context, incoherent. This fragmentation was intensified by the invention of photographs, which perform

> a peculiar kind of dismembering of reality, a wrenching of moments out of their contexts, and a juxtaposing of events and things that have no logical or historical connection with each other. Like telegraphy, photography recreates the world as a series of idiosyncratic events. (p. 73)

New technological imagery did not merely supplement language but replaced it as our primary means "for construing, understanding, and testing reality." Consequently, this focus on image "undermined traditional definitions of information, of news, and, to a large extent, of reality itself" (p. 74).

We were left with a world loaded with "information" that is meaningless because it has no context, can lead to no response, and has no connection to everything else in our arsenal of "facts." A turn toward becoming a people consumed by entertainment was almost inevitable, for, as Postman asks, what do you do with all the information? The crossword puzzle appeared as a first example of the fabrication of a "pseudo-context." Other uses for meaningless information are the cocktail party, radio quiz shows and television game shows, "Trivial Pursuit," and the like. These all furnish the same answer to the question, "What am I to do with all these disconnected facts?" The answer is, "Why not use them for diversion? for entertainment? to amuse yourself, in a game?" (p. 76).

Telegraphy and photography thus prepared the way for television to turn our society into a perpetual chasing after entertainment. As Postman avows,

> a new note had been sounded, . . . a "language" that denied interconnectedness, proceeded without context, argued the irrelevance of history, explained nothing, and offered fascination in place of complexity and coherence . . . a duet of image and instancy. . . .
>
> Each of the media that entered the electronic conversation in the late nineteenth and early twentieth centuries followed the lead of the tele-

graph and the photograph, and amplified their biases. . . . Together, this ensemble of electronic techniques called into being a new world — a peek-a-boo world, where now this event, now that, pops into view for a moment, then vanishes again. It is a world without much coherence or sense; a world that does not ask us, indeed, does not permit us to do anything; a world that is, like the child's game of peek-a-boo, entirely self-contained. But like peek-a-boo it is also endlessly entertaining.

Of course, there is nothing wrong with playing peek-a-boo . . . with entertainment. As some psychiatrist once put it, we all build castles in the air. The problems come when we try to *live* in them. (p. 77)

Modern society began to live in them with the ascendancy of television (p. 78).

As its influence materialized, television revolutionized the structure of our thought. Whereas the printed page revealed a serious, coherent world, "capable of management by reason, and of improvement by logical and relevant criticism" (p. 62), television pictures the world in rapidly shifting images that destroy all the virtues formerly associated with mature discourse. Our "Age of Show Business" is not characterized by these facets of an age of exposition: "a sophisticated ability to think conceptually, deductively and sequentially; a high valuation of reason and order; an abhorrence of contradiction; a large capacity for detachment and objectivity; and a tolerance for delayed response" (p. 63). In fact, television's "surfeit of instant entertainment . . . makes reasoning seem anachronistic, narrow, and unnecessary."[5]

The loss of exposition must be a major concern for the Church, which tries to pass on faith to the next generation, teach creeds, set out the eminent reasonability of belief, and ground children in doctrines that will duly establish them for growth to maturity in truth and hope. Without theological foundation, faith becomes subject to capricious feelings and to life's troubles.

Besides extensively depriving our culture of exposition, television's nature also intensifies the appeal to emotions. Its images distort watchers' ability to reason and justify choices. Earlier advertisements laid out facts so that buyers could make decisions on the basis of qualities in what was

5. Kenneth A. Myers, *All God's Children and Blue Suede Shoes: Christians and Popular Culture* (Westchester, IL: Crossway Books, 1989), p. 171.

23

being sold, but by the turn of the last century "advertising became one part depth psychology, one part aesthetic theory," and reason had to move elsewhere (p. 60). Thus television ushered in a major revision in methods. Indeed, an ad

> is not at all about the character of products to be consumed. It is about the character of the consumers of products. Images of movie stars and famous athletes, of serene lakes and macho fishing trips, of elegant dinners and romantic interludes, of happy families packing their station wagons for a picnic in the country — these tell nothing about the products being sold. But they tell everything about the fears, fancies and dreams of those who might buy them. What the advertiser needs to know is not what is right about the product but what is wrong about the buyer. And so, the balance of business expenditures shifts from *product* research to *market* research. The television commercial has oriented business away from making products of value and toward making consumers feel valuable, which means that the business of business has now become pseudo-therapy. The consumer is a patient assured by psycho-dramas. (p. 128)

Church leaders must see how dangerous such a method is, lest we be tempted to let worship also be "market driven." We permit that to happen when we study what the consumers/worship participants fancy more than we study what is right with God! Then worship, too, becomes pseudo-therapy and not the healing revelation of God.

The cultivation of the television age has enormous consequences for the Church. Will its attitudes and habits imperil the very work we do and prevent us from genuinely being the Church? Since television transforms the method by which people are persuaded of the "truth," how will we inculcate the truths of faith? What questions should we be asking to ponder the means we use to be in the world but not of it, as we seek to appeal to the culture surrounding us?

The Technological Society

Television's influence on our culture's perception of thinking and truth is one of the drastic changes in the social fabric that have evolved with the onset of the technological milieu. More thoroughly than most, Jacques

Ellul fathomed these permutations long before they became fully developed.[6] One of these deleterious transitions that is particularly critical for this book's purposes is the modern loss of genuine intimacy in personal relationships. Other repercussions will be considered in the next chapter because they are more aptly designated as idolatries in our culture that frequently impinge on worship.

As we consider various factors, continually remember that these are not the only elements of our technological society, but simply examples to initiate thinking about many others not named. Moreover, these factors are both symptoms and causes. Part of a never-ending spiral, they have arisen from previous technological developments and societal forces and, in turn, cause other factors that destroy our humanity. They must be named so that we can lessen their negative influences.

As Ellul traces it, the general social fabric of family and community cohesion began to shred in the Industrial Age, when family businesses and farms gave way to factories and corporations. Now the head of the house who went away to work in another place brought home additional psychological strains, numerous relationships that the rest of the family did not share, and extraneous concerns and realities. World War II escalated the process because women left their homes for the workforce outside. As human beings spent less time together with those dearest to them and more time in a wide variety of communities with superficial associations, they lost the opportunity to learn and practice skills of intimacy. A far greater rending occurred, however, with the onset of the technological society, because this new milieu's tools of work and toys of pleasure pull us away from each other. The automobile, instruments of the media, personal computers, and work modems are just a few examples of technological tools and toys that have stolen our intimacy.

Instead of riding on buses or trains, which provide opportunity for genial conversation and social connections, most commuters in our culture take their personal automobiles. Consequently, our society has

---

6. Much of what follows was gathered in previous research focusing on the works of Jacques Ellul and the nature of the technological milieu in light of the biblical doctrine of "the Principalities and Powers." This material will not be footnoted separately because Ellul's references to the subject are scattered throughout his vast corpus. Since my planned book on this subject is not yet written, I must simply refer you now to some of Ellul's works and my dissertation as listed in the bibliography.

not developed the connected intra- and inter-city transit systems that Europe offers — much to the destruction of our ecological and social environment. The automobile lets us live far from our birth families, distant from our places of work and worship, with the result that we inhabit lots of communities, few of which are truly intimate. George F. Kennan cites the automobile as a major "addiction" of our culture and asserts that it "has turned out to be, by virtue of its innate and unalterable qualities, the enemy of community generally. Wherever it advances, neighborliness and the sense of community are impaired."[7]

The isolation engendered by solo commuters is also exemplified by modern architecture in suburbs, where the backyard patio is both a symptom and a cause of non-intimacy.[8] The patio has removed us from the front porch congeniality that characterized architecture and community life in a pre-technological culture. As a child, I enjoyed evenings with my family on the front porch, where we conversed about our day's work and dreams and were visited by neighbors out for walks. My husband and I try to imitate this by means of a swing hanging under our home's front eaves, but few people walk by, we don't live near our closest friends, and the fences and hedges of yards separate us from those next door. Many citizens in modern Western society — pushed by extremes of corporate bureaucracy, the need to climb professional ladders, competition instead of friendship between business or academic colleagues, the frantic pace of the workplace, and many other factors too numerous to catalogue — retreat to a private home life to seek relief from the pressures and threats of work or the fears of random violence. And that violence is often symptomatic of the lack of intimacy and family life, of violent media entertainment, and of the prevalence of technologically sophisticated weaponry.

7. George F. Kennan, *Around the Cragged Hill: A Personal and Political Philosophy* (New York: W. W. Norton, 1993), p. 161. See also an excerpt of this book in Kennan's "American Addictions: Bad Habits and Government Indifference," *New Oxford Review* 60, no. 5 (June 1993): 14-25.

8. The patio points to Lasch's insight that the appearance of a new intimacy in present society "is an illusion. The cult of intimacy conceals growing despair of finding it. Personal relations crumble under the emotional weight with which they are burdened. The inability 'to take an interest in anything after one's own death,' which gives such urgency to the pursuit of close personal encounters in the present, makes intimacy more elusive than ever." Lasch, *The Culture of Narcissism* (New York: W. W. Norton, 1979), p. 188.

Besides destroying our thinking, as previously noted, television also fosters an easy — and mindless — subversion of familial intimacy. Instead of conversing, playing games, or baking cookies together, modern families often merely vegetate in front of the tube — and frequently in separate rooms with unshared program choices. The Walkman pushes this isolation to the extreme as it disengages radio or audiotape listeners from the sounds and ideas that others are experiencing and pulls the listener into a private, vicarious world — meanwhile often causing hearing loss that will lead to later lonely isolation.

I must emphasize at this point that I am not a cranky pessimist opposed to technological innovations. But we must be realistic about what Ellul names the "technological bluff," which blinds us to the mixed bag of positive advances and negative destructions connected with our tools and toys. Indeed, advances in technology bring us many advantages, but the advantages are always coupled with profound losses — primarily the loss of community. The computer is a good example. I am extremely grateful for how it eases the task of book writing — of which I am deeply aware since my first several books were typed and retyped and typed again. However, many workplaces have totally lost face-to-face communication because messages are sent instead over the computer modem. Families are being dismantled because a parent or child is always drawn away to play, work, or experiment on the computer. Confined to my home today because chemotherapy has weakened my resistance to infections, I feel profoundly the isolation of this machine. Separated from friends, I converse with you from my study — but I cannot hear your input nor see your face nor feel your handshake or hug.

Our culture's loss of intimacy has led to serious consequences. One is that many people desperately turn to genital intimacy because their needs for social intercourse are never met.[9] Another result is vicarious living. Talk shows publicly discuss intimate, private matters. People unable to risk open vulnerability with those closest to them instead listen to, or participate in, programs that allow them to speak without revealing themselves or being held accountable to others who love them. Technological factors that reduce skills of intimacy keep many from knowing how to relate to their family and friends.

9. I have detailed this more extensively in my book *Sexual Character: Beyond Technique to Intimacy* (Grand Rapids: William B. Eerdmans, 1993).

Societal and familial loss of intimacy affects the Church, too, in many ways. Living far apart from each other, members of a congregation do not hold each other as their primary community. Consequently, churches do not experience the deep intimacy that could characterize our times together.[10] We might know some facts about each other, but we do not actually know who a fellow congregant really is, so we talk about trivia when we gather. We do not know how to share what genuinely matters, how to deal with the real lives and deep hurts or doubts of honest people, or how to speak the truth. Lacking sincere intimacy in congregational fellowship, we often put false pressure on worship to produce feelings of intimacy. (We will look at this in more depth in Chapter 7.) Alienated by the lack of true "public" worship, many people, conditioned by our culture's sterility, prefer merely to attend, and not participate in, worship. They can get lost in a crowd of passive spectators or worship solely through televised services.

Moreover, the media have stolen our ability to sing together. Teenagers adulate rock stars and listen to their music on Walkmans and on MTV but do not learn to sing themselves. Television robs us of family singing around the piano, and the focus on technological training in schools has joined the media to destroy children's interest in the fine arts of instrumental and choral music, poetry, painting, drama and dance, church symbolism and liturgy. These and many other factors lead to vicariousness in worship. Many churches utilize less communal singing and instrumental work and more solos sung to backup tapes. The lack of training in schools gives us fewer musicians to serve and less interest in retaining the repertoire of the Church's master composers.

But the technological milieu's influence goes far beyond its destruction of congregational participation and of the arts. Most dangerous are the idolatries the milieu engenders. Postman uses the term "Technopoly" to describe a society in which all forms of cultural life are submitted to the sovereignty of technique.[11] Technopoly

---

10. I have tried to counteract this by offering concrete suggestions and questions for personal/congregational reflection in *The Hilarity of Community: Romans 12 and How to Be the Church* (Grand Rapids: William B. Eerdmans, 1992).

11. Neil Postman, *Technopoly: The Surrender of Culture to Technology* (New York: Alfred A. Knopf, 1992), p. 52. Page references to this book in the following paragraphs are given parenthetically in the text.

consists in the deification of technology, which means that the culture seeks its authorization in technology, finds its satisfaction in technology, and takes its orders from technology. This requires the development of a new kind of social order, and of necessity leads to the rapid dissolution of much that is associated with traditional beliefs. (p. 71)

Jacques Ellul named Technique a god and demonstrates, especially in *The Technological Bluff,* how thoroughly it convinces us of its supreme authority.

Though we will consider the idolatries of Technopoly more thoroughly in the following chapter, we should at least mention some of the assumptions of its thought world that are relevant to our topic here. These include beliefs

that the primary, if not the only, goal of human labor and thought is efficiency; that technical calculation is in all respects superior to human judgment; that in fact human judgment cannot be trusted . . . ; that what cannot be measured either does not exist or is of no value; and that the affairs of citizens are best guided and conducted by experts. (p. 51)

We will especially consider the destructiveness of the emphasis on efficiency later. The emphasis on measurement and experts is revealed by the huge push for worship practices to be changed in order to attract large numbers and by the turning of congregations into mega-businesses instead of Christian communities.

Boomers

Drastic changes in social fabric caused by the onset of the technological milieu are intensified by the psychological reverberations of societal events. For those growing up in the sixties — the "baby boom" or "boomer" generation — these tremors were extensive. Wade Clark Roof's chapter entitled "When Mountains Were Moving" characterizes the age of the sixties as a time of great complexity, of nostalgia and optimism, coupled with world-weariness.[12]

---

12. Roof, *Seekers,* p. 32. Page references to this book in this section of the chapter are given parenthetically in the text.

Roof cites Annie Gottlieb's suggestion that the age really began in 1963 with the assassination of President Kennedy and ended in 1973 with the energy crisis and economic recession. These parameters define the sixties as a decade of upheaval plus affluence. To these predominant influences Roof adds the gender revolution and the role of higher education and television (pp. 36-54). Such events and experiences during the critical years of becoming adults caused the character of boomer-generation members to develop in radically different ways. "Even the deeply ingrained cultural narratives on which Americans had for so long relied to make sense of their lives were deeply jarred by the events" of the times, and these "jolts reached to the very foundations of their religious and spiritual understanding" (p. 31). These jolts have enormous consequences for the Church today as it seeks to minister to this generation through its worship.

According to pollster Daniel Yankelovich, the affluence of the times led boomer Americans to ponder more introspective matters. Average citizens of the 1950s and 1960s typically asked if they would be able to be successful or to make a good living or to raise happy, healthy, successful children. In the 1970s, the questions became instead "How can I find self-fulfillment?" "What does personal success really mean?" "What kinds of commitments should I be making?" "What is worth sacrificing for?" and "How can I grow?"[13]

Significant for our purposes, this introspection has great consequences for boomers' relationship with the Church. They have grown up "in a post-sixties culture that emphasizes choice, knowing and understanding one's self, the importance of personal autonomy, and fulfilling one's potential — all contributing to a highly subjective approach to religion" (Roof, p. 30). Chapter 6 will focus on such subjectivism as we look at believers' character formation; here we must grasp some complex elements of this late twentieth-century attitude. Its roots lie in several factors of the modern technological milieu.

As detailed in previous sections, the development of modern means of communication has broadened, but not deepened, our experience. It is not local anymore, but universal. Our interests and influences are multifaceted, not focused. "What is most remarkable about modern people," David Wells observes, "is that they are not in scale with the world they

13. Daniel Yankelovich, *New Rules: Searching for Self-Fulfillment in a World Turned Upside Down* (New York: Random House, 1981), pp. 4-5.

inhabit informationally and psychologically. They are dwarfed" with "nothing to give height or depth or perspective to anything they experience. They know more, but they are not necessarily wiser. They believe less, but they are not more substantial."[14] One result of such dwarfing is that persons can't get their bearings from that huge world which they "know" but which gives them no "point of reference."[15]

Wells blames modernization for the process by which our culture lost God as its point of reference.[16] Modernization's principal effect has been

> to break apart the unity of human understanding and disperse the multitude of interests and undertakings away from the center, in relation to which they have gathered their meaning, . . . by breaking down the central core so that there is nothing to which thought and life return. It has eroded those ideas and convictions, that truth which, precisely because it arose in God and was mediated by him, stood as an unchanging sentinel amid changing circumstances. . . . [T]his flight to the edges, this dispersion from the center, . . . has intruded on evangelical faith even as it has disordered the warp and woof of contemporary life. In the one it leaves a faith denuded of theology and in the other a life stripped of absolutes. . . . Is there not wide agreement that the effect of secularization has been to marginalize God, to make what is absolute and transcendent irrelevant to the stuff of everyday life?[17]

Not only did God become marginalized and irrelevant, but many Americans now find an open hostility between "the religious heartbeat of the country and the nation's cultural institutions." Sixty-two percent of Americans consider television hostile to religion, and forty-six percent think newspapers are.[18]

---

14. David F. Wells, *No Place for Truth* (Grand Rapids: Eerdmans, 1993), pp. 51-52.

15. This phrase comes from Madeleine L'Engle's novel, *The Love Letters* (New York: Farrar, Straus and Giroux, 1966), p. 189.

16. In his newer book (which came off the press too late for me to be able to include much of it here) Wells uses the phrase "the weightlessness of God" to describe the loss of understanding of who God really is. See David F. Wells, *God in the Wasteland: The Reality of Truth in a World of Fading Dreams* (Grand Rapids: William B. Eerdmans, 1994), especially pp. 88-117.

17. Wells, *No Place for Truth*, pp. 7-8.

18. Jeffrey L. Sheler, "Spiritual America," *U.S. News and World Report* 116, no. 13 (4 April 1993): 57.

Another factor in the mix of influences on contemporary religious life is that many people in the sixties were deeply shaken by events such as campus riots, Watergate, and the escalation of the Vietnam war, which put into question the trustworthiness of leaders and officials. As Roof explains, there is

> a question of authority over which boomers are deeply divided. To whom or to what can you turn for reliable answers to religious questions? On what basis are religious beliefs and moral values to be organized? Whose truths are to be accepted? Such questions are vexing in a culture as pluralistic and relativistic as ours, and in an age when traditional authorities have lost influence. The answers to such questions are often divisive and emotion-ridden, and especially so if people try to "impose" their beliefs and moral values on others. Americans hold strongly to the rights of individuals to make their own decisions in moral and religious matters and resist such intrusion in the public arena. (p. 31)

These and many other factors cause the boomer generation to emphasize belief in themselves and their own inner strength. They value independence, but they are often frustrated that their achievements don't match their perceived potential. They have a great tolerance of all kinds of beliefs and behaviors on the part of others, which is closely linked with their own ethic of self-realization, self-help, and self-fulfillment (pp. 45-47).

This (often excessive) search for self challenges enormously what we do in worship. Churches wanting to reach out to this generation must think carefully about forms and styles. As we struggle to ask better questions and to provide more effective ministry, we can be encouraged that many boomers who dropped out of religious institutions years ago are now "shopping around" for a church home. We must be cautious in our planning and changing, however, for the boomers "move freely in and out, across religious boundaries; many combine elements from various traditions to create their own personal, tailor-made meaning systems." Choice, a significant contemporary value, "now expresses itself in dynamic and fluid religious styles" (p. 5). Roof summarizes that from his team's statistical findings and individual accounts emerges a generation

> of diverse seekers who share surprising commonalities. They value experience over beliefs, distrust institutions and leaders, stress personal fulfillment

yet yearn for community, and are fluid in their allegiances — a new, truly distinct, and rather mysterious generation. (p. 8)

How can the Church disarm that distrust? How can we pass on the objective beliefs of our faith that are true regardless of a person's experience?

Other attributes of the boomer society will surface in later chapters. As we tie together this chapter's first three sections, one blatantly obvious connection is the destruction of community and the recognition of its loss. Television brought home to almost every household the disastrous events of the sixties that diminished trust in authority. At the same time, it joined other media and technological innovations in decreasing possibilities for genuine community. The boomer generation increasingly lacked skills for intimacy and turned inward for personal satisfaction. Now a great number of people know that they need community and do not know how to create it authentically.

Postmodernism

Our overview requires one other set of descriptions of the culture in which the Church tries to conduct its worship and for which it seeks to serve. Though many other cultural aspects are worthy of our attention, those included in this chapter primarily affect the Church's worship life. We must particularly notice several especially influential developments that move away from modernism into various strands of postmodernism. Bear with me for several pages as we explore these attitudes and reactions that envelop our present time.

The term *modernism* as first applied to works of art and literature specified certain attributes of style, but often the word refers to the attitudes that underlie that style, which are the products of various factors in the technological milieu. In his momentous paralleling of modernism with mental illness, specifically schizophrenia, Louis Arnesson Sass lists the following attributes of modernism as it intensifies into postmodernism:[19]

---

19. Louis A. Sass, *Madness and Modernism: Insanity in the Light of Modern Art, Literature, and Thought* (New York: Basic Books, 1992). Page references to this book in this section are given parenthetically in the text.

- its negativism and antitraditionalism as that is manifested in "its defiance of authority and convention, its antagonism or indifference to the expectations of its audience, and, on occasion, its rage for chaos" (p. 29);
- the uncertainty or multiplicity of its point of view, which can lead to extreme nihilism (pp. 30-31);
- modernist dehumanization in the form of "a fragmentation from within that effaces reality and renders the self a mere occasion for the swarming of independent subjective events — sensations, perceptions, memories, and the like. The overwhelming vividness, diversity, and independence of this experiential swarm fragment the self, obliterating its distinctive features — the sense of unity and control" (p. 31);
- modernist dehumanization in the contrasting form of the most extreme kind of objectivism. "Here human activity is observed with the coldest and most eternal of gazes, a gaze that refuses all empathy and strips the material world of all the valences of human meaning" (pp. 31-32).

To name the latter two types of dehumanization, Sass uses the term *derealization* and Heidegger's phrase "the unworlding of the (human) world." He emphasizes that in both forms "the ego or self is passivized." In derealization "it becomes an impotent observer of thinglike yet inner experiences — of sensations, images, and the like," whereas in unworlding "it is transformed into a machinelike entity placed in a world of static and neutral objects" (p. 33). The chief characteristic of all the forms listed is disengagement.

From historical and cross-cultural standpoints Sass shows the correlation of increased schizophrenia with these social/cultural factors: weakening of extended family and small community ties in the transition from traditional rural modes to the more impersonal and atomized forms of modern social organization; increasingly specialized work roles and competitive expectations; the loss of supernatural explanations and healing rituals or reintegrative ceremonies; and the increasing "complex, conflicting, and potentially disorienting cognitive requirements" characteristic of more technologically sophisticated societies (pp. 359-65). He deduces that "the ways of thinking, believing, and feeling characteristic of modern Western society are prerequisites for the development of the reflexivity and detachment characteristic of both the schizoid and the schizophrenic condition." This is caused by the disengagement and self-consciousness fostered by the ideas of philosophers such as Descartes, Locke, and Kant and by modern patterns of socialization, which turn human beings away from the search for an objective external order and enjoin us instead "to turn inward and become aware of our own activity and of the processes that form us . . . to take charge of constructing our own representation of the world, which otherwise goes on without order" (p. 369). Sociologist Anthony Giddens has highlighted the "unsettling quality of modernity's 'wholesale reflexivity,'" which has turned against not only all traditions but even "the nature of reflection itself, resulting in the dissolving of anchored vantage points and a universal 'institutionalization of doubt'" (pp. 371-72).

This description of modernity's wholesale reflexivity, of its rejection of objective vantage points in favor of what Martin Luther called being "inward turned," requires those of us who seek to reach out to people in the culture around the Church to consider carefully how genuine worship of God counteracts these tendencies. After his extensive analysis of schizophrenia and modernism, Sass asks these critical questions:

> What, to begin with, does it *say* about modernism that it should display such remarkable affinities with this most severe of mental illnesses, which some have called the cancer of the mind? What does this parallelism suggest about how we should judge the relevant aspects of the modern sensibility? Can we view the alienation and self-consciousness of the modern mind as the inevitable signs of increasing degrees of complexity, subtlety, or insight or must we see them as something far less benign — signs of deep pathology, perhaps, of a disease or spiritual decadence corroding the style and sensibility of our age? (p. 339)

In future chapters we will discuss, as ways to counter modernism's madness, the urgent requirements to keep God as the subject of the Church's worship and to recognize the objective truth of God's revelation. At this point we simply note that one of the present cultural streams in response to modernism is a postmodernism characterized by a new openness to the past. This countermovement, according to Alan Mittleman, recognizes "the hubris and futility" of modernity's project "to conquer, control, and banish the past" and seeks instead "to allow traditions some sway over the present and the future."[20] Sass offers the possibility of this trajectory when he compares philosopher Jacques Derrida and literary theorist Paul de Man to Heidegger, Merleau-Ponty, and Wittgenstein, who attempted "to put us back in touch with ourselves by recalling us to some deep sense of groundedness and unity" (p. 347). This trend offers great possibilities for the Church's worship, especially with its twenty-centuries-long tradition of strong hymnody, scripturally grounded liturgy, and biblically formed community. One example in this country that gives evidence to Mittleman's assertion is the recent wave of converts to, and renewed interest in, Orthodoxy — with all its ancient rituals and liturgy. Another example is the emphasis by the so-called baby busters (or Generation X or the twenty-somethings) on their own need and desire for ties with the past, for community, and for deeper relationships than their boomer parents have.[21]

However, this strand of postmodernism is probably the least powerful, especially among the cultural elite. More highly visible is the stream of postmodernists who take the trajectory of contingency and relativity to a ruthless extreme. A baseball joke makes clear the progression in history from the premodern belief in objective truth to postmodernity's deconstructionism. A premodern umpire once said, "There's balls and there's strikes, and I calls 'em as they is." Believing in an absolute truth that could be found, earlier societies looked for evidence to discover that truth. A modern umpire would say instead, "There's balls and there's strikes, and I calls 'em as I sees 'em." For the modernist, truth is to be found in one's own experience. Now a postmodern umpire would say, "There's balls and there's strikes, and they ain't nothin' till I calls 'em." No truth exists unless we create it.

Gertrude Himmelfarb describes this current in her own discipline of history by noting crucial distinctions between modernists and postmodernists, the

---

20. Alan L. Mittleman's review of Eugene Borowitz's *Renewing the Covenant: A Theology for the Postmodern Jew,* in *First Things* 30 (Feb. 1993): 45.

21. See especially Andrés Tapia, "Reaching the First Post-Christian Generation," *Christianity Today* 38, no. 10 (12 Sept. 1994): 18-23; and William Mahedy and Janet Bernardi, *A Generation Alone: Xers Making a Place in the World* (Downers Grove, IL: InterVarsity Press, 1994). See also Douglas Coupland's two books, *Generation X: Tales for an Accelerated Culture* (New York: St. Martin Press, 1991) and *Life after God* (New York: Pocket Books, 1994).

old-fashioned relativistic relativists . . . and the new absolutistic relativists. Where modernists tolerate relativism, postmodernists celebrate it. Where modernists, aware of the obstacles in the way of objectivity, take this as a challenge and make a strenuous effort to attain as much objectivity and unbiased truth as possible, postmodernists take the rejection of absolute truth as a deliverance from all truth, a release from the obligation to maintain any degree of objectivity or aspire to any kind of truth.

. . . Postmodernism repudiates both the values [truth, justice, reality, morality] and the rhetoric of the Enlightenment — that is, of modernity. In rejecting the "discipline" of knowledge and rationality, postmodernism also rejects the "discipline" of society and authority. And in denying any reality apart from language, it subverts the structure of society together with the structure of language. The principle of indeterminacy is an invitation to creation *ex nihilo.* It presents the historian with a *tabula rasa* on which he may inscribe whatever he chooses.[22]

Himmelfarb then goes on to discuss historians' deconstruction of the "text" of the past and their creation of new histories. Since there is no objective basis for selecting one story rather than another, the only grounds for judging one as better than another are "its persuasiveness, its political utility, and its political sincerity." Because of the race, class, and gender biases now prevalent, she asks, why not change "Everyman/woman his/her own historian" to

"Every Black / White / Hispanic / Asian / Native American . . ."? Or "Every Christian / Jew / Catholic / Protestant / Muslim / Hindu / secularist / atheist . . ."? Or "Every heterosexual / homosexual / bisexual / androgynous / polymorphous / misogamous / misogynous . . ."? And so on, through all the ethnic, racial, religious, sexual, national, ideological, and other characteristics that distinguish people? . . . [This has] the obvious effect of politicizing history. But its more pernicious effect is to demean and dehumanize the subjects of history. To deny the generic "man" is to deny the common humanity of both sexes — and, by implication, the common humanity of all racial, social, religious, and ethnic groups. It is also to deny the common history they were once presumed to share.

---

22. Gertrude Himmelfarb, "Tradition and Creativity in the Writing of History," *First Things* 27 (Nov. 1992): 30 and 33.

Traditional historians, even many radical historians, are troubled by the prospect of a history so pluralized and fragmented that it lacks all coherence and focus, all sense of continuity, indeed, all meaning.

From a postmodernist perspective, this is all to the good, for it destroys the "totalizing," "universalizing," "logocentric," "phallo-centric" history that is said to be the great evil of modernity. Postmodernism proposes instead to privilege "aporia" — difference, discontinuity, disparity, contradiction, discord, indeterminacy, ambiguity, irony, paradox, perversity, opacity, obscurity, chaos.[23]

I quote Himmelfarb at length because her observations show the effects on public life of the loss of a common history. I believe that the Church offers great gifts in its potential ability to honor diversities of history, gifts, race, class, and gender, in the unity of the Spirit and our common history as Christians. But does our worship teach such unity, a sense of our commonality in Christ, and an Absolute that can put all relativities into harmony? In response to the postmodern rejection of all authority and reliability, can the Church offer believable truth, a coherent story that gives meaning in chaos?

We must look at three other strands of contemporary attitudes that arise as responses to the struggle for hope in the midst of the escalating suffering of the present-day world. In reaction to the enormous problems endemic to postmodern culture, Christiaan Beker observes extremes of cynicism and false apocalyptic hopes, as well as attempts (often narrowly privatized) at a middle way. Reflecting on the severity of the suffering, Beker underscores that

both the *quantity* and *quality* of suffering in our world threaten to overwhelm us in such a measure that it seems to evaporate any reasonable basis for hope or at least any reasonable connection between the cycles of individual failure and success, between suffering and hope.[24]

Suffering thus causes many to turn either to "despair and hopelessness" or to "repression, avoidance, and denial." Those who still cling to hope often "conceive of it in highly egocentric ways," such as when people invest in

23. Himmelfarb, "Tradition and Creativity," pp. 33-34.
24. J. Christiaan Beker, *Suffering and Hope: The Biblical Vision and the Human Predicament* (Grand Rapids: William B. Eerdmans, 1994), p. 18.

expensive and private survival technology or "when religious folk among us devise fantasies of heavenly bliss for the few who are chosen." Such activities or plans are designed to avoid any contamination by the realities of our world's suffering.

These extreme reactions are generated because "the spatial and quantitative dimension of suffering [in our time], its worldwide scope, reinforces its qualitative dimension, its experienced intensity." Having himself experienced the horrors of Nazi labor camps and proximity to his own death in war, Beker astutely analyzes our culture's reactions to adversities.

> Indeed, however much we attempt to repress modern questions about suffering and hope, and however much we are sick and tired of the prophets of doom and gloom in our culture, we simply cannot avoid questions about the unparalleled scope and intensity of suffering in our time. The usual response in our culture to these questions seems to be twofold: we repress hope and become cynics or we repress suffering and become credulous ideologues, happily swallowing the images of false hope produced by apocalyptic prophets of doom and by ecclesial and secular technocrats. And when we seek the middle way between cynicism and credulity, we often strive to create private, danger-free zones and egocentric projects of survival.[25]

The loss of hope and cynicism Beker names take many forms in contemporary U.S. culture. Graeme Hunter discusses luck, evil, and victimhood as expressions of this new fatalism. As he insists, "They are what remains in lives when every hope of finding objective meaning is removed."[26] The immense popularity of lotteries, the horrifying escalation of random violence, and the proliferation of media "victim talk" all point to postmodernistic despair.

No one denies the immensity of our world's problems. What can the Church offer in the face of them, in contrast to postmodernist despair? How does our worship deal with the intensity and scope of suffering? Do we proclaim true hope, universally accessible? Are we equipped by our worship to work to ease suffering and to build peace and justice in the world? Or do we merely provide a private happiness, a cozy comfortableness in our own safe sanctuaries?

25. Beker, *Suffering and Hope*, p. 19.
26. Graeme Hunter, "Evil: Back in Bad Company," *First Things* 41 (March 1994): 38.

Before we can start to look at the true hope the Church has to offer and the ways in which we can offer it, we must look at the idolatries that threaten the integrity of our Christian communities. These idolatries are inextricably connected to the aspects of the culture outlined in this chapter, but, even more important, they are the products of the workings of the principalities and powers that try to separate us from the love of God.

3. Outside *the Idolatries of Contemporary Culture*

> Jesus calls us from the worship
> Of the vain world's golden store,
> From each idol that would keep us,
> Saying, "Christian, love me more."
>
> Cecil F. Alexander, 1823-1895

To be *in* the world but not *of* it requires the Church both to understand the surrounding culture and to resist its idolatries. Whereas the previous chapter sketched some key factors in the technological, boomer, postmodern culture that force us to ask better questions about how to conduct worship that reaches out to persons in such a world, this chapter warns against dangers of which we must be aware lest their power take us captive. As Walter Brueggemann makes clear in *Israel's Praise*, the worship of God's people is praise, not only toward God, but also against the gods.[1]

My first impetus for writing this book was the anguish of looking for a congregation and discovering, to my great distress, how extensively

---

1. Walter Brueggemann, *Israel's Praise: Doxology against Idolatry and Ideology* (Philadelphia: Fortress Press, 1988), especially pp. 29-53.

41

society's idolatries have invaded the Church and its worship. Previous study had alerted me to the workings of the biblical "principalities and powers" in the modern technological society — but what this chapter observes does not really depend on focused research. Anyone can notice the flourishing of idolatries both in society and in the Church if one pays attention to them. But are the leaders and worshipers in our churches paying attention? Or are we so captivated by our own gods that we are blinded to their influence?

The God of Efficiency

The escalating disruption of intimacy and community chronicled in the previous chapter is augmented by the technological society's idolatry of efficiency. Our culture is characterized by an enormous push to do everything faster. We want faster vehicles, computers, and cooking equipment. We must solve all our problems with an instant technological fix. Things must be on time. The press for efficiency is compounded by the media, which continue to accelerate the speed of life as news reports get shorter and less substantive, commercials get more hyped, the bombardment of sensory impressions increases in velocity. Recently, in an attempt to find healing laughter to combat cancer, we watched an old Burns-Allen television program on video and were astounded at the slow pace of the commercials. No one accustomed to contemporary society's speed would tolerate such a languorous advertisement. Because the Church seeks to minister to people formed by the technological milieu, it easily succumbs to its principal criterion of efficiency.

When this technological mind-set invades the Church, it can be extremely destructive of true worship in multiple ways — especially if we "must" finish the worship service in an hour. The liturgy becomes clockwork, service elements are eliminated, free expression of praise is stifled, the sermon is cut so brief that no deep biblical explication can occur, hymn verses are chopped off, the Eucharist becomes less communitarian, and there is no time for common prayer and sharing of concerns and thanksgivings. Worst of all, there is no time for silence or the surprising workings of the Holy Spirit.

Second, the bombardment of hyped media impressions creates the need for worship to be similarly "upbeat." There is no place for sorrowful hymns of repentance, mourning dirges for a crucified Savior, despairing cries for hope in the troubles of life, contemplative anthems that call for deeper thinking. The speed of the technological society easily invades all our worship tempos. Many musicians think that the only way to make hymns interesting is to play them faster. When we rush through worship too hastily, the music is sung and the words are spoken so quickly as to preclude much attention to meaning. We lose the majesty of many hymns, the moving pathos of the laments of Lent, the profound significance of the Lord's Prayer and the Creed, the lessons that can be gained by close listening to a slow-paced reading of the Scriptures.

Third, a need for efficiency in "fellowship time" between worship and Sunday school eliminates time for caring. Fellowship becomes a mere matter of coffee and cookies in the narthex between events. Some churches try to deepen these moments by calling them *koinonia* (the Greek word for sharing in common), but it is the same coffee and cookies! We talk about the weather and the latest ball scores, but we don't understand each other as if we belonged to each other, and we don't really want to know the answer to "How are you?" If our worship practices create the sense that the things of God must be tightly timed, this efficiency increasingly destroys our relationships with each other within the Body of Christ. It augments our tendency to think that we don't have enough time to provide transportation for the elderly, to listen to others' concerns, to welcome the child who needs to learn that she is also an important part of Christ's Body.

Above all, the technological society's push for efficiency has robbed most congregations of the Sabbath rhythm, the setting apart of one day in every seven for ceasing, resting, embracing, and feasting, a whole day set apart for God and for each other, a day of delight and healing. Consequently, Christians mimic the frantic lifestyle of the world around them and have no understanding that God has designed a wonderful rhythm of rest and work, of refreshment and then response. In that rhythm, we don't have to rush out of the worship service at precisely noon, since there is no work to do on Sunday. The day is set apart for worship, for relationships, for growing in our sense of who God is and who we are as individuals desiring to become like Jesus and as a community of his people displaying his character to the world.[2]

2. For a thorough explication of the delights of such a day see my book *Keeping the Sabbath Wholly: Ceasing, Resting, Embracing, Feasting* (Grand Rapids: William B. Eerdmans, 1989).

A last instance, intended to lead to personal and communal reflection on examples in your own local situation, is that worship planning and preparation are subjected to the need for efficiency. Pastors are burdened with so much "administrivia" that they have no time to focus, as Acts 6:4 suggests, on prayer and the ministry of the Word. (This change is indicated by the fact that we call their places of work "the office" instead of "the study.") Seminaries spend less time teaching about worship and the heritage of the Church because of all the other curricula demands concerning the mechanics of running a congregation. George Barna, who researches marketing trends, insists that clergy need to keep up with the latest technological developments to use computers and media well in the parish. "Church leaders must be technologically literate," he proclaims, and he adds that "the very fact that the congregation is using the new technology sends an important signal to the surrounding community."[3] Should we not be more concerned to send to the culture around us the important signal that our worship leaders spend their time in personal spiritual preparation, deep study of the Scriptures, and the inefficient work of prayer? Instead, worship — which should and must be the most important work of the Church — gets planned and carried out with less prayer underneath it, inadequate reflection on the texts, little care, minimal substance, and clocked efficiency.

The Idolatry of Money

Closely related to the demands of efficiency is the idolatry of money in our culture and in our churches. Many congregations are divided by arguments over various ways to spend their limited money — a congregation can be split over color choices for new carpet (which really ruins the acoustics of the sanctuary anyway!) — and money becomes more and more limited as lifestyle "needs" take more of parishioners' incomes. Very few congregations and members recognize the biblical priority of worship and the poor in their budgets.

The Jews were commanded (and the Book of Acts shows that early Christians followed their model) to use their tithes for celebrations, caring

---

3. George Barna, *The Frog in the Kettle: What Christians Need to Know about Life in the Year 2000* (Ventura, CA: Regal Books, 1990), p. 49.

for the poor, and paying the professional Levites, priests, and musicians (Deut. 14:22-29). I don't know many congregations in which all the members actually tithe, and I know no churches that spend their tithes biblically. Among the Jews, buildings and accoutrements were all extra gifts, gladly given (see Exod. 35:4–36:7). Think of the musical experiences that could happen in our churches if we spent more to pay good church musicians. Very few parishes have well-paid musicians, and yet music is a major part of the worship experience!

In the world's financial terms, I actually can't afford to be the choir director in my local parish — the pay doesn't cover the amount of time it takes to plan and practice good music — but because my husband's job frees us to give away my income anyway, I can enjoy spending time preparing choir, congregational, and instrumental pieces and special music festivals. I am constantly frustrated, however, that my availability to do such things is so limited because I am gone half the time for speaking engagements. Nevertheless, the situation makes me realize why many congregations have poor music. There is no financial and time commitment to making worship the varied musical experience it must be to evoke a sense of God's majesty, sublimity, and transcendence.

Consequently, the "Paul Manz Institute of Church Music" has been founded to encourage support for a new generation of organists. In *The Christian Century* Martin Marty exclaims, "Such support is urgent, given the barbarianism of our times, churches' frequent preference for mediocre music, and the financial difficulties of would-be musicians and congregations."[4]

A closely related problem with the power of Mammon is that, when church budgets decline, many parishes turn in the wrong direction to overcome the deficit. They push to make worship "attractive" and "popular" in order to appeal to the unsaved public and draw them to our churches. Often, leaders of this movement water down the faith to make it more palatable — and thus contradict the teaching of Jesus, whom the Church is supposed to be following. The gospel is indeed attractive to the unsaved, but we cannot sow it in shallowness if we want to reap deep discipleship. Besides, the Church cares for the unsaved for their sake, not for the sake of churches' monetary gain.

4. Martin E. Marty, "M.E.M.O.: Instrument of Grace," *The Christian Century* 109, no. 36 (9 Dec. 1992): 1151.

Most movements to attract new members emphasize an appeal to the tastes of the public, stressing that music should be like that found in the outside world and that sermons should minister to worshipers' "felt needs." However, the best research calls for an opposite approach. Benton Johnson, Dean Hoge, and Donald Luidens draw this conclusion from their extensive studies of reasons for churches' decline:

> The underlying problem of the mainline churches . . . is the weakening of the spiritual conviction required to generate the enthusiasm and energy needed to sustain a vigorous communal life. Somehow, in the course of the past century, these churches lost the will or the ability to teach the Christian faith and what it requires to a succession of younger cohorts in such a way as to command their allegiance. . . . In response to the currents of modernity, denominational leaders . . . did not devise or promote compelling new versions of a distinctively Christian faith. They did not fashion or preach a vigorous apologetics. . . .
>
> . . . Many of them have reduced the Christian faith to belief in God and respect for Jesus and the Golden Rule, and among this group a growing proportion have little need for the church.
>
> Perhaps some now unforeseen cultural shift will one day bring millions of baby boom dropouts back to the mainline churches. But nothing we discovered in our study suggests the likelihood of such a shift. If the mainline churches want to regain their vitality, their first step must be to address theological issues head on. They must . . . provide compelling answers to the question, "What's so special about Christianity?"[5]

How will we teach Christianity's specialness if the music in our worship services imitates the superficiality and meaninglessness of the general world and our sermons talk about subjects that those in the pew can learn from psychologists, sociologists, and the local television station? I am very interested in using modern music, as future chapters will demonstrate, but our music must contain the *substance* of the faith, the heritage of the Church's uniqueness, the character-forming truths of Christianity. Similarly, our sermons must be focused on the Word of God, which is the "special" domain of Christianity. Our worship services ought not to be designed by what appeals to the masses in order to survive financially;

5. Benton Johnson, Dean R. Hoge, and Donald A. Luidens, "Mainline Churches: The Real Reason for Decline," *First Things* 31 (March 1993): 18.

rather, they must be planned in a genuinely worshipful way that invites persons into the essence of truthful Christianity.

The Idolatry of "the Way We've Always Done It Before"

On the opposite pole of trying too hard to appeal to the masses and consequently losing the substance of the faith is the idolatry of traditionalism, which causes us to do everything as it's always been done, to such an extent that worship remains boring and stale. New wine must indeed be put into new wineskins; to try to nurture revival and to be genuinely open to the new movements of the Spirit require that we not be stuck to old forms that have no life.

This idolatry is not well combated by throwing everything out, however, for there is a great need for continuity in the human psyche; so we must be aware of the danger of swinging the pendulum entirely to the contrary pole. Once again, the dialectics about which we must carefully think require rigorous consideration of both extremes and the many possibilities lying in between.

The God of Vicarious Subjectivism and the Idolatry of "Famous People"

The problem of "attraction" concerns far deeper issues than simply choosing the wrong methods to appeal to the non-Christian or the non-active Christian. At its root is the modern compulsive "need" to be entertained. In the previous chapter this subject was broached by Postman's *Amusing Ourselves to Death*, so I need not belabor the point here, but we should at least note some of the other factors that create this craving for excitement in our society.

I do not intend to give here a definitive explanation; I simply want to paint the general social fabric with some broad brush strokes. As already mentioned, television's constant bombardment leads to personal psyches and a whole milieu that demand constant hype, and children who watch television excessively have smaller brains and are less capable of sustained attention. Moreover, both television and the teaching patterns of many schools destroy children's powers of imagination and creativity.

Much deeper than these factors is our society's loss of a spiritual center. Too many children, teens, and adults don't have any purpose for their lives. They are bored because of a severe lack of meaning, and they are unable to see possibilities for finding it in chores and home activities and jobs and care for others. Many have turned to the accumulation of material possessions as a way to find meaning, but this, too, proves to be empty in the end. As Graeme Hunter asks,

> Can we really expect to wrest a sense of value from our crushing defeat by stubbornly esteeming things that, in truth, are valueless? In the end even this will-to-meaning seems futile. Loud exhortations to value the valueless seem unlikely to keep us from suspecting that our lives are in reality not merely unworthwhile, but absurd.[6]

Few have mentors to guide them in discovering values that matter. Meanwhile, the media deluge us all with images of violence and sexual immorality and materialism, all of which draw us as easy alternatives to our boredom.

All these factors combine, moreover, to make life terribly superficial. Lacking genuine intimacy, many people are desperate to "experience" real life but don't know how to go about it. They have not learned to appreciate the intricacies of symphonic or chamber music, the profundity of genuine works of art, the complexity of classical literature, dramatic mysteries, poetic sublimities, simple and deep delights in nature, scientific wonders, the careful workmanship of crafts, the discipline of playing an instrument, the exquisite pleasure of learning. When I was a child all these things fascinated me, captivated me, filled my hours with vast enjoyment. Now the students in my husband's fifth-grade class are cynical and bored. Most of them have no desire to learn. They spend their recesses fighting with each other, and they cannot treat each other with common civility. Television has made them passive about learning and aggressive about relationships; it has taught them to be rude, to demand their "right" to be constantly entertained without any effort on their part.

Consequently, many people in our society live vicariously. They tune into Walkmans instead of learning to play the piano, escape into pulp literature instead of conversing. They don't experience art or nature, but

6. Graeme Hunter, "Evil: Back in Bad Company," *First Things* 41 (March 1994): 40.

simply take a photograph and walk on. Joey Horstman describes this crudely to shock us into paying attention to, and doing something about, the destructiveness of it all.

> Modern technology and media have proved to be Valium for our leisure time. They have turned the United States into a nation of spectators, more eager to watch life than to participate in it. We want our art, for instance, to provide distraction rather than require concentration, asking it for either escape or knee-jerk political messages. We want shock or sleep. Period. . . .
>
> Perhaps Jean Baudrillard is close to the truth after all when he characterizes ours as the age of simulation. For just as shopping malls simulate the great outdoors, replacing sun and trees with fluorescent lights and green plastic "plants," we simulate danger with amusement-park rides, friends or enemies with talk-radio hosts, rebellion with torn jeans and black boots, sex with lewd phone conversations, revolution with improved fabric softeners, and freedom with the newest panty liner. We simulate real life by eliminating risk and commitment, and end up mistaking what is real for what is only artificial. We exist, that is, encased in a giant cultural condom.[7]

This vicariousness is highly subjective. Everything is directed to the self; one's own ego determines the value of everything. There is little sense of an objective world that offers us gifts to be appreciated as undeserved treasures and of an objective God whose creative grace invites our response.

Recently Myron and I spent my birthday at the Portland zoo, which, among other wonders, features an extraordinary glass house of African birds. In my wheelchair I sat astounded by the birds of many shapes and colors and habits. Because of my visual handicaps, Myron pointed out to me various things that I couldn't see and helped me locate what I couldn't find. We tried to share with others our interest in what we were seeing and hearing, but all sorts of people walked into the building, spent two minutes, and hurried out. They missed everything that could be caught with a little silence, some reflective waiting, and the sharing of community. But they had "done" the zoo — efficiently.

We can observe the same patterns and habits in some congregations.

7. Joey Earl Horstman, "Channel Too: The Postmodern Yawn," *The Other Side* 29, no. 3 (May-June 1993): 35.

Their services and fellowship times contain little silence, reflective waiting, or community sharing. There is not much sense of an objective God, whose majesty demands our awe-full adoration. Instead, overwhelming subjectivism focuses only on the individual's feelings and needs and not on God's attributes or character. Some subjectivity, of course, is necessary; worship cannot be vital without feelings. The problem arises when emotions predominate in mindless subjectivism and God is lost in the process.

To attract people from our culture, some Christian churches depend upon glitz and spectacle and technological toys, rather than on the strong, substantive declaration of the Word of God and its authoritative revelation for our lives. This tendency is blatantly demonstrated by an emphasis on "Entertainment Evangelism," without a correlative process for nurturing those attracted into deeper discipleship. Our relationship with Christ is not superficial entertainment; rather, it is central to life. How can we be fulfilling the purposes of God when we ignore the need for congruence between means and ends?

For example, at the 1987 Vancouver World's Fair, the Christian pavilion's presentation utilized glitzy double-reversed photography and flashing lasers. When I tried to explain my qualms about the production to an attendant who had asked me how I liked their "show," she protested that it had saved many people. I asked, "Saved by what kind of Christ?" If people are saved by a spectacular Christ, will they find him in the fumbling of their own devotional life or in the humble services of local parishes where pastors and organists make mistakes? Will a glitzy portrayal of Christ nurture in new believers his character of willing suffering and sacrificial obedience? Will it create an awareness of the idolatries of our age and lead to repentance? And does a flashy, hard-rock sound track bring people to a Christ who calls us away from the world's superficiality to deeper reflection and meditation? The exhortation of 2 Timothy 2:15 to handle correctly the word of truth must always be our guide when we choose methods — and the recognition that the Greek word *methodia* is used only twice in the New Testament and both times pejoratively makes us cautious lest any of our methods be those of the Deceiver.

The idolatrous adulation of "famous" Christians corresponds to this concentrated subjectivism and vicarious living. Instead of recognizing the value of their own daily experience of following Jesus, some believers falsely elevate big-name stars or let others do the ministry. As a result, performers of contemporary Christian music and hyped-up speakers and writers are elevated to celebrity status. Christopher Lasch makes clear that this idolatry is not the same as "hero-worship," "which esteems the hero's actions and hopes to emulate them or at least to prove worthy of his example." Celebrities are not heroes; they foster instead narcissistic idealization, spectacle, and passivity.[8]

The danger of such "fame" became apparent to me several years ago when a teenager who had heard me speak at a large youth convention saw me in a store in Portland and begged for my autograph. I asked her why my signature was more valuable than hers. We are all equally significant members of the Body of Christ, are we not? We all have crucial parts to play in the Church's ministry to the world. The Church should be the last place where anyone is thought to be more important than anyone else. Yet sometimes congregations who feature lead musicians and singers are tempted to put them on pedestals, with the result that worshipers simply let them perform and no longer participate in communal singing. Or boomers who are too busy to be committed themselves think they can just hire others to do all the work of the Church.

The God of Competition and the Idolatry of Numbers and Success

Our culture is statistical, and, as previously shown, Technopoly aggravates the tendency. As relationships, entertainment, and even the news become increasingly superficial, society looks for ways to signify success. Lacking any tools to grade quality, we have to measure quantity. Moreover, a capitalistic world must necessarily be competitive. Products must outsell all others in order for corporations to survive. Consequently, success is inherently linked in our contemporary mind-set with winning the competition for numbers.

The danger to the Church is enormous and, strangely, often not obvious. Quality suffers when the main concern is quantity. Once, while reflecting with a group on the triviality of a worship song to which everyone in the group objected, I was shocked by the next comment: "But it must be all right. That kind of song in the worship service draws people

8. Christopher Lasch, *The Culture of Narcissism* (New York: W. W. Norton, 1979), pp. 85-86.

like flies." Indeed, flies are drawn to sugar, but we wouldn't give our children sugar for lunch!

Jesus did not measure success by how many disciples he had, and he warned his disciples that the way is narrow. Second Timothy 3:12 insists that all who desire to live a godly life will be persecuted. How destructive it is to genuine discipleship to measure the success of the Church by the numbers of people attracted rather than by the depth of faith and outreach nurtured!

On the other hand, the danger of these idolatries cannot be used as an excuse not to care for the people in the world around us, not to do all we can to attract them to Christ. That concern, however, must always be guided by the goal of faithfulness rather than of numerical success.

The universal Church is harmed when local churches compete with one another to have the most members.[9] Such competition often causes congregations to gain members merely by "sheep stealing" from other parishes, instead of encouraging all the churches to offer their unique gifts and spirit to the world around them in order to draw those who do not yet believe by their diversity.

The Idolatry of Power

Related to everything else in this chapter and involving other dimensions of the Church's contemporary struggles is the idolatry of power. Persons trained to "demand their rights" want the power to set the agenda for the Church's worship. One blatant example of that was the desecration of the communion host and demolition of a worship service in a New York City Catholic parish by a group called "Act Up" as part of their demand to have homosexual concerns take priority in the Church. Militant feminism's demands for inclusive language sometimes negate any consideration for the true meaning and implications of a text and for the Church's heritage. (I don't excuse the un-Christian patriarchalism or oppression of minorities and the poor in the Church's heritage; rather, I wish to preserve the traditions of the *faithful* Church. See Chapter 5 for further discussion of this subject.)

The idolatry of power is often at the root of many congregations'

---

9. See Os Guinness's comments about the idolatry of numbers and its relationship to the need to be in control in *Dining with the Devil: The Megachurch Movement Flirts with Modernity* (Grand Rapids: Baker Book House, 1993), pp. 49-51.

divisions over the style and format of worship services. The war between "traditionalists" and those who advocate "contemporary" styles often becomes a subtle battle for power instead of a communitarian conversation that could result in a blending of the old and new treasures to be found in the Word and in music.

Often the worship of a congregation is undermined by the power of false accusations and deceptions. "Did you hear that so and so . . . ?" "I've heard that many people don't like this style of worship. . . ." Rumor and the tastes of the public become more important in making planning decisions than the skill and training of qualified theologians, pastors, and musicians.

The Workings of the Powers in the Church

We cannot understand all of these idolatries connected with worship unless we recognize that the factors discussed are symptoms of underlying forces of evil that create the immense influence of our cultural milieu on the Church. Since my future book on the nature of "principalities and powers" as they function in various aspects of society is not yet written, this chapter's brief summary will have to do for now to set the stage for further discussion.

The Bible pictures the principalities and powers as created by God for good (Col. 1:16), but now fallen (Rom. 8:19-22). They were overcome by Christ on the cross (Col. 2:15), but they still must be battled (Eph. 6:10-18). What their nature or essence is the Bible leaves ambiguous. The powers are distinct from angels and sometimes are referred to in supernatural ways (such as "in the heavenly places," Eph. 3:10 and 6:12), but they also are referred to in connection with human beings who put Jesus to death — namely, Herod, Pilate, and Caiaphas (1 Cor. 2:8). Probably the best way to put all these aspects together is to recognize that the (supernatural) powers of evil work through human beings, institutions, laws, forces, rulers, or principalities and turn them from their God-given roles into functioning for evil. The creative purposes of God are thwarted when we allow the powers to work with such evil methods as deception, division, accusation, destruction, or power, or as the god Jesus names Mammon.[10]

---

10. Jacques Ellul identifies these six as the functions of the principalities and powers in *The Subversion of Christianity*, trans. Geoffrey W. Bromiley (Grand Rapids: William B. Eerdmans, 1986), pp. 174-90.

The powers function to turn such things as efficiency, money, or fame into the gods of our lives. These are not true gods, but we make them so, and in this we see the influence of the evil powers. Human institutions were created for good, but God's designs have been distorted, corrupted, turned aside into contrary purposes. Even the Church can become an agent of the powers — and that is why I felt compelled to write this book. The problems in worship we are discussing are not just human problems. Certainly we can recognize the forces of evil at work in the Church when the need to do things as they have always been done causes people to accuse others falsely or to act deceptively, to manipulate people in order to gain power. None of us can think about the powers of evil without repentance, for we all must acknowledge how easily they turn us away from living as followers of Christ.

When we "dumb down" the Church, when we fall prey to the idolatries of Mammon or power, when we allow our culture's sloth or efficiency to control us, we serve the purposes of evil and allow the principalities and powers to pervert God's designs for believers' character growth and for their response to God's gifts in reaching out to a needy world with the genuine gospel.

The powers have been defeated at the cross, but we still must do battle against them. I write this book in the sure hope that Christ already won the victory in the battle for our minds and hearts, but with the awareness that we must be vigilant against the powers and idolatries that weaken the Church.

The Power of Death in the Church

The Bible names death as the "last enemy," defeated in the resurrection. The name *death* signifies all types of destruction, so we will conclude this chapter by considering the sorts of things that are being destroyed when the Church falls prey to the idolatries and habits of our culture. Our society is already demolishing children's minds and their consciences through many educational practices, the media, and the lack of parental guidance and discipline. The "culture" of great literature is effaced by condemnation of its "patriarchy" and the substitution of third-rate "politically correct" literature. Great music of past civilizations is rejected; language is lost in the dumbing down of reading material and the news. Most of all, life is being destroyed by the loss of a sense of human dignity; by present attitudes about the value of children, the handicapped, and the aged; and by the random violence of bored kids with too many guns and too much meaningless and hopeless poverty.

We could catalog many other kinds of societal death, but these suffice as a backdrop to the kinds of destruction that exist in our churches. When we allow our society to force us to "dumb down" the Church, we kill theological training, inhibit the forming of character, prevent appreciation for the rich gifts of the Church's past. Most of all, we miss the infinitely faceted grandeur of God and destroy the awe and wonder that characterized worship before God became only a "buddy" ill-conceived and only subjectively experienced.

It is not too late. The meaning and purpose of the Church certainly aren't lost, and what has been destroyed can be recovered. But it will require diligence, careful theological reflection, new training for musicians and pastors, educating the masses, resetting priorities, and, most of all, building a Christian community strong enough to sustain the necessary efforts.

4. Upside-Down: *Worship as a Subversive Act*

God's gift to his sorrowing creatures is to give them Joy worthy of their destiny.

Johann Sebastian Bach, 1685-1750

I initially planned to title this chapter "Worship as an Alien Act," but early reflections proved this title inaccurate.[1] Worship cannot be alien if we wish to reach out to people in the culture surrounding the Church, and, of course, worship uses cultural forms. Jesus called us to be *in* the world, not alien to it. The first chapter of Part II placed us inside the culture to understand it.

On the other hand, we must not be *of* the world. We must resist the world's temptations and remain outside the culture's idolatries, which the second chapter of Part II sketched. If the Church's worship is faithful, it will eventually be subversive of the culture surrounding it, for God's truth transforms the lives of those nurtured by it. Worship will turn our values, habits, and ideas upside-down as it forms our character; only then will we

---

1. I especially thank William Dyrness of Fuller Theological Seminary for making this clear to me and for the choice of the word *subversive*.

57

be genuinely right-side up eternally. Only then will we know a Joy worthy of our destiny.

We seek in our worship the dialectical balance maintained by the Apostle Paul. Lamin Sanneh emphasizes that Paul's legacy to the Church includes

> this exacting vigilance over the true nature of culture. Christian life is indelibly marked with the stamp of culture, and faithful stewardship includes uttering the prophetic word in culture, and sometimes even against it. Paul was a cultural iconoclast in his defiance of the absolutist tendencies in culture, but he was not a cultural cynic, for in his view God's purposes are mediated through particular cultural streams.[2]

In this chapter we will look at several dialectical tensions that must be held in balance in order for worship's subversive work to be effected. We dare not take any of the poles of these tensions to an extreme, for then we will lose the "in but not of" nature of the Church's place in the culture.

Tradition and Reformation

Tradition, along with its correlative authority, was once one of the strongest sinews that held Western society together. David Wells explains the importance of this cord and some of the factors of its loss as follows:

> Tradition is the process whereby one generation inducts its successor into its accumulated wisdom, lore, and values. The family once served as the chief conduit for this transmission, but the family is now collapsing, not merely because of divorce but as a result of affluence and the innovations of a technological age. . . . [F]ilm and television now provide the sorts of values that were once provided by the family. And public education . . . has also contracted out of this business, pleading that it has an obligation to be value-neutral. So it is that in the new civilization that is emerging, children are lifted away from the older values like anchorless boats on a rising tide.[3]

2. Lamin Sanneh, *Translating the Message: The Missionary Impact on Culture,* American Society of Missiology Series, 13 (Maryknoll, NY: Orbis Books, 1989), p. 46.
3. David F. Wells, *No Place for Truth* (Grand Rapids: William B. Eerdmans, 1993),

In its desire to hold on to the traditions of its faith and to pass them on carefully, the Church is, to some extent, alien to this new civilization.

That alienation is aggravated by three factors new to our time. First of all, for the first time in history, a *world civilization* shapes the modern consciousness (p. 89). U.S. television programs, products, and attitudes are ubiquitous throughout the world. Cultures that lack these things desire them (as I learned in Poland, to my great dismay!). Second, the media, which promote and spread modernization's values, "are so intrusive, so pervasive, so enveloping as to render the *experience* of modernity intense to a degree that is without precedent." Third, due to this global, intensive awareness, "we are seeing on a social scale that is without precedent the mass experimentation with and adoption of the values of modernity" (p. 90). Wells insists that these factors are

> experienced by all in the culture. . . . They have generated enormous power in reshaping the inner psyche of both believers and unbelievers. And precisely because modernization has created an external world in which unbelief seems normal, it has at the same time created a world in which Christian faith is alien. It is the inability to resist this oddness that is now working its havoc on the Christian mind. (p. 91)

The Christian faith has always been odd, and we must emphasize the importance of that dialectical pole. However, when churches take this pole to the extreme — becoming completely alien to the culture in sticking to traditions or celebrating them in ways irrelevant to normal life — then Christians separate themselves from the world in a sectarianism, provincialism, or esoteric gnosticism that prevents ministry to the culture from which they remove themselves.

At the other pole of this dialectic is the need constantly to revitalize the tradition, to express the heritage of the faith in new worship forms that are accessible to the world around the Church. The primary key for holding the two poles of this dialectic together is education — teaching the gifts of the faith tradition to those who do not yet know and understand them and teaching those who love the heritage some new forms in which it can be presented to others.

---

p. 84. Page references to this book in the following paragraphs are given parenthetically in the text.

To accent either pole of this dialectic without the other is to lose them both. To utilize only new worship forms without connections to the past heritage is to isolate only a few years out of the 3,500-year history of the Judeo-Christian tradition. Reformation always returns to and deepens the gifts of the original. On the other hand, without reformation the tradition becomes distorted, stale, or dead — or an idolatry.

Throughout this book, therefore, we will try to balance the two poles of tradition and revitalization, old and new. We will preserve the tradition of faith without letting it become ossified and inaccessible. Simultaneously, we want to participate in the present culture without thereby losing our soul.

Truth and Love

Another necessary dialectical tension in the Church's worship places at opposite poles the demands of truth and love. The pole of truth is essential to keep the Church alive with theological content and depth. The pole of love is necessary to minister to those who need that truth. To cling tenaciously to truth in a way that excludes the uninitiated is to lose love in a gnostic superiority. On the other hand, to be driven only by a marketing analysis of what people "need" is to lose the uniqueness of the Church's truth in a false attempt at love. Going to the extreme at either pole loses both poles entirely. Unloving truth is not true, nor is untruthful marketing love at all.

David Wells is perhaps the strongest present advocate for the pole of truth within this dialectical tension. He rebukes fellow evangelicals for failing to see the danger of many cultural values and insists that many evangelicals "believe in the innocence of modern culture and for that reason exploit it and are exploited by it" (p. 11). Consequently, "they are unable to believe in all of the truth that once characterized . . . Protestant orthodoxy." While admitting its weaknesses, Wells longs for the older orthodoxy that was "driven by a passion for truth," which was "why it could express itself only in theological terms" (p. 12).

Wells's passion for truth needs to be balanced with an equally immense passion for love. He does indeed caution us appropriately to avoid an overly simplistic acceptance of technology that does not recognize the values of the attendant milieu. Moreover, he rightly bemoans the loss of

60

biblical fidelity, which reduces the gospel's subversive power. However, his remarks do not seem to contain enough concern for how that truth can be communicated to the modern generation, which has no context for receiving it. The Church needs careful creativity to find the best means for promulgating the truth and educative processes by which we can train the uninitiated in habits for cherishing it.

Unfortunately, many books that emphasize the pole of love within this dialectic discuss reaching the world outside the Church only in terms of marketing strategy. We must analyze the dangers as well as the benefits of this approach before we consider the genuine love that cares for the spiritual needs of those who do not know Christ.

Combining the dialectic of truth and love with the previous tension of tradition and reformation, Leander Keck, former dean of the divinity school at Yale, points out the danger of a marketing approach that rejects the history of the faith. He finds himself estranged from churches because "confidence in the gospel, and in the grand vision of a Christian humanism, was being abandoned, it often seemed, in favor of either narcissistic spirituality or frenetic activity." He recognizes that the identity and mission of congregations has always been, and must inevitably be, "forged in interaction with their circumstances," but he insists that the idea that "the world sets the agenda" is sheer capitulation. He mourns that in the turbulence of the past decades, the "heritage of precedents — the steely as well as the golden" has been neglected, while "plastic, trendy throwaways were improvised instead." Churches have acted

> like inheritors of an estate who camped in the yard because they neither knew nor cared how to live in the house.
>
> Indeed, some authors of best sellers for the religious market and religious leaders themselves were, in effect, if not in intent, telling the churches not to live in the house. Repeatedly, church people were told that what their forebears had emphasized was of dubious value.[4]

Yet church people are often attracted to the marketers' approach because they genuinely want to serve the world around them and are looking for the best ways.

George Barna, a popular leader of the marketing approach to evan-

4. Leander Keck, *The Church Confident* (Nashville: Abingdon Press, 1993), pp. 16-17.

gelism, emphasizes that the Church must respond to the "felt needs" of the baby boom generation, and his research group continues to pour out analyses of those needs.[5] Their work is useful to help churches understand more deeply cultural values and desires. However, the benefit of knowing those "felt needs" lies not in meeting them by "camping in the yard," but in showing people that real needs lie deeper and that the needs they feel are symptoms of more profound spiritual poverty, which can be better met by learning to "live in the house."

Barna's work is immensely appealing; it is full of love for unbelievers and offers great suggestions for reaching out to the world.[6] However, we must read his work with discernment because of his lack of emphasis on the truth side of the dialectic. For example, Barna insists that we must "shed existing attitudes of piety and solemnness, in favor of attitudes of anticipation, joy and fulfillment."[7] Indeed, the Church should demonstrate more openly its hope and gladness; but the gospel's truth also calls for holiness, piety, repentance, and solemnity. Barna seems to have fallen into the present culture's idolatry of happiness.

Similarly, his emphasis on congregations' finding their "market niche," utilizing the media to sustain numerical growth, demonstrating that they are indeed modern in their proficiency with the latest technological developments, and adapting to the lifestyles of the boomer generation all seem to allow the outside culture too much control over what the Church is and to jeopardize the Church's faithfulness. Barna even subtly suggests that seminaries spend time helping future pastors become more technologically adept — in an age when seminaries lack enough time to overcome the biblical and theological deficiencies of many pastoral candidates. Because much of Barna's work is useful for understanding the culture the Church seeks to reach, it is difficult to notice that many of his suggestions pull clergy away from their primary task — and the essential purpose of the Church.[8] Instead of focusing on the gods of the techno-

---

5. See David Wells's critique of Barna in *God in the Wasteland* (Grand Rapids: William B. Eerdmans, 1994), pp. 72-84.

6. See, e.g., George Barna, *User Friendly Churches: What Christians Need to Know about the Churches People Love to Go To* (Ventura, CA: Regal Books, 1991).

7. George Barna, *The Frog in the Kettle: What Christians Need to Know about Life in the Year 2000* (Ventura, CA: Regal Books, 1990), p. 153.

8. For example, Barna elaborates the following seven steps necessary for utilizing a congregational marketing plan: establish a person as the marketing director; create owner-

logical milieu — efficiency, numerical growth, market control, happiness, technological proficiency, and so forth — the pastor and people should focus instead on how they can truly and lovingly reveal God in the Church and to the world. It seems an idolatrous usurpation of the Holy Spirit's control over the effect of God's Word and over conversion to emphasize, as Barna does, that we should "*specify your target market:* Who *[sic]* are you seeking to impact?"[9] Jesus' parable in Matthew 5:14-16 teaches us that we are to be lights in the world. It is God's business to light us, to set us on the lampstand, and to bring the people into the house. Our only duty is to shine forth with the gospel.

Because some strategies to draw crowds to churches might "dumb down" the faith, Barna actually distinguishes between "the tactics required to develop strong spiritual character" and those needed "to generate numerical growth." He acknowledges that "failure to pursue and achieve balance between those competing but complementary interests leads to an unhealthy church,"[10] but he fails to see that the two sets of tactics compete more than they complement each other.

Douglas Webster is rigorously critical of Barna's approach. He insists that this separation of tactics for numerical and spiritual growth is not just a trivial issue, but one that has both immediate and long-range impact. Does God intend such a deployment of two distinct sets of tactics? Webster wonders if marketing is a "value-free, morally neutral technique that can serve the church" and what the consequences are of allowing people to be consumers.[11]

Webster tries to balance the dialectical poles of truth and love for

---

ship of the plan among key leaders; identify resources and conditions needed to move ahead with the plan; identify resources for the plan's implementation; train leaders in the basics of marketing; hold people accountable for their assignments; implement the entire plan. George Barna, *Marketing the Church: What They Never Taught You about Church Growth* (Colorado Springs, CO: NavPress, 1988), p. 121. What if all the time and resources necessary for this procedure were spent in teaching people the faith, the meaning of worship, and what it means to be the Church — and thereby creating in them such a love of God that it would overflow in welcoming the neighbor?

9. Barna, *Marketing the Church*, p. 102.

10. Barna, *User Friendly Churches*, p. 23.

11. Douglas D. Webster, *Selling Jesus: What's Wrong with Marketing the Church* (Downers Grove, IL: InterVarsity Press, 1992), p. 37. Page references to this book in the following paragraphs are given parenthetically in the text.

persons in our culture, without going to the extremes of marketing approaches. He claims that the Church's approach to the culture is "one of the most important issues facing Christians in America" and asks,

> How do we present Christ to a consumer-oriented, sex-crazed, self-preoccupied, success-focused, technologically sophisticated, light-hearted, entertainment-centered culture? How do we strategize, as Jesus did with the disciples, to distinguish between popular opinion and Spirit-led confession? And how does the confessional church, as a community of Christian disciples, engage the world?
>
> Many respected church consultants are offering straightforward, unambiguous answers. They are promoting strategies that encourage churches to establish a market niche, focus on a target audience, meet a wide range of felt needs, pursue corporate excellence, select a dynamic and personable leader and create a positive, upbeat, exciting atmosphere.
>
> But are the Christian marketers asking the right questions? Is the issue for the American church authenticity *or* attractiveness, integrity *or* excitement? Judging from the answers given, the issue must be "how to create a people flow to your church." Or, what is the easiest, most effective, most efficient way possible to attract people, especially baby boomers, to Jesus Christ? (pp. 20-21)

In response to marketers and strategists who want to make church growth easy, Webster thinks it should be made difficult again (p. 22). He opposes the diligent attention to appeal and accommodation with the countercultural emphasis of Christ's kingdom and puts the quest for relevance into greater tension with faithfulness. He asks how "marketing strategies affect the impact of the gospel, the relevance of Christian proclamation, the integrity of the household of faith and the church's commitment to the whole counsel of God" (p. 23).

The greatest danger of a marketing approach to sharing the gospel with the world around the Church is that it treats people as consumers — perhaps religious consumers, but consumers nonetheless. In *The Culture of Narcissism,* Christopher Lasch describes consumers as "perpetually unsatisfied, restless, anxious, and bored." They have been educated by advertising and a milieu that champions consumption as a way of life into "an unappeasable appetite not only for goods but for new experiences and personal fulfillment." Consumption is expected to provide "the answer to the age-old discontents of loneliness, sickness, weariness, lack of sexual satisfaction," the malaise of boring and meaningless jobs, and "feelings of futility and fatigue." At the same time, "it creates new forms of discontent peculiar to the modern age."[12] Since consumption can never keep its promises to fill the aching void in people's lives, to create congregational members who treat religion as another consumer item is to train them not to appreciate the way in which God really does fill our emptinesses.

Webster outlines four crucial ways in which the costs of an approach that focuses on satisfying the felt needs of religious consumers have been underestimated by church marketers. First, he criticizes suburban, market-driven congregations' isolation. Too often "the expenditure of emotional energy, material resources and personal commitment to meet the high expectations of affluent baby boomers diverts resources from global missions and social justice concerns" (p. 90). Webster's concern parallels my own objection to the church growth movement's emphasis on aiming to reach a market matching the congregation — ethnically, socially, and economically. It seems to me that to create homogeneity in the congregation runs counter to the biblical picture of the early Church as a mixture of classes and races, with concern for each other and for the world. It is difficult in many affluent suburban congregations to discuss God's passion for justice in the world — an issue augmented for me by mission work in Mexico, Madagascar, and Poland. Gone are the days of well-attended and effectively inspiring mission festivals.

Webster's second concern is that the church marketing approach depends

> upon time-pressured, family-focused, career-centered baby boomers to meet consumer demand. As older members — those who were reared with a traditional sense of duty and a generous spirit of giving time and money — retire from duty, boomers will face the stress and strain of meeting unrealistic, self-centered expectations. Will they be able to handle the financial and managerial responsibilities necessary to create a full-service Christian subculture without burning out and dropping out? (p. 90)

One congregation that I served in my freelancing exemplified this problem to a frightening degree as the parish suddenly found itself tens of thousands

12. Christopher Lasch, *The Culture of Narcissism* (New York: W. W. Norton, 1979), p. 72.

of dollars short for its budgetary needs and, at the same time, unable to find anyone to serve as officers in eight key positions on the church council.

Third, Webster notices the reversal of attitudes toward popularity caused by the marketing approach. Whereas in the past Christians rejected popularity for the sake of the gospel, now the gospel is sometimes reduced to popularity. Then, if a church is "more like a religious shopping mall than a household of faith" (p. 91), the fourth problem Webster cites becomes more tyrannical as the parish is held hostage to the desires and self-interests of the consumers. Instead of catering to such narcissism, Webster insists, the Church must demonstrate an alternative that frees believers from themselves (p. 92). All four ways in which the marketers underestimate the destructive costs of their approach show that "giving people simply what they want may satisfy certain felt needs but make it more difficult to give them what they truly need" (p. 100).

Besides, it is doubtful that people attracted to churches attempting to meet their needs will really stay. William Hendricks interviewed several persons who became disillusioned with their churches and left. He observes that boomers who remain uncommitted to institutional churches will continue to hop from one congregation to another over time. He expresses deep skepticism that a market-driven, customer-oriented philosophy will attract people into a particular church to stay. Furthermore, committed Christians often leave to look for more than they are given; they seek truth, reality, and authenticity in worship.[13] They want not just superficial consumerism but the "Joy worthy of their destiny."

Genuine love gives people not what they think they need but what they truly need — though, I hasten to add, love will serve them in a way that can be received. Thus part of the pole of love must be the Church's concern for people caught up against their will in modernity's loss of traditional values or postmodernity's complete nihilism; the church must minister in love to those who long to regain their spiritual heritage. As Jeffrey Sheler reports, "The social critics among us, and the consciences within us, increasingly wonder if we have lost our moral compass and forsaken our spiritual heritage."[14] The extensive poll undergirding Sheler's

13. William D. Hendricks, *Exit Interviews: Revealing Stories of Why People Are Leaving the Church* (Chicago: Moody Press, 1993), especially pp. 257-71.

14. Jeffrey L. Sheler, "Spiritual America," *U.S. News and World Report* 116, no. 13 (4 April 1993): 48.

article reveals that U.S. citizens are uneasy with "the perpetual tension between our religious impulses and our unwavering commitment to a secular society. We profess fidelity to traditional morality yet champion individual freedom and resist religious authoritarianism." This tension can be seen in the ambivalence with which people respond to spiritual values expressed by politicians or in the conflict for many between the comfort they find in familiar religious traditions and the uncertainty they experience in living out that faith in a pluralistic and secular society.[15] Congregations must respond to the pain of these tensions and seize the opportunity to be the Church in ministry to many people looking for resolutions to these conflicts.

In an article that appeared shortly after the death of former President Nixon, William Dean commended Nixon for recognizing in 1968 the spiritual malaise of the United States, the violence and nihilism pervading the whole culture. More recently, Cornel West's *Race Matters* and Zbigniew Brzezinski's *Out of Control* blamed spiritual collapse for social failures. In a 1993 speech, President Clinton connected lawlessness and community/family breakdown to a "great crisis of the spirit that is gripping America today."[16] Dean bemoans this distinctively American "flight from ancestral tradition and from eternal and universal meanings, the unchecked investment in the marketplace and in the individual self."[17] The Church must not be so much in sympathy with the culture that it joins the flight from its tradition and the truth of its faith, but at the same time the Church dare not be so alien that we fail to know and share the suffering of those who recognize the immense spiritual loss in that flight.

The Church brings truth and love together best if it genuinely praises God and consequently nurtures the character formation of people. In worship we celebrate the truths of faith in ways that embrace participants in the love of God. The love of the worshiping community, moreover, reaches out to welcome strangers and to instill in them habits of cherishing truth.

15. Sheler, "Spiritual America," pp. 49-50.

16. William Dean, "What Nixon Knew," *The Christian Century* 111, no. 16 (11 May 1994): 484.

17. Dean, "What Nixon Knew," p. 486.

Social Change and Counterculturalism

We can describe Jesus' way to be in the world but not of the world with the dialectical poles of social change and countercultural separation. As with tensions previously discussed, both poles in this one also are vitally necessary, and, again, both poles are lost if either one of them is taken to too great an extreme. The destructive extreme on the social change side is to think that by human efforts we can bring God's Kingdom to earth. Such a messiah complex leads to false pride. We forget that God is the sovereign Lord of the cosmos and that this world is a sinful, broken place, influenced thoroughly by evil powers. As Keck insists, mainline churches "must free themselves from the notion that they have a God-given responsibility for society, and instead claim the freedom to become influential participants in society by being first of all accountable to the gospel."[18] That accountability requires the countercultural pole, which recognizes that we are merely agents to accomplish God's purposes of social change and that Christ has already defeated the powers and will someday bring that triumph to completion.

The destructive extreme at the countercultural pole has already been discussed to some extent in our recognition that the Church dare not be either so alien as to be inaccessible to those still outside it or uncaring about the world's great suffering. Furthermore, when Christians overaccentuate their distinction from the culture surrounding them, they wind up demonizing the world and pridefully thinking that they are not part of its sinful fallenness.

Martin Luther (and Augustine before him) kept this dialectical tension well in balance by means of his formulation of the doctrine of two kingdoms. This doctrine, properly understood, affirms the necessary dialectic of loyalty to society and to the Kingdom of God. Thereby, it provides the Church, as Keck explains, with "possible modes of having a positive influence in society by what the church does and says week in and week out, for it is by patient and persistent pursuit of the ordinary that attitudes are formed and understandings are matured."[19] The doctrine thus has enormous consequences for worship. Worship is the unique praise to God by the countercultural community that equips that community with a

18. Keck, *The Church Confident*, p. 79.
19. Keck, *The Church Confident*, p. 85.

sufficiently deep sense of itself in relation to God that it can go from its worship into the world to effect social change.

Furthermore, God's revelation, conveyed in worship through hymns, sermons, and liturgies, unmasks our illusions about ourselves. It exposes our pride, our individualism, our self-centeredness — in short, our sin. But worship also offers forgiveness, healing, transformation, motivation, and courage to work in the world for God's justice and peace — in short, salvation in its largest sense.

Talking of sin and forgiveness certainly runs counter to the present culture, but the recognition of each and both together is the great gift of the Church's worship to our world's self-understanding. Recognizing the potency of sin and evil but also knowing profoundly the greater power of God's love and mercy frees believers to work for social change without flagging in zeal.

Thought and Feeling

Writing the last section about the pole of social change and its extreme in a destructive pride rebuked me. In the face of cultural "dumbing down," I easily get a messiah complex trying to rescue minds. It disturbs me fiercely that so few people seem to think, and it does not seem possible at this point to stand against the technological tide, to counteract the deleterious effects of our overly subjectivized and trivialized culture. I need worship to put me in my place under the one and only Messiah and to remind me to look for God's methods to maintain the pole of objective thought in our subjectivist society.

The Church cannot save the culture — but Christians could be the best thinkers in the world. Because our relationship with God frees us from having to justify our own existence, we do not have to prove our importance, fit in with our peers, mimic the politically correct, or think according to the current ideologies or idolatries. Our minds are captive only to Christ's lordship; the Holy Spirit empowers us to use the brains God created as well as possible.

Because a mind formed by God's truth comprehends things differently from the contemporary secular mind, we must also recognize the kinds of ideologies that affect the intellectuals of our culture. Anthony Ugolnik summarizes as follows what we have previously discussed about the postmodern mind-set:

Deconstructionist analysis and an enshrined relativism make of every phenomenon but a ghostly apparition, dependent upon the interpreter for meaning. . . . The only certainty in this plastic process is the critic, endowed with the empowering insight to realize that all meaning (except, of course, that which the critic discerns) is a chimera. Nothing could be more despotic than this "democracy of meaning," for in it the Western critic controls the process by which meaning itself is to be discerned. The apostles of "diversity" control the processes by which thought itself is to be judged as "valid." Thus Western secular intellectuals use the mind in much the same way as the Western news media use the camera: selectively, and with the conviction that the tool confers existence itself upon that on which it focuses.[20]

Against such ideologically controlled thought and loss of meaning, Christian worship proclaims the objective truth of the gospel and genuine freedom of thought. Moreover, worship trains its participants in good habits of thinking and reveals a cosmos large enough to ask good questions. Holding up the absolute of God and God's revelation, the Church offers believers a moral compass, a story in which to place their own, a heritage in which to find foundation.

The extreme of the pole of sound thinking in this dialectical tension, however, is for the Church to be only cerebral. The overemphasis on subjectivism evident in some worship services has arisen as a reaction to the cold objectivity of past generations of believers. We Lutherans joke that we can't be otherwise since we are Scandinavian or German, but in his faith Luther himself experienced profound Joy, a glad response to the objective truth of God's grace and love.

The subjective extreme is to depend upon feelings for faith, to let the expression of feelings dominate worship in ways that focus on us instead of on the God we gather to worship. Since feelings are so easily swayed by the circumstances of the moment, they cannot be reliable guides for knowing God. Yet they are important for our response to God and cannot be repressed, ignored, or forced.

Perhaps I overemphasize the thought side of the dialectic, but I do so because my observations reveal that many churches are not aware of the dangers of the super-subjectivism of the present culture. In attempting

20. Anthony Ugolnik, "Living at the Borders: Eastern Orthodoxy and World Disorder," *First Things* 34 (June/July 1993): 16.

to enliven the Church's worship, many try to spice it up with new enthusiasm, engineered with the proper techniques. As Wells rightly insists, that is to apply modernity's solution to a problem that modernity caused. Instead of techniques of revival, the Church needs genuine reformation.[21] We cannot force people to be enthusiastic by insisting that they produce the requisite feelings of happiness, but giving them God's objective truth will lead to subjective responses of gladness and Joy.

Wells outlines the perils of hypersubjectivity by showing that modernity

> obliges us to psychologize life, to look to the states and vagaries of the self for the reality that was once external. . . . [T]his shift from the objective to the subjective, this new fascination with the self, is invariably inimical to biblical and historical faith. Robert Nisbet has argued that this self-absorption, which has been passed off by many as the very essence of evangelical faith, is in fact one of the most telling indications of our cultural decay. He quotes Goethe's comment that "ages which are regressive and in process of dissolution are always subjective, whereas the trend in all progressive epochs is objective."
>
> The subjective obsession . . . [whether] in religious dress . . . [or] in dress that is quite irreligious . . . exhibits the same underlying mentality, the same habits of mind, the same assumptions that reality can be accessed only through the self (and by intuition rather than by thought), the same belief that we can attain virtually unlimited personal progress if only we can tap into our own hidden resources. . . .
>
> [In contrast, the Protestant Reformers] maintained a deep reserve about the self, about the reliability of human reasoning . . . , about human feelings and perceptions. . . . The Reformers held that human beings should be loved but, because they are sinners, they ought not to be blindly trusted. And they granted that personal experience is powerful because it is intense, but they insisted that we should not allow this power to delude us into thinking that experience is always right.[22]

As the following chapter explicates, experience does not always give us truth and knowledge of God. Feelings do not accurately gauge God's involvement in our lives. But feelings are important responses to that

---

21. Wells, *No Place for Truth*, p. 296.
22. Wells, *No Place for Truth*, pp. 144-45.

involvement, so we dare not lose that pole of the thought-feeling dialectic, as the Church often has and does.

We must avoid the dangers both of intellectualism and of emotionalism. To focus on the mind alone won't engage people's will and heart so that they act on what they know. To focus exclusively on training the emotions encourages faith without substance. Genuine worship corrects both extremes, for in it, as Welton Gaddy affirms, "God is to be loved and honored by all of one's being."[23]

Christians can help society recognize the danger of its loss of reasoned discourse in the all-consuming ubiquity of entertainment. By offering worship that educates instead of entertains, that uplifts and transforms through the renewing of the mind (Rom. 12:2), the Church exposes the meaninglessness of our present culture. In his conclusion of *Amusing Ourselves to Death,* Postman summons Huxley again for help with the immense problems he has explicated. He insists that Huxley "was trying to tell us that what afflicted the people in *Brave New World* was not that they were laughing instead of thinking, but that they did not know what they were laughing about and why they had stopped thinking."[24]

By maintaining a vital, balanced dialectic of thought and feelings, the Church displays the shallowness or emptiness of our culture's laughter and trains people in habits for thinking. Genuine worship does, indeed, teach people the depth of truth and enables them to laugh freely with a "Joy worthy of their destiny."

How do we discover and convey that Joy? What does genuine worship mean? Keeping in mind what we have discussed in this chapter about the Church's necessary dialectical balances and in previous chapters about the culture surrounding the Church and the idolatries of that society, we turn in the next part of this book to the specific culture of the Church's worship. What special gifts does that worship have to offer its own participants and to persons in the larger culture?

23. C. Welton Gaddy, *The Gift of Worship* (Nashville: Broadman Press, 1992), p. 67.
24. Neil Postman, *Amusing Ourselves to Death* (New York: Viking Penguin, 1985), p. 163.

PART III

The Culture *of* Worship

5. *God as the Center of Worship: Who Is Worship For?*

Too late have I loved You, O Beauty so ancient, O Beauty so new,
    too late have I loved You!
You were within me but I was outside myself, and I sought You there!
In my weakness I ran after the beauty of the things You have made.
You were with me, and I was not with You.
The things You have made kept me from You —
    the things which would have no being unless they existed in You!

You have called, You have cried out, and You have pierced my deafness.
You have radiated forth, and have shined out brightly,
    and You have dispelled my blindness.
You have sent forth Your fragrance, and I have breathed it in,
    and I long for You.
I have tasted You, and I hunger and thirst for You.
You have touched me, and I ardently desire Your peace.

                                        Augustine of Hippo, 354-430

I apologize for the bad grammar of this chapter's title, but when it is phrased properly the key question loses its punch. The questions "For whom is worship?" and "Worship is for whom?" make God the object of a preposition. The main point of this chapter is that in genuine worship God is the subject — and we are not — so I want to leave the question with its grammatically improper nominative "Who." Augustine's poem makes clear this most crucial criterion for assessing our worship: True worship arises because God calls us. As an echo, our worship directed to God is a gift in response to his[1] gifts. As C. Welton Gaddy details, *"Worship is a gift between lovers who keep on giving to each other."*[2]

God as the Subject of Worship

It is absolutely essential that the Church keep God as the subject of worship since to be Christian means to believe that the God revealed in Jesus Christ is everything to us — Creator, Provider, and Sustainer; Deliverer, Redeemer, and Lord; Sanctifier, Inspirer, and Empowerer. Friendship, instruction, and other aspects of the gathered community are important, but we lose our reason for being if we do not constantly remember that God has called us to be his people and that our ability to respond to that call in worship and life is totally the gift of God's grace.

We who live by the name *Christian* are those rescued from ourselves by the salvation wrought by Jesus. Since salvation is entirely God's gift and not deserved or earned, Christian worship above all makes clear who is the giver of that and every other gift and challenges the world to respond to who he is.

The word *worship* comes from the Old English roots *weorth,* meaning "honor" and "worthiness," and *scipe,* signifying "to create." Of course, we

---

1. Out of my concern to reach the widest audience possible and in keeping with many arguments, especially those of Elizabeth Achtemeier, for retaining the continuity of the Church's heritage, I have chosen in this book to refer to God with the masculine pronouns *he, his,* and *him.* I recognize that these pronouns are inadequate, for God is neither masculine nor feminine, but more than all our words can ever connote (see the conclusion of this chapter for further discussion of this issue). I apologize to anyone who might be offended by my word choices and pray that you will accept my decision to use our inadequate language as carefully as possible for many kinds of people.

2. C. Welton Gaddy, *The Gift of Worship* (Nashville: Broadman Press, 1992), p. xi. Page references to this book in the next two sections of this chapter are given parenthetically in the text.

cannot "create" God's honor because it is inherently God's, but we do devise ways to honor God that bespeak his worthiness, all the while recognizing that our attempts are inadequate, that we will never duly laud the Trinity until we join the saints and angels in perfectly glorifying God forever.

It seems unnecessary to spend time emphasizing that God calls and enables us to worship — that point is made clearly and often by the best liturgical scholars.[3] However, our sketch in Chapter 2 of significant factors in the contemporary milieu highlights how difficult it is to keep God as the subject of worship in the present narcissistic and subjectivized culture.

One example immediately comes to mind. In an Easter extravaganza at a large worship center in a small city, a man entered on a live donkey, representing Jesus' entry into Jerusalem on Palm Sunday. After the equally dramatic presentation of other Holy Week events, the massive choir ended the program with an exultant rendition of praise anthems. However, the biblical emphasis that "the glory of the Lord shall be revealed" had been changed to how "we shall see" his glory. This is not nitpicking, for the same inversion characterized all the worship choruses that day. The focus was on us, instead of on God and what he reveals. Such worship fosters the basic perspective that faith depends on how well we notice God's glory, rather than on the gift of God's revelation that God's grace enables us to receive.

By myriads of means we can keep God as the subject of our worship. The Church's historic liturgy models God-centeredness powerfully — starting with a prelude to offer worshipers opportunity to move away from the distractions of their workday or family-life worlds and into the presence of God. Almost any musical style could be used as long as it is conducive to letting God be the subject. Chorale preludes that remind worshipers of

3. James F. White, in *Introduction to Christian Worship* (rev. ed. [Nashville: Abingdon Press, 1990], pp. 25-30), chronicles the history of worship definitions that emphasize the action of God. Particularly he cites Lutheran Peter Brunner's use of the German word *Gottesdienst,* which connotes both God's service to humans and humans' service to God. However, as White notes, for Brunner the duality of worship "is overshadowed by a single focus, the activity of God both in self giving to us and also in prompting our response to God's gifts" (p. 27). See also Roger D. Pittelko, "Worship and the Community of Faith," *Lutheran Worship: History and Practice,* ed. Fred L. Precht (St. Louis: Concordia Publishing House, 1993), pp. 44-57, and Robert Webber, "The Divine Action in Worship," *Worship Leader* 1, no. 3 (June/July 1992): 7 and 49.

hymns about God are especially effective at nudging an awareness of his presence. The prelude's intent to point the way to God parallels a Quaker exercise known as "centering." As Gaddy points out, Quakers gathering for worship spend time "to get their entire beings focused on God. Each worshiper makes an effort to bring together all emotions, thoughts, and needs and to center them on the Divine Being" (p. 99).

The liturgical invocation beginning worship (often after an opening hymn) again makes God the subject. The proclamation that we are here "in the name of the Father, and of the Son, and of the Holy Spirit" reminds us that the triune God now calls us together to worship him. Only in God's name — that is, in God's character of constant grace — is any worship possible.

Some congregations are replacing the invocation with a casual greeting by the pastor or priest in a false attempt to create "community" and make worshipers feel comfortable. I agree that we must recover the depth of community that formerly characterized the Church, but there are much better ways to do it than to lose the God-centeredness of worship.[4]

It is surely important for the clergy to be friendly with the parish, rather than austere and distant as many pastors once were — but the pendulum has now swung so far in the opposite direction that many congregations seem to have become the private cult of a charismatic leader. I'm stating the extreme case here, but it is because I fear the subtle replacement of the mystery of the Trinity with the pastor's personality in initiating worship. It is almost as if the priest invites us into his living room instead of God welcoming us into his presence. I suggest that a pastoral greeting and the necessary announcements be made first to establish the community and that then the turn into actual worship be decisively made by urging the congregation to let the prelude lead them into God's presence or by a statement like, "Now we give all our attention to the God who has called us here. In the name of. . . ."

Many feminists demand that the Church change the traditional trinitarian formulation of "Father, Son, and Holy Spirit" and say instead "Creator, Redeemer, Sanctifier," but these words signify God's functions and do not name the three persons who unfathomably are yet one. Cogent arguments have been made by many for retaining both the continuity of

4. For ideas, see my book *The Hilarity of Community* (Grand Rapids: William B. Eerdmans, 1992).

the Church's heritage and the biblical language by which God names himself to invoke God's presence. To do so does not foster patriarchalism if the congregation is taught well what the faithful Church has always meant by those words. Martin Luther suggested that whenever we hear the trinitarian invocation we might cross ourselves and remember our baptismal covenant. In those words we were immersed into the 2,000-year-old community of the followers of Jesus. Those words unite us with Christians throughout all time and space.

Many other pieces of a worship service can work to keep God the subject. I especially love the set of liturgical lines, "Glory to you, O Lord" and "Praise to you, O Christ," before and after the Gospel reading. The first line prepares our hearts and minds for the first climax of the service, the words and deeds of Jesus himself. While we sing this line with great gusto, we leap to our feet to exalt Christ and say, "You are honored, Lord! Come to us now and teach us. Tell us again what you have done for us. What a great gift that you come to us this way!" The second line recognizes that what we have just heard is life-changing because Christ, the Word, has met us in the Scripture that testifies of him. "You are worthy of praise, Christ, for you are indeed God in the flesh, and you have come to us in this revelation of truth for our lives." When such lines in the liturgy are well taught, the refrains open our minds to receive the Gospel as the presence of Jesus Christ. He is there to draw us to worship and thoroughly to change our lives by his Word.

If parishes do not use these responses, what other appropriate liturgical rituals might be employed to highlight God's presence in the Word? What symbols convey, and thus heighten, worship participants' anticipation of the encounter with God in the Scriptures? Some churches remember Jewish customs of decorating and unveiling Torah scrolls and stage a Gospel procession. The Orthodox complete this with incense censors, elaborate vestments, and chants.

The accumulation of all such liturgical lines and rituals creates a powerful environment of God-centeredness. Also, even pre-reading children learn to recognize God's presence in symbolic actions and can participate if weekly repetition allows them to memorize liturgical responses. Moreover, this aura is amplified by other elements of the worship milieu, such as the majesty of an organ, symbols on banners and chancel furniture, stained-glass windows, bread and wine, statues and crosses. All of these work together to create the sense that God, who is the subject of what we do, is in this place in special ways. His grace enables us to respond to him with daily lives of total worship.

God as the Object of Worship

Because God is both subject and object, Christian worship is about offerings or sacrifice. Jesus manifested what worship means in his complete act of sacrifice on the cross (Gaddy, p. xvii). The gifts of worship flow from God the subject and return to God as the object of our reverence. As Gaddy summarizes, "The opportunity (privilege) to worship God is itself a gift from God and specific acts of worship are prompted by other gifts from God — spiritual and material. Conversely, the worship of God consists of offering gifts to God" (p. xv). William Temple brings together this movement from God as the subject to God as the object in this beautiful and comprehensive definition of worship as

> the submission of all our nature to God. It is the quickening of the conscience by His holiness; the nourishment of the mind with His truth; the purifying of imagination by His beauty; the opening of the heart to His love; the surrender of will to His purpose — and all of this gathered up in adoration, the most selfless emotion of which our nature is capable.[5]

We will consider later all the kinds of gifts we can offer to God in our adoring response, but first we must make sure of our priorities and labels.

In reply to the question "For whom is worship?" Gaddy insists, "Worship is for God. Only! The chief aim of worship is to please God — whether by adoration and praise, prayer and proclamation, confessions and offerings, thanksgivings and commitment, or by all of these actions combined." The point of worship is to recognize that "God alone matters" (p. 201). Many battles over worship styles would be eliminated if this answer were kept in mind as the foundational criterion for planning what we do, no matter what forms we use.

Many people advocate turning worship into "seekers' services" or "entertainment evangelism." These attempts to reach out to persons who do not know God are certainly laudable — one would hope that we all look for

---

5. William Temple, *Readings in St. John's Gospel* (London: Macmillan, 1940), p. 68; cited in Gaddy, *The Gift of Worship*, p. xvi.

ways to share our faith — but it is a misnomer to call services "worship" if their purpose is to attract people rather than to adore God. Plans for specific efforts to draw nonbelievers to the Church must be accompanied by definite preparations to move those attracted by such evangelistic rallies into services that actually worship God. The key is providing education for new believers to come to know God and what it means to worship.

The New Testament uses many different words to signify worship. Many of them, like *latreuo,* emphasize the religious rites performed to pay homage to or venerate God.[6] Others, such as *proskuneo,* which means literally "to kiss toward" or "to bow down," focus instead on the expression, by attitude or gestures, of allegiance to or regard for the deity.[7] These words convey a profound sense of humble and loving adoration along with appropriate gestures. Other words highlight bringing offerings,[8] which Gaddy sees as central both in biblical times and now.

The centrality of sacrifice in the First Testament[9] "left no doubt regarding the necessity of giving. Though expressed through different forms and acts, offering remained the central activity in New Testament worship as well." But at some time in the Church's history attitudes shifted. "People began attending worship to receive a blessing rather than to make an offering." This destructive change is intertwined with the relegation of worshipers to a passive role. If they had no demand upon them besides attendance and monetary offerings, the true nature of the gift of worship was lost. "All anticipation related to worship came to center on what could be received from an experience (whether or not the music was inspiring, the lessons were edifying, and the sermon was exciting) rather than on what should be expended during a service."

Gaddy insists, instead, that every act of worship should be understood as part of the Church's offering to God. "Any action that does not meet with that qualification does not deserve to be a part of a worship experience."

6. Johannes P. Louw and Eugene A. Nida, eds., *Greek-English Lexicon of the New Testament Based on Semantic Domains* (New York: United Bible Societies, 1988), vol. 1, pp. 531-34, 53.1-15.

7. Louw and Nida, *Greek-English Lexicon,* pp. 540-41, 53.53-64.

8. Louw and Nida, *Greek-English Lexicon,* pp. 534-35, 53.16-27.

9. I prefer to call the first three-fourths of the Bible the "First Testament" or "Hebrew Scriptures" to avoid our culture's negative connotations of the name "*Old* Testament" and to emphasize both the continuity of the covenants in the Bible with Israel and Christians and the constancy of God's grace for all his people.

All the music, from prelude to postlude, offers to God instrumentalists' talents, "producing sounds that please God and serve the purpose of helping people to worship God" (p. 39). Prayers of thanksgiving, confession, and intercession — whether from individuals in silence or spoken corporately aloud — are presented to God as worshipers' gifts. The sermon is not just the gift of the preacher, nor are choral gifts simply the contribution of the choir, but both involve the offering of themselves by all members of the congregation.

Though at certain worship moments gifts of finances, talents, time, and commitments to God are offered, these cannot take the place of participation in every aspect of the service. Because "the entire act of Christian worship is a gift to God of the entirety of the worshipers' lives," Gaddy insists that

> any potential confusion or alteration in the purpose of Christian worship must be addressed and avoided. A constant temptation toward utilitarianism has to be rejected. To use Christian worship for any purpose other than the glorification of God is to abuse it.
>
> God expects a church to meet for divine worship without ulterior motives. Thus, worship is not convened so that church budgets can be pledged, volunteers for ministry enlisted, programs promoted, attendance goals met, or personal problems solved. Authentic worship takes place only in order to honor God. People gather to worship God in order to give everything to God. (p. 40)

Many theologians follow Kierkegaard in comparing worship to the theater. Whereas many worship services allow congregants to be an audience viewing the pastor and musicians as actors, genuine worship happens when everyone knows that God is the audience. Musicians and pastors are the prompters or coaches or stage managers, but all of us are the actors and all our worship acts are directed to God. And yet, we must add paradoxically, because God is the subject, we always remember that we can only be actors because he acted first.

The Loss of God as the Center of Worship

Many factors, both internal and external, contribute to the loss of God as the subject and object of worship. Among the internal forces is the failure to educate well, to teach those in the Church what we do and why when we worship. In addition, the division or even fragmentation of parishes by worship wars prevents thorough discussion of the goal of the worship over which we fight.

Among the major external factors is the great split occurring in the spiritual mind-set of the present culture. Wade Clark Roof analyzes polarities between the new and the more traditional sides of that immense spiritual gulf on the following four issues.[10] Certainly both poles in each set can be taken to destructive extremes, though we will see that the more traditional or conservative pole is more likely to keep God at the center of worship.

Conception of Self

The new generation seeks self-fulfillment, autonomy, a high degree of independence, and the possibility fully to actualize one's potential. Roof gives the example of a person "so concerned with her own pursuits, she is not sure what to make of a question that asks about obligations to others." Care for one's self takes priority over any other roles or responsibilities. More traditional persons recognize that true fulfillment arises largely out of submission to the divine will. A person at this pole will hold herself in check and not allow too much freedom (p. 119). Of course, this pole carried to an extreme can be destructive of worship if a person sees God as an authoritarian ogre who doesn't allow any enjoyment or self-fulfillment. This chapter will discuss later the question of what kind of God our worship portrays. In the dialectic of autonomy and submission, a healthy recognition of God's loving sovereignty will lead to the worship of "gifts between lovers."

Authority

Correlative to the previous point, the new generation places the locus of authority within the self. They demand freedom from all external constraints in order to be able to develop their full potential. A person at this

10. Wade Clark Roof, *A Generation of Seekers* (San Francisco: Harper, 1993). Page references to this book in this section are given parenthetically in the text.

pole understands spirituality in terms of a journey or quest as she seeks truth and meaning within herself. At the other pole "authority rests in an external source: a transcendent God who has saved her through the death and resurrection of Jesus Christ, all of which is revealed in the Bible. We must rely on something more than the fleeting self." Someone at this pole believes that what the Bible teaches is "timeless and objective" (p. 120). Since many people in our culture have lost respect for any authority outside themselves, the Church must carefully explain its worship of God as sovereign over our lives. This aspect of the faith tradition is starkly countercultural, so it is all the more important that the Church translate the truth of God's authority into language that reveals that authority as loving and grace-full.

Meaning Systems

Two different constructions of a meaning system correspond to the two extremes on authority. Roof calls them "mystical" and "theistic," though I prefer to call them "inductive" and "deductive" in order not to confuse modern mysticism with the great mystics of the Church's history. The inductive person wants wholeness and tries by his efforts and out of his own resources to overcome the barriers that separate people from each another and from God and nature. The emphasis in an inductive system is on feelings and life experiences, and thus "explorations" and "journeys" are the means for discovering who one really is. The greatest virtue is being "sensitive and open to [one's] own needs and being open and honest" in order to pick and choose whatever fits one's frame of mind. On the other hand, the theistic or deductive approach centers on belief in God. "God not only influences daily life, but also shapes all of reality and makes life meaningful in some ultimate sense." This kind of meaning system results in loyalty to religious tradition in the face of modern secularity, faithfulness to the covenant with God, and morality rooted in obedience (pp. 120-21).

The opposition of "inductive" meaning focused on the self to a "deductive" mode arising from faith in an absolute God has enormous consequences for worship. Do we worship an objective God, who has revealed himself in his Word, or our own fabrication of God, whom we have constructed out of what fits into our own previously held ideologies? The prevalence of personally constructed meaning systems in modern culture warns the Church of the necessity to scrutinize carefully all that we do in worship to make sure that it reveals God truly. Later in this chapter we will discuss God's nature and our language for God.

Spiritual Styles

The modern quest for harmony results in a spiritual style of letting go of traditions and going with the flow of the culture to blend in with the powers of the universe. A person must free herself from everything, such as guilt or shame or abuse, that is beyond her power to control. At the other pole is a style that takes hold to be firmly in control of what one does in order to have mastery over one's life. A person at this pole sees himself in opposition to the world and stresses personal disciplines such as regular Bible reading and prayer in order to avoid temptations (pp. 121-22). As with all four aspects Roof analyzes, dangers lie at both extremes in spiritual style — at the first pole, going with any flow regardless of its moral and spiritual consequences, and at the other pole, an opposition to the world so intense as to alienate us too much from the culture to be able to relate to persons in it.

These four dichotomies all raise the issue of how, in the midst of a culture moving away from belief in an absolute objective God, the Church can most faithfully let God be the subject and object of our worship. That question is critical, as Roof recognizes, because "virtually all" of the boomers his research group interviewed "see religion less in doctrinal or ecclesiastical terms, and much more in personal meaning terms, and often in vague and generalized moral terms." I am not promoting dead doctrine or narrow denominationalism, but the attitude "It's not so much what you believe, or which religion you follow, it's how you live" (p. 186) entirely misses the point that Christianity means believing in and responding to a God of grace who has revealed himself in objective terms. What we believe is fundamental for how we respond.

Let me explain at this point that when I speak in this book about objective faith, I do not mean merely cold intellectual knowledge. The Word of God carries within itself the power to elicit response, to move the heart and will. The early Lutheran scholar Philip Melanchthon emphasized that the gospel moves us to a faith composed of both "cognitive and affective elements, distinguished yet joined. These elements are *notitia,* 'knowledge,' and *fiducia,* 'trust.'" To know Christ is to be connected to

God's *promise,* and that promise becomes specific in *benefit.* Because the knowledge of God brings with it the "subjective" effect of promise and benefit, it is an *assured* knowledge.[11] I use the word *objective* to accentuate the otherness of this knowledge. We do not manufacture it ourselves, but it is given to us. It is truth proclaimed.

As David Wells declares, "biblical faith is about truth." Since God has revealed himself and narrated his works in the Bible, "it is quite presumptuous for us to say that we have found a better way to hear him (through our own experience) and a better way to find reality (by constructing it within the self)."[12] He summarizes the difference between mind-sets as follows:

> The Christian mind accepts God's pronouncements concerning the meaning of life as the only true measure in that regard; the modern mind rejects such revelation as the figment of a religious imagination.
>
> Today, reality is so privatized and relativized that truth is often understood only in terms of what it means to each person. A pragmatic culture will see *truth* as whatever works for any given person. Such a culture will interpret the statement that Christianity is true to mean simply that Christianity is one way of life that has worked for someone, but that would not be to say that any other way of life might not work just as well for someone else.

Wells compares this relativized conception of truth to the attitude of Elijah or any of the prophets in their encounters with other gods and religions, to Jesus, and to Paul at the Areopagus and concludes, "The reason that they believed in truth in a way that we frequently do not had nothing to do with their parochialism and our relative sophistication but with their understanding of its objectivity and our loss of that understanding."[13]

In the midst of a culture that has lost a sense of objective truth, the Church worships a God who can be objectively known. As the subject of our worship, God draws us to himself by his revelation of himself. We respond with the gift of our praise to the One we know.

11. Michael Aune, "*Lutheran Book of Worship:* Relic or Resource?" *dialog* 33, no. 3 (Summer 1994): 177.

12. David F. Wells, *No Place for Truth* (Grand Rapids: William B. Eerdmans, 1993), p. 184.

13. Wells, *No Place for Truth,* p. 280.

Genuine Praise

In a keynote address on the theme "Declaring God's Praise," James Nestigen of Luther Seminary in St. Paul reminded us of the biblical definition of praise. Based on the liturgical line "O LORD, open Thou my lips," and the response, "And my mouth shall show forth Thy praise," he defined genuine praise as that which comes forth only when God opens our lips. These lines from Psalm 51:15 emphasize the interrelation of God as both subject and object of our worship, for his presence opens our lips to proclaim his glory. We cannot respond to God as the object of our praise unless we first see him, know him, let him be God in our lives. Nestigen protested that "sometimes these days it is hard to distinguish praise from schmooze" and insisted that real praise happens when God becomes God again for us. "Be God to us," we will cry. "Speak your Word so strongly that we can't hear anything else."[13]

I hope churches will continually utilize fresh words and music to praise God, but it worries me that so many new compositions dumb down our perception, knowledge, and adoration of God. A principal cause of such dumbing down is the contemporary confusion of praise with "happiness." Some worship planners and participants think that to praise God is simply to sing upbeat music; consequently, many songs that are called "praise" actually describe the feelings of the believer rather than the character of God. In the extreme, a focus on good feelings distorts the truth of the gospel into a "health, wealth, and victory" therapy. We must recognize this for the idolatry it is. Centering on happiness makes us forget that the world gains redemption not through the Church's glory but through Christ's sacrifice and the suffering of God's people.

As Leander Keck powerfully reminds us, genuine praise of God depends upon truth. It is not just an attitude of appreciation or an emotion of well-being or delight; instead, it acknowledges a superlative quality or deed. Praise does not express our own yearnings or wishes; it responds to something given to us.[14] Thus praise "must contend successfully with

---

13. James Nestigen, keynote address for ELCA Southwest Washington Synod Assembly, May 14, 1994.

14. Leander Keck, *The Church Confident* (Nashville: Abingdon Press, 1993), p. 27. Page references to this book in this section of the chapter are given parenthetically in the text.

alternative impulses, attitudes, and habits of thought. Only so can praising God emancipate us from the secularity that inhabits us." Consequently, to praise the Creator must be recognized as "a discipline, a formative factor in the shape of our lives." Otherwise it becomes "a flight from what we take to be reality, instead of a sustained challenge to it" (p. 29). Genuine praise challenges our secularity and idolatries and narcissism by concentrating, not on our feelings of happiness, but on qualities in God that are truly there, not just there for me (p. 30).

An emphasis on what we "get out" of a worship service — above all, that we feel good about ourselves — displaces the theocentric praise of God with anthropocentric utilitarianism (p. 34). Since the worship of God is an end in itself, "making worship useful destroys it, because this introduces an ulterior motive for praise. And ulterior motives mean manipulation, taking charge of the relationship, thereby turning the relation between Creator and creature upside down" (p. 35).

Instead of trying to force happiness or making the music more upbeat, the Church best renews its praise by gaining a fresh apprehension of God (p. 40). Because we have lacked new visions, we have let modern idolatries reduce God into such an anemic irrelevance that we must entertain people instead of introducing them to God. Keck criticizes the results as follows:

> We have blown up balloons, danced in the aisles, marched behind banners; we have turned to jazz and we have sung ditties whose theological content makes a nursery rhyme sound like Thomas Aquinas. But it is not enough to make things livelier, or set to music our aspirations and agendas. We can do better than that, and we must, for when the truth of God as made actual in Christ and attested in the gospel evokes the truthful praise of God, Christian worship enacts an alternative to the secularism which otherwise deludes us with its promises. (p. 42)

"Praise" that uses only "upbeat" songs can be extremely destructive to worshipers because it denies the reality of doubts concerning God, the hiddenness of God, and the feelings of abandonment by God that cloud believers going through difficult times. I have counseled numerous people whose experience of worship that focused only on happy praise left them with huge feelings of inadequacy. "Why do I feel so discouraged? I know I should praise God, but I just can't," they say. That is because the worship has not dealt with their feelings of guilt, their doubts and fears, their sense of hypocrisy and sinfulness. Many question their faith because they are not able to be as happy as their fellow believers. They can't enter into upbeat worship if their lives are in shambles. Instead of recognizing the inadequacy of worship that teaches only one aspect of our relationship to God, they blame themselves for inadequate faith.

Utilizing the categories of orientation as well-being and disorientation as fragmentation in life, Walter Brueggemann offers this stinging critique of the modern emphasis on happiness and upbeat worship:

> It is my judgment that this action of the church is less an evangelical defiance guided by faith, and much more a frightened, numb denial and deception that does not want to acknowledge or experience the disorientation of life. The reason for such relentless affirmation of orientation seems to come, not from faith, but from the wishful optimism of our culture. Such a denial and cover-up, which I take it to be, is an odd inclination for passionate Bible users, given the large number of psalms that are songs of lament, protest, and complaint about the incoherence that is experienced in the world. At least it is clear that a church that goes on singing "happy songs" in the face of raw reality is doing something very different from what the Bible itself does.[15]

Brueggemann's remarks confirm that churches actually do worship participants a disservice if their praise of God ignores life's harsh realities and God's presence in the midst of them. To be only upbeat is to be unbiblical. In postmodernist escapism, it also ignores the immense suffering of the world.

Closely related to such wishful optimism in worship is the problem that the lyrics of many of the new praise songs are so shallow. Constant repetition of only one attribute of God can lead to profound reflection upon it, as in the gentle choruses from Taizé, but often endless repetitions are only boring failures to create fresh images revealing new aspects of the infinite God or presumptuous rejections of the multiplicity of images found in the Scriptures and in the Church's tradition. To sing over and over again only that God loves us is to miss the truth of God's wrath, the need for our repentance in light of God's justice, and God's mercy and truth in answer to the confusions of a broken and sinful world. Moreover,

---

15. Walter Brueggemann, *The Message of the Psalms: A Theological Commentary*, Augsburg Old Testament Studies (Minneapolis: Augsburg, 1984), pp. 51-52.

mindless refrains about God's love seldom include any elaboration, such as images to tell us how that love is manifested or how we know it.

This same kind of narrowed outlook in worship also occurs if pastors' sermons are based on only one kind of text. We miss "the whole counsel of God" if we neglect various forms of biblical literature, the multiple portraits of God. Worship requires a blend of the infinite attributes of God — focusing appropriately on God's majesty, humility, wrath, grace, hiddenness, ambiguity, love, hate, mercy, creativity, holiness, power, suffering, immanence, transcendence, beauty, glory, and mystery.

The liturgical churches' assigned pericopes lead us into such diversity in our appreciation of God's infinity, but sometimes they abridge a text too much and skip the tough portions of the Scriptures. Also, sometimes assigned texts should be superseded to deal with critical issues of the day and the community. But even then, the issues should not be central; rather, the focus must be on who God is in relation to those issues. The whole point of a sermon is to bring forth God as the subject and object of our praise.

Genuine praise of God involves all our emotions and needs, not by focusing on ourselves, but by proclaiming God's truth and God's attributes and actions on our behalf. Keck complains that all too rarely do worshipers in mainline churches hear "the greatness, the judgment and mercy, freedom and integrity of God brought to bear on the day-to-day. Allusion to God has replaced affirmation and proclamation" (p. 39). Only when we see God as God truly is can we know ourselves aright — and then we can respond with offerings of praise.

Repentance and Lament

Frequently as God reveals himself in all God's truth, our response will be like that of Isaiah, "Woe is me, for I am ruined" (6:5, NASV — Martin Luther translated it, "I am annihilated"). The more we encounter the holy God in our worship, the more we will recognize our utter sinfulness and be driven to repentance. This, too, is an essential part of our praise.

I have heard pastors disparage such hymn lines as "for such a worm as I," and I disagree heartily (and "mindedly"!). I need to know that I am a worm — otherwise I will never experience the incredible freedom and immense Joy of forgiveness. Our culture's emphasis on self-esteem confuses

90

us. We forget that a true sense of ourselves begins with the dialectical interplay of God's infinite grace addressed to our desperate need for it. Then grace sets us free for the most genuine and highest self-esteem.

Some of the best worship gifts are time, silence, and words devoted to repentance within the genuine praise of God. Praise encompassing all of God's character provides a safe haven within which we can face ourselves and acknowledge the truth of our brokenness, rebellions, and idolatries. This is not possible if God is not the subject and object of our praise. If we focus on ourselves, we don't have enough of the truth of God to reveal our inadequacy and alienation.

After worshiping with Christians in Ukraine, Henri Nouwen noted the predominantly penitential nature of Eastern spirituality and its deep recognition of human sinfulness. He exclaims, "There is a great beauty to this spiritual vision because it can show God's splendor and grace in the face of human depravity." The Church in the West has much to learn from our Eastern sisters and brothers, for "the awareness of human sinfulness is hardly existent in the West."[16] My thesis is that we lack such an awareness because we dumb down the truth of God in false efforts to feel better about ourselves. We do not have enough of God — especially the truth of his wrath in the midst of his love — to experience the exhilarating freedom of confessing our sin and the joyous beauty of forgiveness.

Similarly, we need to have enough of God to let us lament. In our present world, in spite of the cultural optimism of the United States, we find ourselves facing the realities of loneliness, unemployment, violence, worldwide political and economic chaos, family disruptions, brokenness and suffering, the fragmentation of postmodern society. Keeping God as the subject and object of our worship enables us to deal with the darkness by lamenting it, by complaining about it. The psalms give us wonderful tools to move from addressing God with pleas, complaints, petitions, and even imprecations to the surprising outcome of praise. Throughout it all, God's presence assures us that we are heard, that something will change — both in ourselves and, through us, in our world.

When in worship we encounter God in all God's fullness, our urgent desperation can be turned to gratitude and a sense of well-being. Walter Brueggemann teaches us through Israel's worship the necessity for laments,

16. Henri J. M. Nouwen, "The Gulf Between East and West," *New Oxford Review* 61, no. 4 (May 1994): 12.

as well as the reasons why contemporary congregations ignore them, in this explication of genuine praise:

> The use of these "psalms of darkness" may be judged by the world to be *acts of unfaith and failure,* but for the trusting community, their use is *an act of bold faith,* albeit a transformed faith. It is an act of bold faith on the one hand, because it insists that the world must be experienced as it really is and not in some pretended way. On the other hand, it is bold because it insists that all such experiences of disorder are a proper subject for discourse with God. There is nothing out of bounds, nothing precluded or inappropriate. Everything properly belongs in this conversation of the heart. To withhold parts of life from that conversation is in fact to withhold part of life from the sovereignty of God. Thus these psalms make the important connection; everything must be *brought to speech,* and everything brought to speech must be *addressed to God,* who is the final reference for all of life. . . .
>
> It is no wonder that the church has intuitively avoided these psalms. They lead us into dangerous acknowledgement of how life really is. They lead us into the presence of God where everything is not polite and civil. They cause us to think unthinkable thoughts and utter unutterable words. Perhaps worst, they lead us away from the comfortable religious claims of "modernity" in which everything is managed and controlled. In our modern experience, but probably also in every successful and affluent culture, it is believed that enough power and knowledge can tame the terror and eliminate the darkness. . . . But our honest experience, both personal and public, attests to the resilience of the darkness, in spite of us. The remarkable thing about Israel is that it did not banish or deny the darkness from its religious enterprise. It embraces the darkness as the very stuff of new life. Indeed, Israel seems to know that new life comes nowhere else.[17]

I have quoted Brueggemann at length because he reveals precisely the shallow fearfulness of some contemporary worship. We avoid life's darknesses because we do not let God be God. We try to control the darkness ourselves, or we must ignore it because our worship does not proclaim God's sovereign control.

I write this as the chief of sinners. The last several years have brought

17. Brueggemann, *The Message of the Psalms,* pp. 51-53.

me one health crisis after another — crippling of a leg and hands, hearing and vision losses, frequent wounds that won't heal, intestinal disfunctions, immunity deficiency, nerve deterioration, cancer. Too easily in the darkness I try to be in control, to manage by exercising enough or taking good care. But when darkness strikes again, my efforts to control it pervert personal worship and make God too small. I need public worship to bring me a holy and merciful God who shows me my sinfulness and yet offers the possibility of repentance and forgiveness. I need worship that lets me lament and find in that cry God's caring presence. I need an assembly of people who ask God to be God in their lives and thereby proclaim God's power, faithfulness, and gracious healing.

To praise God in the midst of suffering or confusion is to declare, in Keck's phrase, the ultimate "Nevertheless!" It is to cling to faith in a God of grace despite apparent evidence to the contrary.

Worship Styles

When we agree that God must be the subject and object of our worship, we discover that the bitter war between "traditional" and "contemporary" styles misses the real issue. Both can easily become idolatrous. Many defenders of traditional worship pridefully insist that the historic liturgy of the Church is the only way to do it right, while their counterparts advocating contemporary worship styles often try to control God and convert people by their own efforts. Neither pride nor presumption can inhabit praise; both prevent God from being the subject and object of our worship.

Enthusiasts for contemporary worship are right in seeking to reach out to persons in the culture around us and in rejecting tradition that has grown stale. Those who value the Church's worship heritage are right to question the faithfulness and integrity of many contemporary worship forms and to seek a noticeable difference in worship that underscores the Church's countercultural emphasis. Only in a dialectical tension of tradition and reformation can we ask better questions to insure that worship is consistent with the nature of God as revealed in the Scriptures and in the person of Jesus Christ.

Debates about worship style usually arise because, in their desire to reach out to the culture surrounding us, parishes are striving to make worship meaningful to that society. Gaddy insists that this approach asks the wrong questions.

> Occasionally I am asked to speak or to write on the subject of how to make worship meaningful. I am troubled by assumptions behind those requests. First is the conviction that generally worship is uninteresting. Second is the suggestion that worship can be made interesting by human ingenuity and creativity. Both ideas are as mistaken as they are common.
>
> I am always pleased to address the topic of meaningful worship. However, I work with the assumption that worship is meaningful. To explore meaningful worship is to examine worship. Corporate experiences claimed as worship and complained about because of their lack of meaning are misnomers. Authentic worship is always meaningful worship.
>
> Quests for meaning in worship are best served by discovering how to worship with integrity. Determining the nature of true worship is much more important than exploring the ways humans can bring novelty to worship.[18]

Gaddy then sketches several principles, adherence to which is necessary for genuine worship. He insists that a concern for meaning will be well served if we start with a study of these principles. Worship must center on God, glorify Christ, involve people, express praise, communicate the truth of the Bible, encourage faith, promise redemption, reflect the incarnation, build up the Church, instill vision, make an offering, nurture communion, and evoke an "Amen" (pp. 200-20). We will explore many of these principles in later chapters of this book, even as we have seen in this chapter the truth of Gaddy's insistence that meaningful worship centers on God and expresses praise.

Worship style isn't really the primary issue that it has become. Instead of getting caught up in the traditional-contemporary debate, we must always ask whether a style is really conveying the presence, the self-giving of God. Catholic campus chaplain Michael Hunt has surveyed student participants for many years and asserts that, when asked why they attend mass, they almost unanimously respond, "God." Since Catholics don't "publish sermon topics or emphasize guest speakers" and "the music is

---

18. Gaddy, *The Gift of Worship*, p. 200. Page references to this book in the rest of this chapter are given parenthetically in the text.

often very routine," there is "little ambiguity about the point of the mass. It is God."[19]

The Kind of God We Worship

At this point I must insert a word of caution because, as we seek to keep God the subject and object of our worship, it is critical to think through carefully the kind of God we portray. A vivid early scene in "Brother Sun, Sister Moon," a movie about Francis of Assisi, shows how, before he came to a genuine faith in Jesus, he looked at the dominical crucifix and the priest's trappings and saw only a God of cruelty and abusive power. Such images of God lead to correlative responses. For example, sociological studies have shown that in more fundamentalistic churches that accentuate a rigidly authoritarian picture of God and hierarchies of power, there is much hidden family abuse.

What kind of God do our worship practices portray? Is God shown chiefly in judgment or in grace, in power or in mercy? Does our God come to us primarily in law or gospel, in rules or in compassion? Are the humility and servanthood of Jesus portrayed truthfully so that worshipers strive to become like him, willingly offering themselves in service to God and others in all of life?

David Wells complains of contemporary churches that lose "the traditional vision of God as holy." Divorced from God's holiness,

> grace is merely empty rhetoric, pious window dressing for the modern technique by which sinners work out their own salvation[,] . . . our gospel becomes indistinguishable from any of a host of alternative self-help doctrines[,] . . . our public morality is reduced to little more than an accumulation of trade-offs between competing private inter-ests[,] . . . our worship becomes mere entertainment.[20]

Certainly we have all observed such destructive results from that divorce.

On the other hand, holiness cannot be truthfully portrayed without the accompanying dialectic of gracious love. In fact, most weaknesses of

19. Michael J. Hunt, C.S.P., *College Catholics: A New Counter-Culture* (New York: Paulist Press, 1993), pp. 34-35.

20. Wells, *No Place for Truth,* p. 300.

95

worship arise when we forget the constant dialectics of God's character. Holiness without love incites terror; love without holiness invites libertinism. Worship that focuses on God's transcendence without God's immanence becomes austere and inaccessible; worship that stresses God's immanence without God's transcendence leads to irreverent coziness.

As Gaddy emphasizes, "Every word and act in worship constitutes a witness about God as well as an offering to God. The manner in which God is worshiped is a message about how God is perceived, how God's holiness is to be reverenced and approached." We want, therefore, to give God not only "what is best, what God deserves, what is consistent with God's nature," but also "that which most accurately reveals the nature of God to others. People will have difficulty understanding that God's Being requires reverence if they know worship services that are not reverent." On the hand, if we offer that reverence "perfunctorily [or if] hymns are sung routinely," if we neglect the confession of sins or of faith, then "the message conveyed is that God doesn't care, that God is not concerned with the integrity of worship" (p. 186).

One of the best aids to creating worship that portrays the dialectical attributes of God, that praises the totality of God's being, is the liturgical year.[21] Beginning in Advent's season of repentance, which confronts us with our desperate need for a Messiah, God comes to us in mercy, in sovereignty over time, and with the promise that Christ will come again. The Christmas and Epiphany seasons convey God's grace, tenderness, and splendor. Lent reveals the faithfulness of God's suffering on our behalf through the immensity of Christ's sacrifice. Easter demonstrates God's power and victory over the principalities and powers. Pentecost brings us the mystery and wonder of God at work in us. The nonfestival half of the Church year then celebrates many other attributes and actions of God in its focus on segments of Christ's teaching and life.

In the calendar's ordering, Scripture readings and sermons, liturgical responses and art, hymns and instrumental pieces all contribute to displaying the whole character of God. A great gift of the Church's musical heritage is that so many excellent pieces were composed specifically to convey the truths of these different seasons. The Church needs new com-

---

21. See White, "The Language of Time," in *Introduction to Christian Worship*, pp. 52-87, and James L. Brauer, "The Church Year," *Lutheran Worship: History and Practice*, ed. Fred L. Precht (St. Louis: Concordia Publishing House, 1993), pp. 146-74.

positions that display more thoroughly the multiple aspects of God's character — and our Church year heritage could guide composers and poets well.

Mystery, Awe, and Reverence

With brilliant insight, Martin Luther began each of his explanations of the Ten Commandments with the phrase, "we should fear and love God that. . . ." This wonderful phrase captures so well the dialectic of human beings' relationship with God. Our alienation from God necessitates fear, a truthful recognition of how much we deserve God's wrath — but immediately we also see the opposite pole, that God instead deals with us in gracious love and invites us to respond in love. We dare not lose either side of this dialectic. If we forget God's wrath, we make grace cheap. Without God's loving mercy, grace becomes far too expensive. Only in the constant pulling of both poles do we understand the costliness of grace in the suffering of God. Only in that dialectical tension can we really experience the genuine "fear and love" of God, which is more than awe and reverence, but less than terror. Then we will bow before the mystery and never treat our relationship to God with flippancy.

This sense of God's greatness, fullness, and mystery is often missing in modern worship. Certainly the course of time gives place for all kinds of worship moods and attitudes, for God is an infinitely diverse God. But I am disturbed that the awesomeness of God is repeatedly swallowed up by coziness. Not only the Church but God himself is dumbed down, made too small, trivialized.

Martin Marty addressed this subject profoundly in a lecture entitled "Holy Ground, Sacred Sound." He warns that we easily lose our sense of awe through "chuminess" or "chattiness," and he criticizes the reduction of "sacred sound" to marketing. Referring to Rudolf Otto's phrase *mysterium tremendum et fascinans* in *The Idea of the Holy*,[22] Marty offers several images for response to the sacred, which is often associated, for example, with shattering light. We are blinded by the holy. Even angels are usually pictured with large sleeves to shield against the light. Taking off his shoes,

22. See Rudolf Otto, *The Idea of the Holy*, trans. John W. Harvey (London: Oxford University Press, 1923), pp. 12-40.

Moses at the burning bush shows us the need for a sense of holy ground, a space for the sacred to break through — and it does, sometimes even in our agonies. Marty highlights the necessity for sacred sounds to convey a sense of the holy and chided those who complain, "Don't let the organ interrupt my trivial line of thought."

Because we resist salvation and won't let grace really be entirely grace without our synergistic human efforts, we need to focus in our worship on more than God's incarnation and humanity. We must also be aware of God's otherness, and for that we require a sense of holy ground and sacred sound. The Other addresses us in an alien voice — not to terrify, as we have already noted, but as an Other evoking the dialectical response of fear and love.

For this reason, Marty insists, worship cannot be determined by the market. The marketing approach, of course, draws crowds, but it is "so fully adapted to the not-yet-born-again" that worship becomes "measured by the aesthetics and experience of those who don't yet know why we should shudder."

Our culture of technopoly and unlimited choice, as outlined in Chapter 2, rejects awe because it involves the reduction of the human, the purging of our pride. In a society that exalts the individual, we don't want to be reduced, to be vulnerable to God. Instead, we want to be in control. Marty suggests that one of the gifts of organ music is that we cannot be in control (which I take to mean that the organ ushers us into the presence of God and an awareness of various divine attributes by means of its diverse sounds — majestic, mysterious, massive, ethereal, thundering, pastoral, trumpeting, meditative, plaintive, jubilant). The Church's organ repertoire can convey all sorts of aspects of God — the horror of the Passion, the glory of the Resurrection, the nothingness of suffering, the exhilaration of Joy. Certainly there is no single way to be in the range of awe, but, as Marty stresses, "there'd better be awe."[23]

Language for God

I remember having a lively debate with my high school freshman English teacher because I wanted to use the word *awe-full* instead of *awful* in a

---

23. Martin E. Marty, "Holy Ground, Sacred Sound," lecture given at Zion Lutheran Church, Portland, Oregon, November 14, 1993.

composition. That conversation introduced me to semantics and began a lifelong pursuit of the precise words required to convey the truth I believe. The process of naming God, however, leaves me undone, for all our words are inadequate for God. How can we capture the wonder inspired by the great "I AM" in human, finite words?

Many worship wars arise over the matter of what to name God. Perhaps those wars are sometimes unnecessarily prolonged because we forget that it is *God,* after all, about whom we are speaking — and God is awe-full.

Certainly the most bitter debates ensue because of the English language's lack of suitable pronouns for God and the predominance of masculine images for God in the Scriptures. In an effort to be neutral we wind up saying such things as "God reveals God's self in God's Word." If we say instead "God reveals himself in his Word," we are accused of being patriarchal or exclusivist, and we are severely denounced by many in the religious guild. That condemnation is soundly based, for certainly in much of its history Christendom has been patriarchal and demeaning of women. However, the present rejection of masculine pronouns and images for God is perhaps causing us to lose, not only the wholeness of Scripture and its truths about God, but also our ability to apply the Scriptures in contemporary society.

I have chosen to address this issue at length here because our naming of God is basic for worship and for keeping God its subject and object. I could easily dismiss the issue by insisting that masculine pronouns and images are the ones the Scriptures use and we should be faithful to the names by which God Godself has revealed God's self — but the honest complaints against patriarchy, the genuine oppression of women in many churches and by many Christians, the serious questions about how to use the Scriptures in contemporary worship, and the troubling problems of language are far too important for such a dismissal.

Those who subordinate the subject of language for God to political agendas sometimes accuse those who wish to preserve the biblical language of "defending an outdated structure of patriarchal power." That is not usually the case. "Rather, what is being defended is the connection between today's worship and yesterday's revelation. The biblical symbols make that connection."[24]

Before going further, I should confess my presuppositions. I believe that the Scriptures are God-inspired. Fundamental for me is the declaration

24. Ted Peters, "Worship Wars," *dialog* 33, no. 3 (Summer 1994): 171-72.

of 2 Peter 1:21: "Not by human will has a prophecy ever been brought about, but possessed by the Holy Spirit, human beings have spoken on the part of God." Consequently, I believe that God-inspired writers were able to rise above their patriarchal culture. In other words, *God got what God wanted* (which was not permanent patriarchy) as human writers spoke on God's behalf and recorded in human language and imagery the insights of their Spirit-possessed and -empowered state.

Many would disagree with the previous paragraph because the Bible seems to be so patriarchal, but is that an accurate assumption? In the deliberate placement of the biblical order, the canon begins with a liturgy and a narrative of creation and the story of the fall, all of which manifest a remarkable egalitarianism. Genesis 1 emphasizes that the image of God is both male and female. Both genders of humankind are equally blessed and commanded to be fruitful and to care for the earth and all the creatures in perfect harmony.

Genesis 2 names the woman *'ezer* (Helper), a word usually used for God in the Hebrew Scriptures. This surprising title contradicts a patriarchal culture by elevating the woman's imaging of God, the Helper Superior. The woman is called a Helper Corresponding, imaging the care of God in a human, rather than divine, way. Moreover, in Genesis 2:24, the normative declaration, "A man must leave his father and mother and cleave to his wife," also counteracts a patriarchal culture, which would command the wife instead.

Genesis 3 describes the dominion of men over women as a sign of sinfulness and a violation of God's creation design. The rest of the Scriptures demonstrate time and again how the brokenness of the world is manifested in all sorts of human inequalities and oppressions. Then the New Testament particularly emphasizes that the new order brought about by Jesus eliminates race, class, and gender distinctions so that once again, as in God's original design, there is neither Jew nor Greek, slave nor free, male nor female.

The question then arises, why does God reveal himself most often in masculine terms and only occasionally in feminine ones? In an article in *The Christian Century,* John G. Stackhouse, Jr., presents lucid and thorough arguments for his thesis that the images of "lord" and "lover" were the best for God to convey to the cultures of the two Testaments these two complementary main points: God's transcendence and God's deep care for humans.[25]

25. John G. Stackhouse, Jr., "God as Lord and Lover," *The Christian Century* 109, no. 33 (11 Nov. 1992): 1020-21.

100

It seems to me important to add to Stackhouse's two this third main point that God also intends to convey: we human beings are sinful and can only live well by means of the salvation and modeling of God. This point is equally essential because the whole Christian story centers around the fact that God's transcendent sovereignty and God's immanent care for human beings required their salvation through Jesus Christ and the possibility for a new creation to counteract their fall into sin. Human brokenness necessitates images for God that offer models to human beings of how to live according to God's creation design. God is not only "lord" and "lover" in relation to human beings; God also sets human beings free from sinfulness and teaches and empowers them to be caring masters and faithful spouses. Because of human sinfulness, the images for God in the Bible offer models intended to be corrective of human behavior.

Throughout history, as Genesis 3 and Romans 8 emphasize, all of creation has been in travail, unable to be what God designed it to be, because of the brokenness engendered by human rebellion. Human beings have especially violated God's plan for harmony and mutuality. Consequently, all images for God offer us correctives, visions of how to live out our new creation. God's image as the Perfect Father is certainly such a corrective.

I delight in the Scriptures' feminine images for God, but for years I've wondered why God chose to reveal himself more often as Father, since that image has led to such ungodly patriarchal oppression. Perhaps Isaiah 49:15 provides a key to the mystery. God asks rhetorically, "Can a mother forget the baby she has borne?" We all respond, "Of course not!" Tragically, in our present culture drug problems, the stresses of a technological milieu, extreme disarray in families, and other factors do sometimes cause mothers to forget their children. Generally, however, in the history of the world's various cultures, it is an exception rather than the rule if women don't properly care for their children. Fathers, on the other hand, are often absent, frequently emotionally distant, sometimes negligent. In the Greek and Roman societies of biblical times, elite men might attend orgies with educated, high-class prostitutes while their wives were kept hidden at home to raise good children. Even more so today, as we see from the statistics of absentee fathers and single-mother households, fathers are more likely than mothers to forget their children. Among other reasons, God reveals himself as Father to teach us his design for human families. The Hebrew image of "womb-love" (the principal First Testament word for God's compassion) functions similarly, but women seem to have done a better job of following God's nurturing design. To the question "Can a woman forget the baby she has borne?" we still answer, "No, not usually."

The image of Father, therefore, accomplishes three important purposes: it reveals God as lord, lover, and model. The divine Father stands in a transcendent, yet caring relationship with his children and thereby models the perfect combination of authority and intimate tenderness that human fathers need to care best for their children.

Jesus incarnates and culminates the biblical imaging and revisioning. Besides demonstrating perfect masculinity in his relationships with both men and women, Jesus points primarily to the image of a heavenly Father and invites his disciples to know their almighty God in such an intimate way. Moreover, his life and teaching (and that of the rest of the New Testament) help us to see how all the biblical images serve to clarify our understanding and to correct human behavior. God is the loving King who uses his authority to seek the well-being of his subjects. God is a Mother who never forgets her child, the Lion who acts like a Lamb, a caring and disciplining shepherd. God is a wooing husband who sets his spouse free to be holy (and wholly herself), a Warrior who forms his people to be peacemakers.[26] God reveals God's self in many images and narratives that nurture in us a godly character.

By this time many readers might be objecting that it is damaging to call God *Father* when so many women have been abused by fathers, spouses, and lovers. I have seen instead how extremely destructive it is to abused women to deny them the One who best models caring, tender, gracious manhood and fatherhood. When we deal with women whose lives have been severely shattered by men who fail to follow the image of God, we can help them best by restoring the security of a true and gently loving Father, as well as Mother. Our human psyche needs both father and mother. If our human situation has robbed us of one or both, then fatherness and/or motherness must be restored for healing.

Our human failures to bear the parenting image of God necessitate that we all turn to God for forgiveness. The rhetorical question "Can a woman forget the baby she has borne?" is followed by God's comforting declaration, "Yes, but even if she does, I will not forget you. I have engraved you on the palm of my hands." We can assure our children that whenever they are distressed by our human failures the truth of God's perfect

---

26. See my article "What the Bible *Really* Says about War," *The Other Side* 29, no. 2 (March-April 1993): 56-59.

Father/Mother love and care is larger. We know that God's parenting care will not fail; the evidence is there for us to see in the way he has carved us into the Son's hands on the cross. In clear communication with our children, Christian parents will ask for our failures to be forgiven, as we continue doing the best we can to bear the image of God more faithfully in our fathering and mothering.

The world needs this biblical revisioning of masculine terms. Stackhouse ends his article on the value of the biblical images of lord and lover with a warning to take great care in reconstructing theology lest we lose key elements of the biblical truth by rejecting certain images. He concludes that we must know

> that God is not male and that the biblical accounts need reinterpretation from points of view other than that of the traditional, privileged male. But let us also appreciate the multidimensional images of the Bible that contain important truths. If we're going to go beyond biblical images as we attempt to speak in contemporary terms, we must make sure that our alternatives maintain the best elements of the biblical system and in their appropriate relations. This is always the challenge in improving upon the tradition of our elders (let alone upon the revelation of God): it often emerges that they knew more than we might think, and we would do well not to dispense quickly with their wisdom.[27]

Stackhouse's plea must be widened to insist, not only that we need our elders' wisdom for our own sake, but also that the Church has a great gift to offer the society around us in the many pictures of God that help us recover our true humanity. We want our worship to portray the fullness of those biblical pictures, and we want to follow their model in ordering our own lives in the new creation wrought by Christ. Within the Christian community these images teach us to be an alternative society, rejecting the world's injustices and inequalities in order to be women and men according to God's creation design for human mutuality and harmony.

We need all the images for God in the Scriptures — bright Morning Star, Alpha and Omega, Vine, Gardener, Rider of the White Horse, Bread of Life, Paraclete — that still do not encompass all that He/She is. Particularly we dare not lose the contemporary recovery of feminine images.

---

27. Stackhouse, "God as Lord and Lover," p. 1021.

However, I have read many feminist lambastes that go overboard, rejecting all images for God except feminine ones, which results in much inappropriate and absurd language for God and makes a mockery of God's true character. Lest the pendulum swing too far, we must take care to maintain the positive masculine biblical images and not be too lazy to educate people to understand them and their value — especially because God chose to reveal himself in terms that contradict and overcome the sinfulness of human behavior and the brokenness of human relationships.

Finally, let me stress again the necessity and privilege of bearing in our parishes the Church's continuity and its insights in knowing God. We stand on the shoulders of the giants before us to see more clearly than we could by ourselves. As the Christian community, we celebrate the universal Church both historically and geographically. Throughout the ages and throughout the world God's people have baptized believers in the name of the Father, the Son, and the Holy Spirit and welcomed them into this unique community who claim that God is one, yet three persons. Every time I hear the Church's historic invocation, stemming from the command of Matthew 28:19, I wonder at the mystery of it all. I rejoice also that saints throughout the world (including my friends in Poland and Madagascar) are saying the very same thing, so that we are bonded across space in the global community of those who submit to that mystery. Together we worship — and God is the subject and object of our praise.

6. The Character of the Believer: Having Content or Being Content?

O God, teach me to see You, and reveal Yourself to me
     when I seek You,
For I cannot seek You unless You first teach me,
nor find You unless You first reveal Yourself to me.
Let me seek You in longing, and long for You in seeking.
Let me find You in love, and love You in finding.

Ambrose of Milan, 339-397

Ambrose's poem invites us to keep God as the subject of our worship and reminds us that to do so will change our lives. When God comes to us in all the fullness of who God is, our character will be transformed. Consequently, if our worship practices accord God the proper place and scope, who we are and what we are becoming as Christians will be rightly developed.

However, notice that I phrased the paragraph above in terms of "we." Who you are as an individual believer depends greatly upon the character of the community of believers in which you are nurtured. How faithfully does that community incarnate God's presence and pass on the narratives that reveal God when they assemble together? It really isn't possible to discuss this chapter's subject, the character of the individual believer, independently of the subject of the next — nurturing the Christian community's character. We will discuss individual believers first, though, since our present culture thinks about Christianity in such terms and because so many societal factors militate against the formation of Christian character. In a society that values show and appearance more than character and internal integrity, congregations often fail to consider worship's role in nurturing participants' character.

People Are God's Method

When I was studying the relationship between worship and ethics for my doctoral exams, I asked a Jewish professor how Judaica envisions the correlation. Some faiths see spirituality and ethics as two sides of the same coin; some place spirituality/evangelism as primary with ethics/social action as a secondary outflow; others advocate social responsibility almost to the exclusion of concern for spirituality. The professor laughed. "There is no difference between worship and life," he said. "Both are the same thing — fulfillment of Torah."

Christians need to recover that Jewish unity, for all that happens in life is our worshipful response to God and God's revelation, and the specific response of our worship practices influences both directly and indirectly who we are as we worship in the rest of life. Various elements of worship create certain perspectives and understandings about God and specific attitudes and habits of being, all of which affect how we think, speak, and act. It is crucial, then, that leaders of the Church study carefully our underlying theology of worship and the specific worship practices that result, for they do, indeed, determine who we are. How (and whom) we worship nurtures personal character.

As we develop this book's theology of worship, remember that every action of our lives molds our character. If I constantly curse, I become a foul-mouthed person. If I want to be a kind person, I must make daily choices that lead to kind actions. Morality is best formed not by dwelling on rules (deontological ethics) or by considering our actions' outcome (teleological ethics) but by making use of all the means in the Christian community to nurture a godly character, out of which moral choices will be well made. Christian character is nurtured by all the scriptural narratives and rules, our images for God, specific worship practices, prayerful consideration of means and ends, tiny choices in daily life, the values of the community, and our interactions with its members. All these things together contribute to who we are, how we live.

Some churches scramble to find better worship "methods" to increase their membership or stewardship or educational effectiveness. We must constantly remember as we seek to be God's Church that most of all God wants holy people. As the great man of prayer E. M. Bounds says, "People are God's method. The church is looking for better methods; God is looking for better people."[1]

That is why I strongly advocate Sabbath keeping (an entire day set apart to learn more thoroughly who God is and the kind of character he wants to develop in us) and Christian schools (to train children to recognize God's presence in all their subjects and in every area of life). Specifically, we must recognize that every aspect of the time we spend together in the worshiping Christian community influences the kind of people we are becoming. Some of the negative influences are very subtle — which makes them all the more dangerous. We must work explicitly to counteract those destructive influences.

Narcissism in Contemporary Society and Worship

Perhaps the most dangerous of the subtle influences on contemporary worship practices is the self-centered bent of the modern world — caused by the societal streams and idolatries sketched in Chapters 2 and 3. The technological society increasingly isolates us from one another, with a resulting focus on individual selves and needs, not the good of the community. Furthermore, technicization destroys human skills for intimacy, though the speed, mobility, and fragmentation of modern life leave most persons desperately hungry for the very intimacy they do not know how to create. Even more deadly is the sense that we can solve all our problems with new technological advances, that we are masters of our destiny. This aggravates the already prevailing rejection of God, institutions, and authority that characterizes the modern cosmology.

1. E. M. Bounds, *Power Through Prayer,* ed. Penelope J. Stokes (Minneapolis: World Wide Publications, 1989), p. 13.

Christopher Lasch's *The Culture of Narcissism* clarifies that this new emphasis on the self is not just the timeless selfishness of human beings reclothed, but a new self-hatred, derived from "quite specific changes in our society and culture" — including "bureaucracy, the proliferation of images, therapeutic ideologies, the rationalization of the inner life, the cult of consumption, and in the last analysis . . . changes in family life and . . . changing patterns of socialization."[2] Lasch's is the most thorough clinical and etiological analysis of modern narcissistic culture — a recognition of which is crucial for resisting the focus on self that invades much of contemporary worship. The Church must combat the constant influence of this cultural mind-set on our character and its subtle expression in Christian worship.

For example, read thoughtfully the following words of an opening song used in worship at a regional denominational convention I recently attended:

> I will celebrate, sing unto the Lord.
> I will sing to God a new song. (repeat)
>> I will praise God, I will sing to God a new song. (repeat)
>> Hallelujah, hallelujah, hallelujah,
>> Hallelujah, I will sing to God a new song. (repeat)
> I will celebrate, sing unto the Lord.
> I will sing to God a new song. (repeat)
>> (Repeat All)

God is never the subject in this song, but with all the repeats "I" is the subject 28 times! With that kind of focus, we might suppose that all the "Hallelujahs" are praising how good I am (without any *we* of community!) at celebrating and singing. I poke fun at this ditty because it is not immediately obvious that the song really does not praise God at all. The verbs say *I will,* but in this song I don't, because, though God is mentioned as the recipient of my praise and singing, the song never says a single thing about or to God. If an unbeliever heard the words, she would have no idea of why God is praiseworthy or of who God is.

Furthermore, in the rest of the service there was not one song that

---

2. Christopher Lasch, *The Culture of Narcissism* (New York: W. W. Norton, 1979), p. 32; see especially pp. 31-51. See also Paul C. Vitz, *Psychology as Religion: The Cult of Self-Worship,* 2nd ed. (Grand Rapids: William B. Eerdmans, 1994), especially pp. 49-51.

said anything about the God we were supposedly praising — all the songs were about us. The sermon was remarkably forgettable, the litany focused on all the suffering in the world, and the Scripture lesson was one verse long. Nowhere was God the subject except in brief passing. How can we have the courage to face all the world's suffering if we hear nothing about the Cosmic Lord who cares about it and is at work to bring about his justice? How will we sing to God a new song if we haven't learned anything about him, if we have not met him in this worship time, if he has not been the subject?

Compare the song above to such opening hymns as "Holy, holy, holy Lord God Almighty" or "Jesus Christ is risen today. Alleluia." Such hymns focus on God as the subject. They call us by his holiness to awe and draw us by the death and resurrection of Christ to salvation, renewed life, and praise. When God is the subject, our character is formed in response to his.

In contrast, focusing in worship on me and my feelings and my praising will nurture a character that is inward-turned, that thinks first of self rather than of God. Though many modern songs actually praise not God but how well we are loving him, this tendency isn't found only in modern music. The old camp song "We Are Climbing Jacob's Ladder," for example, does the same thing. We sing that we are climbing higher and higher in our relationship with God, rather than that God comes down to us in his revelation of himself. Such a theme teaches us to depend on our feelings or efforts, rather than on God's gift of grace, in assessing our relationship with God.

The contrast is well illustrated by the difference between the biblical word *heart,* stressing will and intentionality, and the modern English metaphor *heart,* referring to feelings. When the Psalmist says, "I will praise Thee, LORD, with my whole heart" (9:1), he means that he will continue deliberately to praise God (whether he feels like it or not) because God is praiseworthy. Since often the texts of our culture's music very subtly keep the attention on ourselves, it is crucial that the Church utilize words that draw our attention to God's attributes and interventions in our lives and world. Though certainly present in many contemporary compositions, such a focus is more often found in soundly doctrinal hymns from an age with a more God-centered cosmology.

It is urgent that the Church recognize how easily we assume the self-centered mind-set of the culture that surrounds us and work more deliberately to reject it. In 1983 James Hunter analyzed releases from eight of the most prolific evangelical publishers and found that 97.8 percent of their titles concerned the self, in "an accentuation of subjectivity and the virtual veneration of the self, exhibited in deliberate efforts to achieve self-understanding, self-improvement, and self-fulfillment."[3]

This focus on the self is a curious inversion, for in losing God as subject we lose exactly what we need to find genuine self-identity. David Wells criticizes the inroads of this cultural distortion in the United States as follows:

> It is not good character that we value as much as good feelings. . . . [I]t is a remarkable development. Is not the self movement evidence of our collective unhappiness and insecurity? It is only the hungry, after all, who are always thinking of food. . . . It is only the unhappy who are constantly preoccupied with happiness, only those crippled by a sense of their own insubstantial self who expend their lives in its pursuit. Why, then, are many turning to these symbols of our cultural failure and fear for the materials with which to redefine evangelical faith?[4]

The self focus beginning to characterize many churches "has been highly successful," but "its costs are apparently not self-evident." It causes people "to seek assurance of faith not in terms of the objective truthfulness of the biblical teaching but in terms of the efficacy of its subjective experience." Thus outreach to nonbelievers asks the wrong question — "not whether Christ is objectively real but simply whether the experience is appealing, whether it seems to have worked, whether having it will bring one inside the group and give one connections to others" (p. 172).

Genuine knowledge of God involves "an experience of his grace and power, informed by the written Scriptures, mediated by the Holy Spirit, and based upon the work of Christ on the Cross." However, this experience should not, in and of itself, become the *source* for knowing God, nor should it be the means by which we commend that knowledge to others. Biblical witnessing always pointed to the objective truth of Christian faith.

3. James Hunter, *Evangelicalism: The Coming Generation* (Chicago: University of Chicago Press, 1987), p. 65, as cited in David F. Wells, *No Place for Truth* (Grand Rapids: William B. Eerdmans, 1993), p. 176.

4. Wells, *No Place for Truth*, p. 172. Page references to this work in the rest of this section are given parenthetically in the text.

Now witness instead points "to our own faith, and in affirming its validity we may become less interested in its truthfulness than in the fact that it seems to work. Evangelical hymnody today is changing direction to reflect this experience-centered focus" (p. 173).

To remain the Church we must sustain orthodoxy and frame Christian belief doctrinally, but Wells warns that this requires "habits of reflection and judgment that are simply out of place in our culture" — and increasingly are disappearing from the Church, too (p. 173). Our society seeks rapid gratification — immediacy of feelings, rather than the slowness of learning. As credit cards enable us to possess without waiting, so churches give the message that "we can likewise have divine results, without having to wait — indeed, without even having to think." As Wells summarizes, this development in faith is due to "the powerful undercurrents of self-absorption that course through the modern psyche. . . . The self therefore becomes pivotal" (p. 174).

Wells's insights give strong directions for theological consideration. Worship practices that only evoke good feelings and thereby foster a character that seeks instant gratification might be enormously successful at first, but the costs, though not immediately obvious, may be high. The very methods that attract crowds might also prevent the development of habits of reflection and learning. A focus on self and feelings limits the nurturing of a godly and outreaching character.

Moreover, a focus on good feelings actually distorts the biblical message and thereby distorts the development of genuinely *Christian* character. This is because the "self movement" is founded upon the common assumption of the perfectibility of human nature. As Wells explains, the biblical gospel

> asserts the very reverse — namely, that the self is twisted, . . . maladjusted in its relationship to both God and others, . . . full of deceit and rationalizations, . . . lawless, . . . in rebellion, and indeed that one must die to self in order to live. It is this that is at the heart of the biblical gospel, this that is at the center of Christian character. . . . It is perhaps paradoxical that self-denial should build character and that self-fascination, more than anything else, should undercut it. (p. 179)

How ironic and tragic it is if worship practices foster self-idolatry instead of genuine praise of God! Only when worship brings us into the presence of the Jesus who called us to deny self can our character as his followers be truly nurtured.

Christian character cannot be built if we "exchange enduring qualities for a spate of exciting new experiences," if we are "guided by a compass
of circumstance rather than belief" (p. 180). As Wells warns, a Christian
faith that is

> conceived in the womb of the self is quite different from the historic
> Christian faith. It is a smaller thing, shrunken in its ability to understand
> the world and to stand up in it. The self is a canvas too narrow, too
> cramped, to contain the largeness of Christian truth. . . . [G]ood and
> evil are reduced to a sense of well-being or its absence, God's place in
> the world is reduced to the domain of private consciousness, his external
> acts of redemption are trimmed to fit the experience of personal salva-
> tion, his providence in the world diminishes to whatever is necessary to
> ensure one's having a good day, his Word becomes intuition, and con-
> viction fades into evanescent opinion. Theology becomes therapy. . . .
> The biblical interest in righteousness is replaced by a search for happi-
> ness, holiness by wholeness, truth by feeling, ethics by feeling good
> about one's self. The world shrinks to the range of personal circum-
> stances; the community of faith shrinks to a circle of personal friends.
> The past recedes. The Church recedes. The world recedes. All that
> remains is the self . . . a paltry thing. Simply put, the psychologizing of
> faith is destroying . . . Christian habits of thought because it is destroying
> the capacity . . . to discern between good and evil, to think about all
> of life in terms of God and his purposes, to construct a way of being
> that accords with his Word, and to contest the norms of cultural plausi-
> bility. . . . And when people are no longer compelled by God's truth,
> they can be compelled by anything, the more so if it has the sheen of
> excitement or the lure of the novel. . . . (pp. 182-83)

Perhaps Wells overstates his case, but he does so to warn us, and I
have quoted him at length because the warning seems so urgent. A
worship emphasis on the self has long-term consequences that are not
apparent but are hidden by their seeming success. Self-centered worship
does indeed appeal to the boomers, who, as we saw in Chapter 5 from
Roof's analysis, find their source of authority and meaning in themselves
rather than in an objective God. What worries me is that many congregations are hurriedly switching their worship practices (throwing out
hymnbooks, for example, in favor of music that is overly self conscious)
in order to "grow" their churches — without adequate consideration of

112

the long-term, negative results in the character of the worship participants.

Having said that, however, I must now immediately move to the other pole of the dialectic. We cannot only emphasize truth without attendant concern for feelings — especially if, as a result, that truth is conveyed in stale or stilted ways. Our worship practices must embody the truth in ways that relate to people, that invite them to experience the truth firsthand and not simply as irrelevant tradition. Roof highlights the importance of authentic religious experience for the boomer generation. What happens in many churches often seems to them "far removed, if not downright alien, to life as experienced outside; the institutional languages of creed and doctrine often come across as stale and timeworn — hardly conducive to 'firsthand religion.'" Yet many boomers "yearn deeply for a religious experience they can claim as 'their own.'"[5]

The difficulty for churches is to find worship practices that invite boomers to experience the truth of God without the self-absorption that distorts it. How can we convey God's revelation to those who regard their own self-discovered experiences as superior to truths handed down by the creeds of the Church? I am convinced that we don't serve our narcissistic culture best by conforming to its demand for psychologizing self-help projects and highly subjective worship forms. It is imperative, though, that the objective truth of the gospel be conveyed in ways that "relate to people's everyday experiences and . . . their deepest feelings and concerns."[6]

The Longing for Moral Authority

One especially prominent concern of the boomer, postmodern, technologized society is its search for moral authority.[7] As random and gang violence, drug and alcohol abuse, teen pregnancy and abortion, and political and economic malfeasance escalate, Americans increasingly recognize that many of our social ills are integrally related to the loss of moral foundations.

A 1993 national poll discovered that "while nearly 2 out of 3 Amer-

5. Wade Clark Roof, *A Generation of Seekers* (San Francisco: Harper, 1993), p. 68.
6. Roof, *A Generation of Seekers*, p. 68.
7. See Neil Postman, *Technopoly* (New York: Alfred A. Knopf, 1992), p. 160.

icans say religion is gaining influence in their personal lives, a comparable number say it is losing influence on the country in general." We must ask what kind of influence religion is gaining in their lives if "almost 90 percent (including 85 percent of those who describe themselves as not very religious) say the nation is slipping deeper into moral decline." Reporter Jeffrey Sheler asks, "If spiritual values are strong, shouldn't the moral tone of the nation be on a more even keel?" Sheler recognizes that moral values are lost when genuine religious belief is lost. He quotes Billy Graham, who says that most Americans " 'believe the Bible, but they don't read it or obey it.' Pollster George Gallup Jr., whose organization has tracked U.S. religious behavior for over 60 years, agrees," saying that the United States is " 'a nation of biblical illiterates. . . . The stark fact is, most Americans don't know what they believe or why.' "[8]

Wade Clark Roof reports that 70 percent of the boomers his team surveyed favored a "return to stricter moral standards." Because families are the arena for instituting rules of biblical authority and living out the Christian life, boomers expressed great concern "about the breakup of families and of what is happening to children" — blaming television as "a major culprit." Christian boomers recognized that the core of the problem is "a crisis of commitment: People do not take seriously their vows, their duties and obligations — to others and to God." Since many boomers understand that the moral authority they seek is not offered in public schools, which increasingly emphasize human reason and value neutrality in the classroom, they are turning to home schooling or developing new Christian schools.[9] These expressions and actions of concern suggest to the Church that boomers are looking for more substance, the truths of God, rather than the self-help illusions of society.

For that reason the Church must not become infatuated with the culture's self-absorption. The only way to offer the world an alternative, the moral foundation of God's truth, is if the Church and its members are distinctly different — if we are formed with the character of persons following Jesus. Our culture's moral crisis points to humanity's sinfulness and need for God. If worship reveals the fullness of God, we will be formed to become like him.

8. Jeffrey L. Sheler, "Spiritual America," *U.S. News and World Report* 116, no. 13 (4 April 1993): 56-57.
9. Roof, *A Generation of Seekers*, pp. 96-97.

However, many believers' character seems to be moving in the opposite direction — choosing personal happiness over God's purposes. A national survey

> discovered that no fewer than seven out of ten Christians are prone to hedonistic attitudes about life. The study found, for example, strong support among Christians for the sixties notion that an individual is free to do whatever pleases him, as long as it does not hurt others. Two out of five Christians maintain that such thinking is proper. . . . A similar proportion of born-again people deny the possibility that pain or suffering could be a means of becoming a better, more mature individual. . . . [T]hree out of ten Christians agree that "nothing in life is more important than having fun and being happy." . . . Regarding materialism, the statistics are nearly identical. Two out of three Christians express such love for money, possessions, and other material objects that their Christianity cannot be said to rule their hearts.[10]

How are our worship and educational practices failing that they do not form Christians who follow Jesus in his willingness to suffer for the sake of God's kingdom? How can we crave money and possessions and still follow the One who had nowhere to lay his head?

What great gifts the Church offers the world if it nurtures persons of godly character who devote their financial resources and time to God's purposes of caring justice. The Church offers great alternatives to our society's economic attitudes and practices.

The same is true for politics. Modern society so desperately needs public servants of integrity, municipal stewards who stand for what benefits the common good, politicians of virtue. Just as Martin Luther wrote treatises for the nobles and princes of his day, couldn't the modern Church nurture godly character in its members so that they reach out to their society with virtue?

My book *Sexual Character* extensively outlines the virtues needed for marriage and friendship, so I need not elaborate them here. Besides human relationships, we could mention many other life aspects in which our world is starved for persons of solid godly character — godliness that is manifested not just in moral behavior but in their whole character

10. George Barna and William Paul McKay, *Vital Signs: Emerging Social Trends and the Future of American Christianity* (Westchester, IL: Crossway Books, 1984), p. 141.

of trust, stability, virtue, and will. Most of my counseling is with persons who are dissatisfied with the shallowness of their lives; people in our society crave better values, more genuine pleasure in life, more satisfying goals. We who are God's people *know* how to find life's real meaning — which is not merely morality, but the fullness of relationship with God. Worship is meant to usher us into God's presence so that we can delight in that relationship and consequently be formed to live according to God's best purposes.

Nurturing Character Formation

God's best purposes for us involve the highest self-identity — not to be satisfactorily found by endlessly pursuing self-improvement, but received as a gift of grace. However, the gift of self in God's grace cannot be received unless we get rid of our self-centeredness. Worship offers the perfect balance because "Christian identity begins with the death of the empirical ego in baptism." Then, as baptized, forgiven, and thereby truly whole persons, we are free to pursue God's best will in every aspect of our lives. "Christians therefore are neither consumed with realizing their identity as the end and purpose of life, nor do they desire to throw the self away because it is either evil or an illusion."[11] Worship nurtures this dialectical sense of ourselves when it is planned and practiced with God as the subject and the nurturing of believers' character as a primary goal. The culture *of* worship thus offers an alternative to the culture *in* which the Church seeks to serve.

It is crucial to stress character formation[12] because believers do not enter into the life of Christ through a system of rules (as in deontological ethics) or even by naming the goals of this life (as in teleological ethics). We are formed by Christ's presence in the Word and in the community. We experience God's life in the narratives of the Church and seek to follow God's designs. Our motivation for obedience is never rules or laws but the positive invitation of God's grace at work through us by God's power.

11. Patrick R. Keifert, *Welcoming the Stranger: A Public Theology of Worship and Evangelism* (Minneapolis: Fortress Press, 1992), p. 88.

12. See a more thorough explication of an ethics of character in my book *Sexual Character* (Grand Rapids: William B. Eerdmans, 1993), pp. 32-38.

To form character, the means must match the ends. If we want deep faith, we must be nurtured by deep experiences of its reality. That is why it is so essential to plan worship well, for we must be concerned with how every action in the process of the faith journey affects the development of our character.

Particular behaviors arise out of the kind of persons we are. If we habitually concentrate on ourselves, we will be more selfish with others. If God is the subject in our worship, our behavior will reflect God's actions in us. Paul writes that as we behold the Lord's glory we are all "being transformed into the same image from one degree of glory to another" (2 Cor. 3:18).

Models in our environment form us. Our behaviors form us — they arise from our character, and repeating those behaviors will reinforce character in turn. Our milieu forms us — that is why we must ask careful questions about how much we should allow the ethos of the culture surrounding the Church to affect what we do in worship. Especially because we live in a milieu that bombards us with its false conceptions of the world, of self, and of truth, we must be very careful and purposeful in fostering biblical perspectives.

Against the toxicities of our milieu (outlined in Chapters 2 and 3), the Church creates an alternative society. Each believer needs to be en-folded in a caring community of faithful people who offer guidance, wisdom, the perspectives of the Scriptures, and love to nurture character growth. (We will pursue this in more depth in the next chapter.)

Our primary source for character formation is the Word of God. As God's people, the Christian community will continually ask how that Word guides us in seeking the truth about our humanity and God's design for it. What is revealed by the biblical accounts of God's people in their ethical choices, in their instructions to each other? What virtues are displayed? What commands are issued that we ignore to our peril? How does the Bible give us courage to stand against false values and idolatries in our society because it announces to us the defeat of the principalities and powers? How can the worship of the community especially pass on the narratives and the hope that form us in faith? How does worship invite us to respond to the Word in faithfulness?

In an article about her mother written as part of a series on "spiritual mentors," Elizabeth Achtemeier describes her childhood attendance at worship every Sunday and concludes as follows:

I did not know at the time that all those experiences were sinking into my bones — that I was learning the language of prayer and hymnody, of doctrine, scripture and liturgy. But I was. I was slowly but surely being taught the language and worldview of the Christian faith which has nourished me all my life long.[13]

Of course, Achtemeier's experiences began in her home, for her mother did more than take her to worship every week. A child's faith nurturing begins with bedtime prayers, Bible-story books read on a parent's lap, mealtime devotions, family conversation about God, faithful parenting and modeling of the Christian life. Our churches must more consciously educate parents to nurture their children's faith through simple conversations, activities, and modeling.

Similarly, the Church must teach children what it means for the community to gather in worship. Let us teach them why we do what we do in specific worship practices and thereby enable them to enjoy the depth of symbols, the awe of ritual, the value of silence, the importance of the Bible to teach us how to be God's people, and the critical need for us to be different from society.

Our worship cannot accomplish such character formation if it falls prey to our society's self-absorption. As Keck explains, whom or what we praise

is an important clue to one's character. The object of praise reveals what one deems praiseworthy, what we value and perhaps aspire to be like. But even if we do not aspire to sing like Pavarotti, in praising his rendition of a difficult solo we show that we value excellence. And whoever does not value excellence, especially if it is achieved by discipline, will not strive for it in one's own life. Whether by affirmation or by aspiration, the praised both reveals and shapes the praiser.[14]

Keck continues by emphasizing that a community teaches us the discernment necessary for praising what is excellent (more on this in the following chapter), but here we simply note the importance of worship that praises

13. Elizabeth Achtemeier, "An Excellent Woman," *The Christian Century* 110, no. 24 (22 Aug.–1 Sept. 1993): 808.

14. Leander Keck, *The Church Confident* (Nashville: Abingdon Press, 1993), pp. 27-28.

God, his attributes and will and truth. Then what we praise will shape us to be like God.

Worship forms subtly influence the kind of people we are becoming. As Elizabeth Achtemeier's comments emphasize, all the elements of a worship service immerse us in the heritage of the faith — its stories and convictions. Martin Luther advocated twice daily worship services in which Scripture was read and interpreted (preaching), with responses of psalms, hymns, and prayers. He insisted, "Thus Christian people will by daily training become proficient, skillful, and well versed in the Bible. For this is how genuine Christians were made in former times . . . and could also be made today."[15] We must always ask how well our worship practices are training participants with tools of Word and song and prayers to make "genuine Christians" in postmodern times.

All aspects of our worship — what we say and how we sing, the accoutrements of the worshiping place, our interactions within the community — nurture in us a specific kind of character. We must therefore be constantly asking how our worship reveals God and what kind of people we are becoming, because the perspectives and understandings about God and the specific attitudes and habits of being that are created by all the elements of worship services affect how we think, speak, and act as we worship in the rest of life.

Besides forming character especially by the type of things we do and say in our worship gatherings, every aspect of a congregation's community life is part of the nurturing process. We nurture growth in faithful life in our educational programs, youth group meetings, boards' and committees' tasks, congregational business meetings, social work projects, stewardship drives, prayer services, choir practices, day care programs, and dinners. It is very important that all members of the congregational staff and all its leaders are conscious of the goal to nurture character by what we do together. Such a consciousness will influence our attitudes as we deal with each other and keep us mindful of the behaviors that influence positive growth in our own virtues and in the godliness of those who observe us and hold us as models.

Our world urgently needs the kind of personal character that Chris-

15. Martin Luther, "Concerning the Order of Public Worship" (1523), trans. Paul Zeller Strodach, in *Liturgy and Hymns*, ed. Ulrich S. Leupold, vol. 53 in *Luther's Works*, gen. ed. Helmut T. Lehmann (Philadelphia: Fortress Press, 1965), p. 12.

tian worship and community life nourish. The critical scarcity of quality leaders in our society is obvious. As Keck warns, "Even the most progressive legislation will fail if the people who administer it are incompetent, are deficient in character, and lack moral conviction." How will such quality leaders be produced? "On demand? What institutions and experiences will form their character, shape their vision, and sensitize their consciences to the moral dimensions of life and work? Who will nourish the qualities that make for trustworthy leaders?"[16] We therefore expand our primary question about worship and ask, What kind of people is our worship forming — not only for the sake of the Church, but also for the sake of the culture around it?

Memorized Tradition

One of the most important tools for nurturing lifelong character growth is the memory. Many years ago I visited weekly in two convalescent centers in Moscow, Idaho, and Pullman, Washington. Several Alzheimers' patients resided in these homes, some whose minds were totally gone. Yet among those patients were some who, as soon as I began to sing "What a Friend We Have in Jesus," would join in and sing all three verses without a missed word. They could pray the Lord's Prayer, say the Apostles' Creed, and sing other hymns with me, before their minds wandered off. Research studies show that the earliest memories are retained longest in people's minds. How important it is, then, to fill children's memories with hymns, songs, prayers, Scripture verses, and creeds!

I want to emphasize this point doubly because of my own experiences with chronic illness and life-threatening crises. Last year a retinal hemorrhage in my good eye made reading barely possible only for very short periods with a double set of magnifiers. During seven months of near blindness, I thanked God constantly for my eight years at a Lutheran elementary/junior high school, during which I memorized hundreds of hymn verses and passages of the Bible. This background enables me to participate almost fully in worship even when I cannot see the words. In times when I have been near to death, those songs and texts have flooded my brain and brought enormous comfort and strength.

16. Keck, *The Church Confident,* p. 93.

In crises, old age, blindness, or other infirmities, our faith and hope continue to be nurtured by what we have stored in our memories.[17] Let us make sure that what we put into children's memories are things of substance, pieces of the Church's heritage that have stood the test of time and suffering.

Having observed hundreds of worship services throughout the United States, I am troubled that in so many "contemporary" services the children are not able to participate at all. These services do not include memorized liturgical pieces every week so that the children can anticipate them and join in. When I was three I knew different liturgies and could sing the whole service every Sunday or at evening vespers. Consequently, worship was much more meaningful to me, for I could truly be part of it. It makes me profoundly sad to observe young children entirely uninvolved throughout a worship service — because either there are no non-reading parts for them to do or their parents do not help them participate.

With amusement I remember that the first word I learned to read was *Selah,* because the congregation of my youth often read psalms in worship services. As my mother followed the text with her finger for my benefit, I began to notice a word sometimes printed off to the side, a word I didn't understand. Listening carefully, I soon became involved in psalm reading; watching for one of those words in the margin, I could shout "Selah" with the congregation whenever mother's finger pointed to it. Silly — but I was participating in psalm praise with my Joy-full Selahs and felt a part of the community.

Moreover, memorized pieces of tradition are vital for connecting us to the rootedness of our faith and to the knowledge of God that has endured throughout time and space. In times of fear, we need the assurance that God has intervened in the history of his people and continues to do so. Gail O'Day gives an example that shows the value of tradition in enabling us to remember the language of faith and to experience the grace-giving, life-changing presence of God. She explains how Second Isaiah preached

> the salvation oracle from Israel's liturgy to reteach his fellow exiles their own language. Second Isaiah's theological genius and pastoral creativity

17. For example, see Barbara Myerhoff's story of Sylvia, the Sabbath Bride, in *Number Our Days* (New York: Simon and Schuster, 1978), pp. 259-60, and all of chapter 7, "Jewish Comes Up in You From the Roots," pp. 232-68.

were to appropriate the words *do not fear* from the liturgy of the temple and make them the stuff of proclamation. In the liturgy, the words of the oracles were not simply an urging for the petitioner to be fearless, a reminder that the petitioner should merely get tough and show what he or she is made of. Rather, in the moment when the salvation oracle is spoken, with the articulation of God's word of "fear not," *fear is removed.* A real change is wrought by virtue of God's assuring word, evoking God's assuring presence. It is the moment of speaking that permits the petitioner to engage in a life of new possibilities.[18]

Similarly, God's Word in my memory has brought God's presence. Hearing the oracles of the liturgy is empowering as it renews in us the language of faith.

Many people argue that memorized traditions get too stale and boring and cause adults not to get involved. We can counteract this if we continually teach what parts of the liturgy mean, use seasonal and other suggested variations, and choose alternate settings and new music. The secret to lively worship that also builds memory is a constantly tested dialectical balance between old and new, memorized and fresh — the heritage of the faith in new wine skins.

Not Style, but Substance

By pointing out the value of memorized pieces of tradition I do not mean that only "traditional" worship develops character. Memorized pieces can — and must — occur in every kind of worship service. Obviously, various styles suit different kinds of people. The most important question for planning worship to form personal character is not that of style but of substance.

Faithful worship styles pass on different elements of faith's substance. Baptist Michelle Bobier explains that she frequently worships also with Episcopalians because of her longing for beauty and ceremony that will affect not only her spirit but also her senses and body. She finds scriptural foundation for this in that

18. Gail R. O'Day, "Toward a Biblical Theology of Preaching," in *Listening to the Word: Studies in Honor of Fred B. Craddock,* ed. Gail R. O'Day and Thomas G. Long (Nashville: Abingdon Press, 1993), p. 23.

the Bible is not itself without ritual. Far from it. The Old Testament is filled with descriptions of ornate ceremonies, replete with gold, incense, and vestments. Granted, most of the New Testament is pretty spare, but once you get to Revelation. . . . [T]he Lord gave us those glimpses of gorgeousness throughout Scripture because He knows that some of us, at least, need it. We need it for our souls.[19]

Her conclusion emphasizes these values in the various styles of worship:

I am taught and challenged and set free in my Baptist church, which is simultaneously austere and raucous, its white walls ringing with laughter. At the same time, sometimes on the same day, I am calmed at the Episcopal church, and brought to a place of peace. The two traditions coexist side by side within my mind and heart, ministering to the disparate parts that make up the person I am becoming.[20]

We ask the wrong questions about worship if we concentrate only on matters of style. Rather, style must be determined by faithful answers to the necessary question, What kind of people are we forming?

Worship that entertains an audience instead of praising God is certainly inimical to this substantive purpose. Entertaining worship is deadly to the formation of character, for, as the Bible shows, "forms of media favor particular kinds of content." Postman explains that the second commandment of the Decalogue, which prohibits the Israelites from making concrete images of anything, assumes *"a connection between forms of human communication and the quality of a culture."* The God of the Jews and then of Christians was different from the gods of other cultures in that this God exists "in the Word and through the Word, an unprecedented conception requiring the highest order of abstract thinking." Since "the media of communication available to a culture are a dominant influence on the formation of the culture's intellectual and social preoccupations,"[21] we must be very careful to avoid forms of communication that dumb down or trivialize the content of our worship.

Let us overstate the case to stress the danger. As John Alexander mocks,

19. Michelle Bobier, "A Baptist Among the Episcopalians," *New Oxford Review* 59, no. 6 (July-Aug. 1992): 16.
20. Bobier, "A Baptist Among the Episcopalians," p. 16.
21. Neil Postman, *Amusing Ourselves to Death* (New York: Viking/Penguin, 1985), p. 9.

Daily flossing and Right Guard, it seems, rather than truth or justice, are the weapons necessary to defeat Satan and his decidedly unsanitary and uncouth army. We decorate Sunday school rooms to resemble the cozy artificiality of morning talk-show sets. We adopt the sound-bite techniques of political advertising to avoid offending or even challenging our constituency, and we evaluate our ministers on their ability to convincingly imitate network news anchors. "And now over to brother Jim in the choir loft for an update on 'The Old Rugged Cross.'"

And then we wonder where our youth get the idea that worship and entertainment are inseparable.[22]

The entertainment mind-set is evidenced when people attend worship for "what I will get out of it." In such an approach, God is not the center of worship; we are. Such worship does not create a special time and place for God to confront us, for us to be with God in a set-apart and faithful way. The result of true worship will be that God will change us, transform us, fashion our character after God's holiness — but only if we worship God and not ourselves, if we attend worship services for the love of God.

People Want and Need More

Persons whose lives are being nurtured toward godly character will not be satisfied with worship that merely entertains or is dumbed down. Recently our congregation's youth group, who always lead worship one Sunday a month in months that have five Sundays, got very excited in planning a service for Reformation Day. They were astonished to discover all the hymns by Martin Luther in the *Lutheran Book of Worship*. In choosing the music for the service they picked substantive hymns rather than the superficial camp songs that are often sung in youth services. We accompanied a few hymns with guitars and "A Mighty Fortress" with the organ, a trumpet, and a choir descant. We used various styles of music, all with solid meaning, and the youth verbalized their appreciation for its depth.

I discovered the same interest in the deep heritage of the faith when

22. John Alexander, "Jobs against the Church," *The Other Side* 29, no. 4 (July-Aug. 1993): 53.

I did a series of children's sermons two years ago (see the Appendix). One Sunday the children and I listened to three different kinds of organ preludes — a hymn chorale, a trumpeting processional, and a Lenten meditation — and talked about how preludes help us prepare for the theme of the worship service. The little children were fascinated by the organ and listened carefully when I told them several ways in which they could prepare for worship — by praying before the service for God to help them listen well, by meditating on the music to prepare their emotions and minds for the day's theme and message, or, when they got older, by reading the hymns before the service started so that they could participate better in the singing. Many parents told me after that service how much it helped them to learn to prepare.

My point is that people *want* worship to be more meaningful, but they often need careful instruction to make it so. Children, teenagers, young adults, senior citizens — all will gladly receive more depth, especially because so much in our world is superficial and trivial or else deep in a way that is painful and tragic. How disturbing it is that many congregations dumb their worship down to society's level instead of letting worship uplift the congregants' souls and minds and spirits! What kind of character is being formed in the persons who participate in such flimsy worship?

The argument is usually made that we must "meet people where they are" or "be all things to all people." Indeed we must intentionally relate to people in accessible ways, but this does not mean that we should dumb everything down to be appealing and then not try to lift worshipers beyond the lowest common denominator. As Os Guinness insists, it is "perfectly legitimate" to "convey the gospel in cartoons to a nonliterary generation incapable of rising above MTV. . . . But five years later, if the new disciples are truly won to Christ, they will be reading and understanding Paul's letter to the Romans."[23]

I am especially concerned about these questions of worship for the very reason usually cited as support for turning to less substantive forms — namely, concern for unbelievers. Let us continually remember that unbelievers are brought to Christ 95 percent of the time not by style of worship but by friends. Consequently, our worship must be such that

23. Os Guinness, *Dining with the Devil* (Grand Rapids: Baker Book House, 1993), pp. 28-29.

125

it nurtures the kind of welcoming character that will reach out to the unsaved with the gospel. Churches are not doing a very good job of forming that kind of character, according to a recent poll conducted by the Institute for Research in Social Science at the University of North Carolina in Chapel Hill. The study concluded that "Jesus' scriptural admonition to 'make disciples of all nations' ranks far down the list of important church functions." A lack of mission/evangelism consciousness is evidenced by the fact that "today only 32 percent of the nation's Christians outside the South — and 52 percent of Southerners — consider converting people to the faith a 'very important' activity for the church."[24]

How can our congregational members become more mindful of the needs of others for faith and hope? We certainly cannot foster such awareness if our worship falls prey to the dominant "self" movement of our society and concentrates on our own feelings or experiences. Rather, our worship must keep God as the subject, for such worship cannot help but invite us all into God's self-giving character, into God's concern for the lost, into the incarnation of the gospel through our lives. How can we grow into God's likeness if we do not concentrate in worship on who God is — in all of our struggles and concerns?

As Walter Brueggemann summarizes, the main difficulties of Christian faith are "the problem of *trusting a God* who seems not available, and the problem of *caring for a neighbor* who is experienced as enemy."[25] We need worship in which we can encounter God and learn that God is trustworthy, that God is large enough to care for us in everything. We need worship that teaches us God's concern and welcome for all of our neighbors and invites us to participate in God's purposes on their behalf. We need worship deep enough to change us, strong enough to kill our self-absorption, awe-full enough to shatter the little boxes into which we try to fit God, and thorough enough to address the world's needs because God is already at work to meet them.

God gives himself to us in worship — in Word, community, and the sacraments. As we receive God's presence, our character is formed. "As

---

24. "Converting Others Not a High Priority," *The Christian Century* 111, no. 19 (15-22 June 1994): 601.

25. Walter Brueggemann, *The Message of the Psalms: A Theological Commentary,* Augsburg Old Testament Studies (Minneapolis: Augsburg, 1984), p. 81.

Alan Jones, a priest, friend, and spiritual guide, once said as he held up the bread at the Eucharist and quoted Augustine: 'Be what you see. Receive who you are!' "[26]

26. John H. Westerhoff III and John D. Eusden, *The Spiritual Life: Learning East and West* (New York: The Seabury Press, 1982), p. 59.

7. The Character of the Church as Christian Community: What Is at Stake?

We pray to You, O God, who are the supreme Truth,
    and all truth is from You.
We beseech You, O God, who are the highest Wisdom,
and all the wise depend on You for their wisdom.
You are the supreme Joy, and all who are joyful owe it to You.
You are the greatest Good, and all goodness comes from You.
You are the Light of minds, and all receive their understanding
    from You.

We love You — indeed, we love You above all things.
We seek You, follow You, and are prepared to serve You.

Alfred the Great, King of England, 849-899

Correlative to my emphases both on keeping God as the subject and object of our worship and on how worship forms the character of individual believers is the essential question of how our congregational gatherings for worship form the parish community. The biblical picture of the Body of Christ is the preeminent image for guiding this aspect of our theological formulations. This metaphor primarily reminds us that Christ is the Head; he must remain the focus, and his self-giving presence determines everything that we do.

The Worshiping Community Depends on Christ the Head

The only thing that the Christian community can do that no one else in the world can is praise its Source. That is why the Church's gatherings for worship dare never lose God as the subject and object of our praise. In Martin Marty's memorable phrase, worship is "pointless, but significant."[1]

The contemporary demand to find a "marketing niche" actually threatens genuine Christian community, for the purpose of true worship is to offer to God what will be pleasing to God. Welton Gaddy insists, "Worship experiences are inappropriately constructed (and spiritually dangerous) if their aim is congregationally directed." Confusing worship that pleases God with "entertainment in which people, with God's help, seek to please other people . . . is to risk doing great harm to the spirituality of all the people involved."[2]

Gaddy best elaborates the necessity for the Church faithfully to worship only God and how such genuine worship shapes community identity as follows:

> The true identity of the church is never in question. But it is almost always in danger of revision. From both within and outside, constant pressures push and pull at the church, favoring directions which, if followed, will alter its nature. Only in the ownership of God can a church keep in touch with its divinely ordained identity and the strength needed to maintain it. Persuasive arguments aimed at redefining the nature of the church are plentiful. Powerful forces are bent on establishing a new orientation for the church. The confidence in and commitment to the identity of the church which come from Christian

1. Martin Marty, "Holy Ground, Sacred Sound," public lecture at Zion Lutheran Church, Portland, Oregon, Nov. 14, 1993.
2. C. Welton Gaddy, *The Gift of Worship* (Nashville: Broadman Press, 1992), pp. 35-36.

worship are essential to the successful resistance of such influences. . . . In worship the church is identified as the people of God committed to the lordship of Christ. Shaped by experiences of worship, the church exists as an extension of the ministry of Jesus, a communion that is a contradiction to society. In its worship, the church realizes the resourcefulness of its corporate life and thus acknowledges its promise as a community of giftedness.[3]

In Chapter 5 we discussed the crucial requirement that the Church find its true identity in God's ownership and headship. This chapter will explore the themes of the Church's identity, ministry, and giftedness, but first we must look at the pressures that push and pull at the Church and recognize the damage to community caused by our culture's narcissistic self-absorption.

Cultural Narcissism Inimical to Community

The Christian Church's identity as a community is a given in the Bible and even in parish conversations, for we talk glibly about being "the Body of Christ." However, we scarcely recognize the immense difficulty of creating genuine community in our narcissistic culture. For years I have experimented with vocabulary and repeatedly observe how rarely contemporary Christians think in terms of "we" instead of "I." I wrote *The Hilarity of Community* with study questions to try to foster specific, tangible actions for deepening community life, but I have not had nearly as much response to that book as to others. In the first place, most churches fail to admit how much they have to go against the cultural flow to become a genuine community; and second, few are willing to expend the effort it takes to develop the necessary commitment.

We must honestly ask if the cultural odds are too much stacked against the formation of genuine Christian community. Such books as Richard Sennett's *The Fall of Public Man* (1978), Christopher Lasch's *The Culture of Narcissism* (1979), Robert Bellah and his colleagues' *Habits of the Heart* (1985), and William Dyrness's *How Does America Hear the Gospel?* (1989)[4] would seem to suggest so.

3. Gaddy, *The Gift of Worship,* pp. 52-53.
4. See especially pp. 96-105 in William Dyrness, *How Does America Hear the Gospel?* (Grand Rapids: William B. Eerdmans, 1989).

Wade Clark Roof's research on the boomer generation reveals how cultural narcissism invades the culture of the Church and turns it away from biblical community. Boomers, having left churches in the crises of young adulthood, are now becoming concerned about spiritual growth, but they seek it in psychologizing forms that isolate the self. Roof explains that a "psychological language of 'choices' and 'needs' replaces older-style religious obligations as a basis for getting involved in a congregation."[5] Those duties were primarily communitarian — commitments to each other and to tenets of a commonly held faith. In contrast, boomers shop around as consumers for a parish that emphasizes "feeling" religion. Of course, faith does stir up feelings; but what is backwards in such congregations is the loss of those communally held beliefs which create the feelings. We have already seen in previous chapters how this privatized religion changes the approach to truth from an objective grounding to a "more instrumental understanding of what it does for the believer, and how it can do what it does more efficiently" (p. 195).

We have also previously seen that this simplification of religion alters the very notion of the self, so that people think that the self can be improved and, above all else, that it must be satisfied, even though "the self's appetite is insatiable." Contemporary pluralism "feeds into this 'new voluntarism' by demonopolizing any single version as *the* religious truth and by making a wide variety of religious options open to everyone" (p. 195). Consequently, boomers pick and choose their beliefs from a wide variety of sources, which results in a "multilayered spirituality" characterized by a quest, not for systematic theological grounding, but for personal fulfillment and authenticity (p. 201). What congregations fail to convey is that a life grounded in Christianity's theological basis offers the best possibility for genuine fulfillment, and that a community of faith nurtures in its members the most authentic character.

One very harmful aspect of a narcissistic society is its rejection of the past. Lasch observes that "the cultural devaluation of the past reflects not only the poverty of the prevailing ideologies, which have lost their grip on reality and abandoned the attempt to master it, but the poverty of the narcissist's inner life." Society trivializes the past "by equating it

---

5. Wade Clark Roof, *A Generation of Seekers* (San Francisco: HarperCollins, 1993), p. 192. Page references to this book in the following paragraphs are given parenthetically in the text.

with outmoded styles of consumption, discarded fashions and attitudes," and consequently "people today resent anyone who draws on the past in serious discussions of contemporary conditions or attempts to use the past as a standard by which to judge the present."[6] This attitude is surprising — and dangerous — in the Church, since who we are depends on remembering the past, but it has become dominant nonetheless.

Even in the Church — and especially in the "worship wars" — we see what Lasch calls "the fashionable sneer that now automatically greets every loving recollection of the past" and that exploits "the prejudices of a pseudo-progressive society." Historically, however, we know that many radical movements drew "strength and sustenance from the myth or memory" of the past. "This historical discovery reinforces the psychoanalytic insight that loving memories constitute an indispensable psychological resource in maturity."[7] Thus, for the sake of its memory and its community — which are inextricably intertwined — the Church must resist our society's narcissism.

Instead of giving in to that cultural narcissism, churches could serve our society best by recovering what it means to be a community of faith (as discussed below). However, as Richard Lischer complains, "the 'community of memory' [Robert Bellah's phrase] in which members are nurtured in tradition has given way to the 'life-style enclave' in which convenience and a common mode of consumption are the most important factors." The result is that congregations no longer are alternative "contrast-societies but mirrors of the individualistic culture that surrounds and infects them."[8]

Can this narcissism be overcome? I am convinced that it can — and that worship which keeps God as the subject is the most important key, for God is the Creator of community and the preserver of the Church. Just as worship that centers on God will nurture godly character, rather than just "good feelings," in individual believers, so worship that draws all its participants into a common understanding of God will develop vibrant communities — and then the communities in turn will also deepen the character growth of their members.

6. Christopher Lasch, *The Culture of Narcissism* (New York: W. W. Norton, 1979), p. xvii.

7. Lasch, *The Culture of Narcissism,* p. xvii.

8. Richard Lischer, "Preaching as the Church's Language," in *Listening to the Word: Studies in Honor of Fred B. Craddock,* ed. Gail R. O'Day and Thomas G. Long (Nashville: Abingdon, 1993), p. 120.

Narcissism in parishes is both a cause and a result of community deterioration. Because churches are not truly communities, many believers seek fulfillment elsewhere. I share Arthur Just's conviction that "if a renewal of biblical theology allows the people of God to see themselves first and foremost as a community of saints, then they will no longer tolerate metaphors of their life that reflect the individualism of today's culture which has become pervasive in their lives."[9]

Now at the turn of the century, the Church, if it strengthens itself to be genuine community, has a wonderful opportunity to respond to deep longings in the culture that surrounds it, for people are not really satisfied by the effects of their narcissistic self-absorption. As Robert Bellah and his colleagues note, "American cultural traditions define personality, achievement, and the purpose of human life in ways that leave the individual suspended in glorious, but terrifying, isolation."[10] When the flash of glory fades, the individual often discovers the empty loneliness of her own personality, the transitory nature of achievement, and the vacuousness of selfish purposes.

There is a growing desire for community in American culture. President Clinton tapped into it in his campaign speech at the University of Notre Dame when he declared, "Most of all we are in a crisis of community, a spiritual crisis that calls upon each of us to remember and to act upon our obligations to one another." He recognized that the purpose of community "should be to call us to pursue common values and common good, not simply in the moment of extreme crisis but every day in our lives, starting right now, today." In commenting on this speech, Bellah and Adams noted that Clinton understood, "at least on a rhetorical level, that community has a moral dimension, that it demands the recognition of interdependence."[11] The Church is a critically needed community since it provides the truth of God as a basis for its moral dimension. Its worship, therefore, must proclaim, not merely feelings, but the core values of the community as it is centered in relationship with God.

Even the church marketers recognize the golden opportunity —

---

9. Arthur A. Just, "Liturgical Renewal in the Parish," *Lutheran Worship: History and Practice,* ed. Fred L. Precht (St. Louis: Concordia, 1993), p. 28.

10. Robert Bellah et al., *Habits of the Heart: Individualism and Commitment in American Life* (Berkeley: University of California Press, 1985), p. 6.

11. Robert N. Bellah and Christopher Freeman Adams, "Strong Institutions, Good City," *The Christian Century,* 111, no. 19 (15-22 June 1994): 605.

though I disagree at key points with their strategy for creating community. As Barna and McKay assert, "*The Christian community may be the most important component of all.* Millions of Christians feel they are waging a solitary battle. Sadly, loneliness is every bit as common among Christians as among the unsaved." Among the advantages they list from creating a vibrant community are bonding, fellowship, encouragement, accountability, and implementation of scriptural principles. In other words, genuine Christian community issues in changes in "belief, conduct, and speech"[12] — that is, in formation of character.

Democracy, Public Opinion, and Syncretism

Before we consider what the Christian community is — and how that both defines and is defined in its worship — we must warn against perversions of community. Since the Church is formed by its relationship with Christ, it is not — though it is usually mistaken to be — a democracy. The earliest Christians made their decisions through intensive discussion and prayer until they could say, "It has seemed good to the Holy Spirit and to us" (Acts 15:28).

Such a decision-making procedure eliminates two major problems in churches. First, congregations could prevent divisiveness if they avoided majority-vote decisions that create winners and losers. How much better it is if parishes can look for solutions that bring factions together instead of polarizing them. How many "worship wars" could be prevented if congregations discussed all the options and found as much as possible on which to agree!

An opposite problem avoided by Spirit-led consensus is finding solutions only in popular opinion. This is dangerous in the Church, for God's people above all should seek to be faithful to their Head and not be swayed by the whims and fads of the culture around them. Parish discussions certainly have a different character if everyone who submits ideas to the procedure can honestly say, "This is what I think the Holy Spirit is saying." This procedure deepens our sensibilities, forces us to learn to be more attentive, and trains us in habits of obedience.

12. George Barna and William Paul McKay, *Vital Signs* (Westchester, IL: Crossway Books, 1984), p. 147.

The nondemocratic process of listening together to the Holy Spirit is especially helpful in the worship war between advocates of high culture and those who want the Church's music to match what they hear outside the Church. The commonality of the discussion will preclude elitism, and the guidance of the Holy Spirit will thwart "popular" perversions of the gospel.

The procedure of searching for consensus under the Holy Spirit's guidance will properly incorporate the gifts of the community — as gifts to be shared for the upbuilding of all, rather than for the self-fulfillment of the gifts' possessors. In a common search for the Holy Spirit's purposes concerning worship, for example, those with gifts of wisdom and faith, those who know the Church's heritage and history, and those with theological and musical training will be respected for the necessary insights they bring to the discussion and as gifts given by God to the community to equip it for greater faithfulness.

I am certainly not advocating a rigid authoritarianism that is itself inimical to the gospel, but it does seem to me urgently necessary to bring the Church back to faithfulness in listening to the Holy Spirit rather than to mass opinion. We have let the democracy of the culture around us prevent the Church from being its own culture — a genuine Christ-following community.

David Wells criticizes democracy's effect on Church leaders as follows:

> In a democracy, every person's vote has the same weight, regardless of how well or badly informed it is. . . . Common access to truth is understood to mean common *possession* of truth. If everyone's intuitions . . . stand on the same plane, it is assumed that they are all equally valid, equally true, and equally useful. . . . Church leaders should fulfill their responsibilities within the limits of popularly held ideas . . . [which is very] different indeed from the One who . . . never once tailored his teaching to what he judged the popular reception of it would be. . . . There can be no leadership without a vision of both what the Church has become and what, under God, it should be.
>
> . . . I am *not* arguing that Christian faith should be held captive to the interests only of high culture. . . . My point is that Christian faith should not be captive to anyone. It should not be driven by the felt needs of the masses . . . [or] the prejudices of elites. . . . [I]t is Christian truth that should be taking captive culture both high and low, the elites and the masses, the special interests of the rich and poor, men and

women, racial minorities and majorities . . . teaching and explaining what has not been so well grasped, where the demands of God's truth and the habits of the culture pull in opposite directions.[13]

I have quoted Wells at length because his comments relate to so many of the worship wars. However, as usual he overstates his case, stressing truth while not acknowledging the need for a balancing love that cares for the concerns of the various groups he mentions.

That is why I advocate Christian community as the overarching entity embracing leadership. As the community educates its leaders in the members' concerns, the leaders can more lovingly educate the community in the truth in which they have been trained. Such an understanding of the Body avoids the excessive individualism, the tyranny of majority rule, and the oligarchies of self-serving elites that characterize the culture surrounding the Church.

These precautions against allowing democracy and mass opinion to control the Church are urgently necessary in this boomer age, when many returnees to the Church bring an avalanche of opinions and choices in the "multilayered spirituality" Roof describes. Without Spirit-led community and theologically trained leadership, churches stand in danger of syncretism, the appropriation of ideas and practices from various spiritual traditions without adequate discrimination of their truth.

Bernard Green asks insightful questions to prevent syncretism.[14] Let us broaden his comments by replacing specific Roman Catholic terminology with the Catholicity of Christianity, for what is at stake is our fundamental Christian identity. "Are we a community whose teachings and practices are based on our faith in the veracity of the original witnesses, or one that draws its beliefs and practices from a smorgasbord of ideas and personal experiences?"

This issue is crucial because it involves the core spirituality of the Christian community, which is a living tradition rooted in explicit historical experience. To be a Christian means "to be a committed member of a community of faith with its own specific beliefs, practices, and institutional

13. David F. Wells, *No Place for Truth* (Grand Rapids: William B. Eerdmans, 1993), pp. 214-16.

14. Bernard D. Green, "Catholicism Confronts New Age Syncretism," *New Oxford Review* 61, no. 3 (April 1994): 18. Quotations from this article in the following paragraphs are from scattered places in pp. 19-21.

disciplines," which transcend the particular colors and forms of local culture because the community is centered on Christ, the universal Head.

Because people in our culture are "physically and socially mobile," they become "religiously mobile" by dabbling in various spiritual styles. They want to be free and not "to be 'tied down,' to take a definite stand." Green criticizes this popular notion of religious "searchers," "those who have freed themselves from the limitations that commitment to a historical tradition involves." How can a search be valuable unless it includes "the capacity to commit oneself to specific truths which answer the search when they are encountered"? To be a Christian is to believe that the core truth of human life is found in Jesus Christ as the Church presents his life and teaching. "One thereby enters into a very distinctive view of life." Since the Christian "stands committed to a body of religious truth to which he is even willing to witness," now the search becomes different — to "understand more fully the content of the faith and how to live it out."

Instead of perverting faith's truths by adding incompatible elements, Christianity synthesizes many peoples and cultures while maintaining its own clear identity; it "extends its inner self to incorporate every people and culture, yet it discriminates what it assimilates in accord with its own identity." The Church critically "learns from and also reforms and develops the cultures it encounters."

Synthesizing and syncretism are radically different, but Christianity's thrust toward the former causes the latter always to be a potential problem. Therefore, whatever Christianity absorbs from a culture must be transformed in a way that enhances rather than dilutes its own identity. Christianity's identity and self-understanding are never put in question, for it is capable of absorbing whatever is best and true in other traditions and cultures.

This distinction between synthesizing and syncretism is critical as we question the community's worship. Are our worship practices faithful to the distinctive way of life of the Christian community into which faith places us? How can we best absorb the verbal, ritual, and musical forms of the culture that surrounds us without losing the unique identity of the community's culture? These questions can only be answered rightly if God remains the subject and object of our worship and if, consequently, we remember that the character of both individual members and the community at large is at stake.

The Community's Life

Our faith story is that of God's self-giving presence and intervention, which call us and form us to be a community in response. God comes to us in the "distinctive talk" of the Church's preaching and liturgy. According to Karl Barth, that talk will both reflect and promote the Church's common life as the people of God.[15] The very nature of Christianity itself demands this. God chose a people, the Jews, through whom he would accomplish his saving purposes. Christ came from this people, lived among people, chose people to carry on his mission, died for people. His chosen people were gathered together when the Holy Spirit came to empower them for ministry to every other people.

Richard Lischer names Gerhard Lohfink as one who demonstrated how much New Testament Christians lived according to "the praxis of 'togetherness'" by pointing out the ubiquity of the Greek pronoun *allelon,* translated "one another." He cites Romans 12:10 (twice), 16; 15:7; 1 Corinthians 11:33; 12:25; Galatians 5:13; 6:2; Ephesians 4:2; 5:21; Colossians 3:13; 1 Thessalonians 5:11 (twice); James 5:16 (twice); 1 Peter 4:9; and 1 John 1:7 as a few examples (pp. 114-15). Certainly, as theologians from Origen to Stanley Hauerwas have emphasized, one of the greatest gifts the Church can give to the world around us is simply to be the Church.

The community renews this identity as Church by assembling for worship. We cannot speak our distinctive talk unless we gather around God's Word and sacraments (p. 115). However, through practices already discussed in this book and other practices emanating from theological schools, preaching and song have changed from the *church to church* focus of the New Testament to a *person to person* approach. "The *formation* of a people has been replaced by the *persuasion* of individuals" (p. 119). The experience of the Word, which Barth named as God's breaking into human reality, has become a call to individual repentance, an announcement of personal justification, or "a summons to authentic existence. It leaves the hearer not with a new way of life or a new 'world' to inhabit, but a new status before God" (p. 121). We must recover biblical community life, for "neither Bultmann's call to authentic existence nor liberalism's reliance on experience creates an imaginative world of the church in which Christian hearers can find a home" (p. 122).

15. Barth, cited in Lischer, "Preaching as the Church's Language," p. 113. Page references to this article in the following paragraphs are given parenthetically in the text.

139

Consequently, my call for renewal in this book is an urgent plea to recognize that the Church as community is at stake in how we worship. Our preaching and hearing of the Word, the way we use liturgical forms, our participation in the sacraments, our song, art, and architecture all contribute to create the sense that God is with us (plural) and that we respond by dwelling in his new world.

Worship as a Public Invitation

In our desire to deepen community life, we must avoid one specially strong misconception derived from our culture's pervasive narcissistic attitudes. Worship leaders and participants alike base their expectations for worship on a false perception of "the intimate society."[16] The resulting "ideology of intimacy," Richard Keifert explains, has these three tenets:

> it posits that an enduring, profound human relationship of closeness and warmth is the most — or even the only — valuable experience that life affords. Second, the ideology supposes that we can achieve such an intimate, meaningful relationship only through our own personal effort and will. Third, it assumes that the purpose of human life is the fuller development of one's individual personality, which can take place only within such intimate relationships. This ideology of intimacy distorts contemporary understanding and evaluation of Christian public worship.[17]

Fundamentally, this ideology causes us to think that participants in a worship service must feel cozy and close to each other. This fallacy prevents worship from being truly *public* and open to those who are not part of the community.

The Christian community does develop warm and caring relationships that are nurtured in times of fellowship. However, worship is for God and should not depend on cozy feelings either toward each other or toward God — although the result of good worship will be a deepening of both. In fellowship times, we welcome strangers best by conversation and actions that focus on them. In worship, contrarily, we welcome them best by worshiping God in a public way.

16. See a thorough explication of this notion in Richard Sennett, *The Fall of Public Man: On the Social Psychology of Capitalism* (New York: Random House, 1978). See also Lasch, *The Culture of Narcissism,* pp. 27-30.

17. Patrick R. Keifert, *Welcoming the Stranger* (Minneapolis: Fortress, 1992), p. 24.

Genuine worship that "welcomes the stranger" can only happen by means of objective proclamation — for no one can enter into the feelings of others, nor will newcomers feel that they belong to an already established group.

> Indeed, the response of hospitality to the stranger can by no means be limited to the specific one-on-one friendly encounters we usually imagine by this metaphor. Hospitality to the stranger is critical to public life by definition, because it is precisely the interaction of strangers through a common set of actions that constitutes a public.[18]

For this reason, our theologizing must search for the best means to keep worship public. My emphasis on God as subject underscores the same point. How can worship best convey God's self-giving presence to a stranger in our midst?

The Christian heritage of liturgical rites and responses has functioned in such a way throughout the ages. That heritage also serves to widen our concept of community.

The Heritage of the Faith

A crucial part of making the worshiping people a community is acknowledging our unity with the entire Church, the Body of Christ, throughout time and space. Though we thoughtfully put the wine in fresh wineskins by using new forms, new melodies, new instruments, new instructions about the meanings of the old, we always preserve faith's heritage, the fundamental core of the historic Church. We don't put the wine in worn-out skins, but we do remember that it comes from grapevines that have been tended and nurtured for years. Again we see the critical need for a very careful dialectical balance — keeping the heritage of the faith and offering it in new forms faithful to that heritage. Our heritage in the story of God's presence among his people throughout the ages and nations must be carried in ways that are consistent with the story itself.

Bernhard Christensen, in exploring the treasures of spiritual classics, comments on how the *Book of Common Prayer* carries our heritage in a style

18. Keifert, *Welcoming the Stranger,* p. 8.

always clear and beautiful, often noble and sublime. . . . The most basic reason for its worldwide and enduring appeal is unquestionably its thoroughly *biblical* character. From beginning to end, in both thought and language, it is based upon Scripture. In fact, approximately two-thirds consists of actual quotations from the Bible. And the remaining materials, the prayers, the orders of worship, the occasional services, even the creeds and catechism — are cast largely in Scriptural wording. It could almost be said that the Prayer Book is the Bible arranged and paraphrased for devotional use.

Closely related to the biblical character of the Prayer Book is the fact that it is *churchly* in its whole spirit and orientation. Its authors, rather than simply devising new forms, drew freely upon more than fifteen hundred years of the worship experience of the church. The result is a work of profound, tested spiritual substance. The devotional life which it recommends is not of any individualistic sort. It is the book of *common* prayer. Its major services of prayer are intended to be conducted when the people of God are assembled in his house.[19]

Christensen comments that to use the *Book of Common Prayer* is "rather like coming into a great cathedral where solemn music is being played, or like experiencing a true friendship, which ripens with the years."[20]

Long ago Percy Dearmer wonderfully emphasized this significance of the Church's heritage. He exclaimed that in its recorded words we have

the accumulated wisdom and beauty of the Christian Church, the garnered excellence of many saints. We are by them released from the accidents of time and place. Above all we are preserved against the worst dangers of selfishness; in the common prayer we join together in a great fellowship that is as wide as the world, and we are guided, not by the limited notions of our own minister, nor by the narrow impulses of our own desires, but by the mighty voice that rises from the general heart of Christendom.[21]

19. Bernhard Christensen, *The Inward Pilgrimage: Spiritual Classics from Augustine to Bonhoeffer* (Minneapolis: Augsburg, 1976), p. 67.

20. Christensen, *The Inward Pilgrimage*, p. 68.

21. Percy Dearmer, *The Story of the Prayer Book* (New York: Oxford University Press, 1933), p. 11.

More recently, church music professor Paul Westermeyer analyzed three new service books — the Presbyterian *Book of Common Worship*, the *Book of Worship: United Church of Christ*, and *The United Methodist Book of Worship*. He notes that various scholars might argue about disparate details, but he insists that the interesting questions are the "broader ones." These three service books all

> point to the deep structures of word and sacrament and to the church at prayer across large sweeps of time and place. Though they are sensitive to their own milieu and to their specific allegiances, they point to more enduring realities and to the church's deepest instincts about worship. These instincts transcend time, place and ecclesial affiliations.
>
> Consequently, the services in these books are not likely to be popular in the sense of having immediate appeal. They are popular in that they represent the "common" prayer of all sorts and conditions of faithful Christian people over long stretches of time. This means that they call into question the sectarianism of American Protestantism, which now is more likely to flare up within denominations and congregations than between them. They certainly call into question current attempts to make worship a marketing tool.
>
> The liturgical instincts which these books represent reflect the Reformers' concern that worship belong to the people. All three make it clear that worship is not the priest's, pastor's, musician's or lay leader's property. It belongs to the community as a whole and assumes their engagement. These books protect the community from its leaders' whims and are in the people's best interests. . . . They seek to embody the Christian faith in its fullness so that the people can celebrate that fullness without the truncations and modifications each of us introduces when there is no check on pursuing our own favorite themes.[22]

As these three writers stress in different ways, the heritage of the Church is crucially necessary to preserve genuine "community" worship — worship that is not the property of its leaders, worship that crosses lines of time and space, worship that involves us in each other and not in our own private mullings, selfishness, or falsely cozy "personal relationship with Jesus."

---

22. Paul Westermeyer, "Three Books of Worship: An Ecumenical Convergence," *The Christian Century* 110, no. 30 (27 Oct. 1993): 1056.

The fact that the Church's identity as Christian community is at stake lends burning urgency to the call for renewal that preserves the heritage of the faith. Many people unknowingly influenced by narcissistic modernism want simply to throw out the "old-fashioned and outdated" without understanding the danger of destroying the Church's legacy. This failure to pay attention to the Church's history leaves us with inadequate tools to create the best new forms.

Os Guinness perceives the accelerating rate of change in the Church to be what Nietzsche calls "feverishness." Rather than letting the roots of faith come to flower and produce fruit, "feverishness is the condition of an institution that has ceased to be faithful to its origins. It is then caught up in 'a restless, cosmopolitan hunting after new and ever newer things.'" Such a pursuit of relevance, Guinness concludes, "thus becomes a prime source of superficiality, anxiety, and burn-out."[23] It certainly is the opposite of the biblical call to rest, to remember, and to reflect upon what is remembered. In order to be the Church "at a time when so many of its actual historic links are being weakened," we "must be a community of memory by perpetuating the narratives of the past, by telling stories that bring the past into the present."[24]

The Church's Tradition and Creativity

Many think that new creativity depends on dispensing with old traditions. This arises from factors we have already reviewed — movement away from the classic understanding of worship as a community's praise of God to a new individualized expression; rejection of doctrines as a means for finding our way in favor of emancipation from connections with institutions; the boomers' search for a church to meet their needs instead of commitment to the Church through which to serve.

Getting rid of the old traditions, of course, also means getting rid of denominational loyalties. Many congregations now name themselves

23. Os Guinness, *Dining with the Devil* (Grand Rapids: Baker Book House, 1993), p. 63, quoting Frederich Nietzsche, *Untimely Meditations* (Cambridge: Cambridge University Press, 1983), p. 74.

24. Robert Wuthnow, "Church Realities and Christian Identity in the 21st Century," *The Christian Century* 110, no. 16 (12 May 1993): 521.

such things as "Community Fellowship of Joy" so that there is no apparent connection to a denomination. The nature of the worship service in such a congregation cannot be differentiated by any doctrinal sense or any links to a coherent system of thought and practice. As Kenneth Woodward of *Newsweek* writes, criticizing Robert Schuller's recently formed "Churches Uniting in Global Mission," a national coalition of 200 pastors of "the most dynamic and successful" congregations,

> the aim of this determinedly antidenominational network is to lure baby boomers back to church by welcoming all comers regardless of their beliefs and appealing to their lack of theological convictions. This, of course, is precisely how American denominations got started — by belittling the competition. The difference is that the old-line Lutherans, Calvinists and Anglicans saw themselves as heirs to coherent traditions they thought worth passing on. Even when competing for converts, they put doctrinal and devotional integrity before success. "To give the whole store away to match what this year's market says the unchurched want is to have the people who know least about faith determine most about its expression," warns American church historian Martin E. Marty. The mainline denominations may be dying because they lost their theological integrity. The only thing worse, perhaps, would be the rise of a new Protestant establishment that succeeds because it never had any.[25]

We must ask if church effectiveness and preserved traditions are mutually exclusive and whether traditions prevent genuine creativity. What is lost in the process if we throw away traditions for the sake of success and novelty?

One of the great myths of contemporary marketing analysis is the idea that churches fail because of their ties to traditional belief and practice. On the contrary, sociologists with hard data about why churches decline reveal a different picture. Benton Johnson, Dean Hoge, and Donald Luidens found that decisive, "orthodox Christian belief" was necessary "to impel people to commit their time and other resources to a distinctively Christian regimen of witness and obedience in the company of other believers." The kind of congregation that does not have "an empowering system of belief" — that merely "supports honesty and other moral virtues" or "encourages tolerance and civility in a pluralistic society" — "does

25. Kenneth L. Woodward, "Dead End for the Mainline?" *Newsweek,* 9 Aug. 1993, p. 48.

not inspire the kind of conviction that creates strong religious communities."[26] In other words, to create long-term loyalty, churches need to offer orthodox substance, a system of belief that is strong enough to be empowering. Notice also these sociologists' emphasis on community. Only as the Body of Christ, carrying together the faith that is being passed on, can we know faith in a coherent way.

This does not prevent creativity. Another myth frequently espoused in modern marketing analysis is that tradition deadens the possibility for newness. This myth has some foundation in the presence of so much stale tradition, but the problem is with the staleness and not with the tradition.

Mary Ann Glendon, professor of law at Harvard, traces the roots of this myth to the beginnings of the Renaissance, when "with that heady estimation of human capacities came a certain sense of liberation from tradition, custom, and the group." However, "it was not until the Romantic era that creativity came to be identified in many quarters with individual originality, and later yet that disdain for tradition became a tradition in itself." This trajectory has reached its extreme in our time, when "the tradition of antitraditionalism would have it that *homo sapiens sapiens* can cancel its debts to the past, and that we too can bring wonders out of the void."

Glendon examines, challenges, and proves wrong the idea that tradition is antithetical to human creativity, "along with its usual underlying assumptions that tradition is necessarily static, and that the essence of creativity is originality." She asserts that to "anyone with a scientific bent" her "project will seem to be an exercise in the obvious," for, as Stephen Toulmin, Thomas Kuhn, and others have made clear in the history of science, "nearly every great advance has been made by persons (typically, groups of persons) who simultaneously possess two qualities: a thorough grounding in the normal science of their times" and "the boldness to make a break." Glendon then proceeds to discuss her primary concern — "the progress of antitraditionalism in the human sciences, where what counts as an advance, or creativity, is more contestable, and where many eminent thinkers now devote much of their energy to attacking the traditions that have nourished their various disciplines."[27]

26. Benton Johnson, Dean R. Hoge, and Donald A. Luidens, "Mainline Churches: The Real Reason for Decline," *First Things* 31 (March 1993): 16.

27. Mary Ann Glendon, "Tradition and Creativity in Culture and Law," *First Things* 27 (Nov. 1992): 13.

It is right to reject moribund tradition — its keepers have not had the boldness to be creative with it. On the other hand, those who spurn tradition itself, instead of the atrophy of tradition, forget that real creativity is impossible without the grounding in truth that tradition conveys. Avery Dulles explores poet Charles Péguy's comments on this connection between creativity and tradition:

> Tradition must renew itself by constantly returning to its own original inspiration. Tradition is thus . . . a resource. Péguy was apparently the first to use in French the term *ressourcement*, in the sense of the self-renewal of a people from the original sources of its own life. . . . Against a superficial and imperfect tradition, Péguy maintained, there is no remedy except to reactivate a deeper and more perfect tradition, and to sound the depths from which a richer humanity can well up. . . .
>
> . . . [T]o let the past live, one must grasp its spirit and adapt its forms. . . . On a superficial level, fidelity may be understood as adherence to the approved forms. But on a deeper level, the faithful adherent is one who penetrates to the meaning, the principle, the intention. Only the latter type of fidelity is open to progress and development. . . .
>
> Paradoxically, therefore, the most innovative artists and scientists have often been the most deeply traditional. Each renaissance has been, at root, a *ressourcement*. . . . So, likewise, the theologians who have made the greatest contributions by their personal genius have taken pains to labor within the tradition. What would Luther have been without Augustine, Newman without Athanasius, or de Lubac without Origen?[28]

Building on this foundation, Dulles specifically discusses the Church's worship, for its liturgy is "a privileged locus of tradition" in the Church's life. Dulles cites Polanyi's dialectic of "dwelling in" and "breaking out" and observes how traditional worship rites train and activate participants' "tacit powers" so that they experience new discoveries "in a moment of ecstasy produced by dwelling in spirit 'within the fabric of the religious ritual, which is potentially the highest degree of indwelling that is conceivable.' "[29]

Genuine tradition is sure enough to allow us to dwell in it, but it is

28. Avery Dulles, "Tradition and Creativity in Theology," *First Things* 27 (Nov. 1992): 23-25.

29. Dulles, "Tradition and Creativity in Theology," pp. 25-26.

also open enough to let us break out into new expressions. So much is lost if churches arbitrarily throw out all the tradition in response to marketing myths, yet those who seek to preserve the tradition for the sake of the community are often derided as old-fashioned or merely elitist in taste. Thus it becomes extremely difficult to fight the modern trivialization that is happening in churches for the sake of newness. As Richard John Neuhaus asserts, "Effective resistance to innovation, when one is convinced that resistance is called for, requires courage and imagination. It also requires being embedded in a community that has an identifiable history that is sustained by authoritative claims to truth."[30]

Because a supportive community is crucially necessary and because the very narcissistic innovations that must be resisted destroy that community, those who seek to bring their home parishes to a better understanding of what it means to worship often suffer personal derision and lack any community support. Several of the individuals described in Hendricks's *Exit Interviews* left churches for just that reason. Sometimes in their attempt to make worship "exciting" parishes lose the very members who can best teach them about true worship. Even more important, those congregations lose their source of stability — the continuity, durability, and fruitfulness of the Church's heritage.

We can judge the vitality of maintained tradition by its fruitfulness. Does it give rise to new expression? Does it relate to the life and situations of those who come to worship? Are the presence and action of God clearly conveyed so that those who participate in the tradition can experience God's self-giving addressed to them and respond with praise? Is the tradition both carried by the community and a source of character growth for the community?

God calls us to be discerning. As Douglas Webster declares, "Spiritual direction is often a call back to the basic faith and to practice that shapes and strengthens the church as the body of Christ. . . . Discernment is not so much an intellectual exercise as a discipline of faithfulness."[31]

30. Richard John Neuhaus, "The Innovationist Edge," *First Things* 27 (Nov. 1992): 66.

31. Douglas D. Webster, *Selling Jesus* (Downers Grove, IL: InterVarsity Press, 1992), p. 139.

Passing On the Faith

The question of passing on the faith connects this chapter and the previous two. The faith is not worth passing on if God is not its subject and object. We can only pass on the faith if it has nurtured our character to be its carriers and if we are part of a community, the Church, that has carried the faith down through the ages. Worship is a crucial key, for in worship we experience the presence of the self-giving God to create and nurture our faith. Worship forms us; all the elements of the service develop the character of believer in us. And worship forms the community if it unites us in common beliefs, traditions, renewal, and goals. Worship schools us in the language of faith as we listen and sing and participate in its rites.

The major reason why tradition often grows stale is that we have failed to educate worshipers to know why we do what we do and who we are as a community carrying the faith together. Moreover, we have not taught the vibrancy of renewed worship rooted in the heritage of faith and expressed in new forms. We must constantly be teaching people what is happening and why, as well as who and whose we are.

Who does such teaching? We might think it is the job of a congregation's clergy and musicians and education leaders, but it is really the responsibility of the entire community to hand on the faith to the next generation. I once surveyed a confirmation class of seventh and eighth graders. Their responses matched exactly — every kid who loved the liturgy was the child of parents who sang it. One boy, whose father usually stood silently gazing elsewhere, exclaimed that he hated the worship service, but could give no specific answer when I asked why.

The problem for many who don't like worship is that they don't understand it. We have not taught the meaning of symbols, the reason for certain actions or responses, the value of doing things in certain ways. As a child I never liked the slow movements of piano concertos. I liked the flashy parts, the thrilling impossibility of moving one's hands so fast over the keys. Not until I was more mature did I learn to appreciate the greater difficulty of capturing the kind of expression that is only possible in slowness. To appreciate genuine worship, no matter what style or form, requires training, sensitivity, and patience with mysteries of God that are beyond our ken. Worship that is too easy cheats us. It deprives us of the grandeur of an infinite God.

Our narcissistic culture makes it difficult for many to get outside of themselves, to appreciate ideas and ideals that are larger than they are. Worship must, therefore, be invitation — invitation to the profound Joy of the presence of God, to involvement in a community of praise, to disciplines that nurture personal and corporate growth in character.

The invitation of worship is most often accepted because of the model of others. Almost 60 percent of citizens in the United States attribute their current religious beliefs to the example of their parents.[32] Because so many children in our culture are raised in homes that do not set the example of spiritual devotion, the Church must encourage its more mature members to provide mentoring to families, fathering or mothering for children in single-parent households, extra teaching and time beyond Sunday school and catechism instruction. The whole community must always be in a process of growth to become more grounded in the faith it seeks to pass on and to practice its proclamation.

Unfortunately, many congregations move in the opposite direction of the one they should pursue because increasing numbers of people are transient and infrequent participants in religious communities. Instead of retelling the stories of the faith both to remind community members of the meaning of their life together and to invite newcomers to begin to learn that meaning, "now churches shy away from such stories because they know newcomers will not understand."[33] The result is that the community owns less and less of a story to which all — mature believers and learners alike — can be committed.

If we give people less of a gospel, they see no reason to be Christian. Kenneth Woodward's *Newsweek* report summarizes the mainline churches' problem:

> These churches have lost their children. Few baby boomers raised in Presbyterian families, for example, have become adult Presbyterians. Rather than join other denominations, surveys show, fully 48 percent opt out of churchgoing altogether. "There used to be an ecology that nurtured the faith of children through parents, Sunday schools, youth conferences, summer camps and church-related colleges," observes [John M.] Mulder [president of Louisville Presbyterian Theological Seminary]. But in the last 25 years, the Presbyterians and other mainline

32. Jeffrey L. Sheler, "Spiritual America," *U.S. News and World Report* 116, no. 13 (4 April 1993): 50.

33. Wuthnow, "Church Realities and Christian Identity," p. 521.

denominations have diluted these programs. "We provided our children with a theological rationale for embracing secularism," says the Rev. William Willimon, Methodist dean of the chapel at Duke Divinity School.[34]

When we give people an inferior gospel, we also fail to train their capacity for judging truth and for seeking the best expressions of it. What we do and the worship forms we use are critically important because they shape the community's "capacity to discriminate and discern excellence." These skills are "learned and warranted in a community of discourse." Unless worship is careless or trivialized, "the acquired capacity manifests disciplined habits of seeing and valuing, which reflect the ethos of a knowledgeable community."[35]

Every community that gathers for worship could be like the people of Berea, who searched the Scriptures to confirm everything the apostle Paul said to make sure it was the truth (Acts 17:10-12). Each community is part of the constant process of preserving the faith throughout time and space. As Paul Mankowski reminds us,

> every article of faith we have, no matter how obvious or how arcane it may appear, has run a gamut of fatal threats throughout the centuries, and has been vouchsafed to us, *multa interalia,* by bishops and censors and canonists and judges. . . . [T]he teachings of the Church have to be reappropriated in every generation — unglamorous work! — and protected from contamination, neglect, and the random predations of those Williams of Newcastle [a monk who distorted Council decrees] that stalk the pages of the history of doctrine in every age like a recurring nightmare.[36]

What would happen if we challenged our churches with this commission, if we reminded worship participants that they are responsible for keeping the faith intact to pass on to the next century? Could we enable them to pay more careful attention to how our worship and community life faithfully protect it?

34. Woodward, "Dead End for the Mainline?" p. 47.
35. Leander E. Keck, *The Church Confident* (Nashville: Abingdon, 1993), p. 28.
36. Paul V. Mankowski, "The Skimpole Syndrome: Childhood Unlimited," *First Things* 33 (May 1993): 28.

Yet the opposite is happening in the educational channels of the Church. This is illustrated by the shift in the contents of *Christianity Today,* a leading evangelical journal, between 1959 and 1989. In those thirty years advertising increased from 3-7 percent to 30-48 percent. News increased from 20 percent to 40 percent, but exposition of the Bible and explication of biblical doctrine decreased from 36 percent to 8 percent![37]

Today the statistics are even less encouraging. A recent survey conducted by the Barna Research Group discovered that few adults in the United States could "explain the meaning of commonly used religious terms such as the Great Commission (9%), John 3:16 (35%), evangelical (18%), or the gospel (37%)." We might expect such figures from our post-Christian culture, but among those who identified themselves as "born again" the statistics were alarmingly dismal. Only one-quarter could define the Great Commission and only half knew John 3:16.[38] At a time when fewer believers are rooted deeply in the essential truths of the faith, we must make sure that we do not dumb down our educational programs or our worship as we seek to reach out to the culture around the Church.

Our religious symbols are key tools for passing on the faith, but, as we shall see more thoroughly in Chapter 10, they also are in danger of trivialization in the culture of technopoly. That is why my plea is so urgent for churches to think carefully before they throw away their worship rites and liturgies and arts, their traditions of faith, their community stories and habits and language. Without the symbols developed over the centuries, we have fewer means to hand over the truth of the gospel to the next generation — and if we are not careful, we will have no substance in our faith to pass on.

By passing on the faith in worship, the Church especially nurtures the character of believers. The Christian community fosters that transformation also in many other ways. We hear and study in Bible classes the narratives that teach us who Jesus is and what his people are like. In the community's fellowship we experience the incarnation of those virtues. In the community's discipline we are rebuked and warned and instructed and loved when we choose values other than those of the Kingdom of God. In the community's strength we are bolstered with courage to continue

37. Wells, *No Place for Truth,* p. 209.
38. Barna Research Group, *National and International Religion Report* (March 21, 1994), as cited in *Discipleship Journal* 14, no. 4 (July/Aug. 1994): 14.

holding fast to the truth about our life in God in the face of the conflicting perspectives of the technological milieu. Because the Christian community is an alternative milieu, many facets contribute together to nurture godly character. But this will not happen automatically; it must be intentional and consistent and pervasive and strong and beautiful to provide an appealing alternative to our society's milieu.

Dialectics Necessary for Genuine Community

Let us look more intentionally at the dialectical balances required to create and preserve genuine community life in a worshiping, character-nurturing congregation. Probably the most important dialectical balance already emphasized is retaining the heritage of the faith while using fresh forms to express it. Diversity can be achieved in many ways — by using a multiplicity of liturgical forms (the 1969 *Hymnal of the Moravian Church,* which goes back to the Prague hymnal of 1501, contains 200 pages of liturgies for various seasons and moods); by varying the same liturgy's musical style (the *Lutheran Book of Worship* has three different musical settings for the communion liturgy with suggested variations at many points); by using a variety of musical instruments (in one celebration this year we sang various verses of one hymn with trumpet and organ accompaniment, with flute and guitar accompaniment, with trumpet descant, with only men or only women singing — all according to the content of the verses); or by interspersing newly composed liturgies with the familiar ones.

Above all, the worship forms we use must foster "the work of the people" and not be subject to the whims of the leaders. I cannot stress enough the requirement for worship to remain the people's work, the praise and prayer of the community gathered to offer itself as a living sacrifice. Our culture's entertainment mentality is so easily imbibed; recently I witnessed a "worship service" in which the participants did not say or sing one single line!

"Entertainment worship" must be countered by nurturing in the community members an understanding of the dialectic of the congregation being the actors who worship God and God being the Actor who reveals himself in that worship to his people. This is serious business — both because God is worthy of the very best praise and worship we can create

153

and because we so desperately need God's revelation in order to be formed as a people who can think well in a world that denies his revelation. To be intentionally serious about worship need not lead to boring or stiff worship. Only with great seriousness about the content of our worship can we discover its immense Joy and freedom.

Many other dialectical balances enable corporate worship truly to build the character of the community. Robert Mulholland lists the following:

> elements of interaction with others balanced with space for individual reflection; worshipping God with our bodies and senses balanced with opportunities to listen and respond to the whispers of the Spirit; loving God with our minds by careful thinking upon the issues of our discipleship as the body of Christ in the world and loving God with our hearts through affective responses to God and others; an orderly and disciplined liturgy balanced by openness to the movement of the Spirit.[39]

Besides Mulholland's dialectics of listening and responding, mind and heart, will and body, discipline and spontaneity, this book comments elsewhere on others, as do my other books on Sabbath keeping[40] and on Christian community.[41] I emphasize all of these in order to make it more possible for each Christian to live out the dialectic of being personally, individually, uniquely important for the well-being of the whole community while yet understanding oneself not in individualistic terms but as an integral part of the community's wholeness.

Accoutrements That Affect Community

In order to do everything we can to foster worship participants' sense of community, we should be aware of subtle aspects of architecture and design

---

39. Robert M. Mulholland, Jr., *Invitation to a Journey: A Road Map for Spiritual Formation* (Downers Grove, IL: InterVarsity Press, 1993), p. 72.

40. See my book *Keeping the Sabbath Wholly* (Grand Rapids: William B. Eerdmans, 1989), especially for discussion of the dialectics of grace and response and of God's rhythms for our lives.

41. See my book *The Hilarity of Community* (Grand Rapids: William B. Eerdmans, 1992), especially for an understanding of the need to build genuine community in the local congregation and for practical study questions to help build it in your setting.

in our worship space and even of behaviors in our worship time that are inimical to genuine community. Sometimes we can eliminate these factors; if not, we can only counteract them with practical tactics or explicit teaching.

Unfortunately, the old cathedral style of architecture in which most of our naves are built militates against a sense of a worshiping *community* in whose midst God is present. Rather, the long narrow nave with a raised chancel for the pastor fosters the idea that the pastor performs the service or that God is represented by only one person in the community. If the pastor becomes the staged actor and all the congregation members the audience, this nurtures the attitude that during the week the pastor does the ministry while the rest of the people go about their daily lives. What can we do, if we have such a building, to develop instead the vital sense that all of us act in the worshiping Body, that the participation of each person is essential for the Body to be complete? How can we best teach pastors and musicians to serve only as stage directors of the action? How can we keep God as the object or audience of our praise, even as he is, paradoxically, the acting subject?

Our sense of community is heightened by architectural designs such as round buildings with worshipers on three sides of the altar or with the baptismal font placed in the center of the Body. If a parish's old building aggravates the stage sense of worship, a committee might generate ideas for improving the worship ambience. Perhaps the pews could be placed at a different angle so that congregants see more of each other than the backs of necks; perhaps the Scripture lessons could be read from the middle of the people, or more members could be involved in various parts of the service.

The entire ambience of the worshiping place affects our sense of the whole community, often in ways that might never occur to us. David Hendricksen insists in an unpublished paper that since the Church's business is *corporate* worship, everything in the church building itself must be intended to enhance community. Consequently, since room acoustics directly affect the worship life, acoustics are a spiritual and not just a musical issue. Hendricksen notes the fact that carpet is a very effective means of deadening a room acoustically, and he describes several negative spiritual consequences. For example, during hymns, members hear only themselves and the organ, because the sound of others' singing is soaked up. Most people are embarrassed to sing alone, so they will sing with progressively less gusto until some might quit entirely. A dead room also leads to mumbled spoken prayers and liturgical responses. As a result,

155

people feel more isolated and begin to sit further apart. We might therefore consider in our congregations whether we should remove thick carpet and heavily padded pews that stifle the sound in our sanctuaries and cause worship participants to be more removed from each other.[42] In what other ways might we improve the acoustics of our worship place to facilitate singing together?

The scriptural image of the Body urges us to nurture each person's gifts for the sake of the functioning of the whole. Romans 12, 1 Corinthians 12, Ephesians 4, and 1 Peter 4 all teach that God's grace comes through varieties of gifts, the contributions of all the members of the Body. The belief that all of life is worship and the conviction that we are a worshiping Body are both especially nurtured if the worship place makes visible the various gifts of many people — for example, crafted wood carvings and sculptures, specially built chancel furniture, banners, pottery vessels for the Eucharist elements, homemade bread and wine, handwoven baskets for offerings, homegrown flowers, and so forth. What other visual elements can we use as symbols that we are a people together, a community using our gifts in response to God?

It is essential that we teach congregants how these physical aspects of the community's space affect our worship. We can put notes in the worship folder to remind participants of various members' gifts that are visible or tasted. Children's sermons can focus on such gifts as the symbols on homemade banners or the beauty of God visible in homegrown flowers. By such messages we nurture in children a sense of the many ways in which they can participate in and contribute to the Body's wholeness. We want every aspect of worship — not only what we say and sing, but how we interact and the ways in which the environment affects all our senses — to underscore the awareness that all of life is a response to a gracious God who frees us to use our gifts together.

One contemporary tendency that is subtly destructive of genuine community is the growing practice of applauding when choirs or individuals sing. Affirming these participants' use of gifts should be done after the corporate service, for applause really disrupts the worshiping community in two ways. First, the ones applauded become the center of attention instead of God, to whom they offer their gifts. Second, applause heightens

---

42. David Hendricksen, "Observations Regarding Worship, Carpet, and Music," unpublished paper.

the attitude in other members that they are not as important in the Body as those with special musical gifts. We want our practices instead to create the sense that *all* that we do is worship. Some people worship by singing; others, by listening. All of us worship in our daily jobs, our family life, the offering of our gifts for God's service.

I object strongly to applause during worship because in many churches I have witnessed the two disruptions mentioned, although I also agree that sometimes a spontaneous burst of applause can be healthy. However, such outbursts of applause are frequently arbitrary, recognizing some singers or instrumentalists but not others, often without attention to the amount of care and effort expended. In one parish, for example, some young girls who had not spent any time practicing sang badly off-key during the offertory and were applauded, while the adult choir, which sang beautifully after extensive practice, was not applauded, nor was the young trumpeter who played melodies and descants for several of the hymns in the festival services. The applause for poor singing encouraged mediocrity and lack of effort and left many excellent and hard-working musicians feeling totally unappreciated.

I'd rather have no applause in worship than a failure to recognize that all congregants offer their best — by serving on the altar guild, sweeping the carpet, making a banner, singing the liturgy with gusto, listening closely to the sermons, reading well, and taking old bulletins out of the hymnbooks. One friend suggested that instead of applause, the pastor could make a comment of gratitude for the use of specific gifts and the congregation could say, "Amen" — but I must add to this suggestion the hope that the pastor would, throughout the year, mention all kinds of gifts being used to serve God so that the congregation could get a greater sense of the wholeness of the Body.

The Community Reaching Out:
The Courage to Sing and Preach the Faith

Being a genuine community is especially important as congregations seek to reach out to the boomer generation. As Wade Clark Roof emphasizes, "There are no simple formulas, no simple set of criteria that will explain why some congregations attract boomers and others repel them. The chemistry between congregation and people is much more complex and far more unpredictable."[43] Consequently, we dare not reduce our plans for reaching out to focusing on one single factor, such as style of music. Roof elaborates some of the factors involved and thereby points to the critical need for genuine community. His research team discovered that boomers go to congregations that

> have something distinctive about them — good worship, good programs, a particular social cause, a warm and accepting environment. Whatever the religious background, integrity is crucial. And in all these places there are conflicts — latent, if not always manifest — between the loyalists who never left and the returnees who have just come back, and between boomers and an older generation. How these tensions and strains all work themselves out affects the ethos of a congregation.[44]

We must add, moreover, that the ethos of a community greatly affects how well the congregation works out those tensions. How well the congregation asks itself about keeping God as the subject of worship, nurturing the character of the believers, and developing the community life of the people together will have great consequences for their ability to work through the tensions and strains.

Every aspect of behavior, space, and style is immensely important because the entire character of the Church is at stake in our worship. Is the Church the living testimony to God's saving work in Jesus Christ and to God's presence in our worship? By what is the character of the Church formed — by market forces and strategies or by the two Testaments of God's revelation?

Paul Westermeyer laments that "the spirit of the times calls us to catch the worship bandwagon that is pulled by marketing," and he adds, "to the extent that that is permitted to happen, the church will be impoverished."[45] If we want to prevent the Church from becoming merely market-driven, we must recognize our calling to be an alternative society, God's "peculiar" people. We can best reach out to the world around us by truly being who we are as a community of faith in response to God. As Richard Lischer emphasizes, "The way the church 'talks to itself' at wor-

43. Roof, *A Generation of Seekers,* p. 204.
44. Roof, *A Generation of Seekers,* pp. 211-12.
45. Westermeyer, "Three Books of Worship," p. 1057.

ship ultimately constitutes its witness to the world."[46] We will need great boldness to sing and preach the faith in a post-Christian society. Our worship and education must nurture in us the courage to sing of hope and love in a world short of both.

In a world characterized by gender wars, it is a shame that the politics of language is very divisive in many local churches and national denominations. In an article describing various methods for healing the language rifts (such as using new feminine or neutral names for God, adding feminine images, and healing distorted patriarchy), Catherine Mowry LaCugna recognizes that at root the problem is deeper than language. She suggests that the Christian community is to be "the icon of the Trinity where there is sheer joy in mutual love, the fullest possible exchange and interdependence among persons. Just as there is no room for division or inequality or hierarchy in God, the same must be true among the followers of Christ." LaCugna insists that we gain nothing if "language for God is made inclusive, but is uttered by a non-inclusive community."[47] We need the presence of God to give us courage to discuss the language of our worship so that it is inclusive of women, biblically faithful, and constructive for the community's unity.

In a racially divided and ethnically fractured world, it is brave to sing of the unity of all people in Christ. Churches do well to add to their hymnody songs from other lands in other tongues to practice that inclusiveness. For our community life to reflect genuine unity will require new awareness, deeper intention, careful practice, worshipful expression.

In a world that kills the weak through mindless abortions and in a cultural climate growing more and more favorable toward euthanasia, the Church must take pains to welcome to its worship life the handicapped, the infirm, the senile, the disordered. What provisions do we make in our sanctuaries so that the hearing or visually impaired are not excluded from the community? Are we preventing children from growing up in the language of worship by banishing their cries, relegating their songs to special programs, not involving them in the practices of worship? Do we provide transportation, hospitality, entrance ramps, and alternative seating

46. Lischer, "Preaching as the Church's Language," p. 117.
47. Catherine Mowry LaCugna, "Freeing the Christian Imagination," *dialog* 33, no. 3 (Summer 1994): 194.

so that no one is denied access to the community's gatherings? Do we educate well so that worship-illiterates can join in?

For the sake of community inclusiveness, what do we do with our worship? Is it geared, as the marketing engineers urge us, to a homogeneous unit? Do we only emphasize the individual's relationship with God and make a person feel comfortable because the congregation meets that person's felt needs? Or do we invite members and visitors to be part of a larger whole than themselves, participants in a Church that exists throughout all time and space?

How can we design our worship to be truly inclusive, not only in our language, but also in our welcoming of all races and all people whose lives have been broken? We need continuity with past traditions, as well as with the present global community. We need, as Brueggemann explains, the public imagination of the psalms.

> Given our privatistic inclination, we do not often think about public disasters as concerns for prayer life. . . . We have nearly lost our capacity to think theologically about public issues and public problems. . . . The psalms [of communal lament] are statements about the religious dimension of public events of loss. They permit us to remember that we are indeed public citizens and creatures and have an immediate, direct, and personal stake in public events. The recovery of this mode of psalmic prayer may be important if we are to overcome our general religious abdication of public issues and the malaise of indifference and apathy that comes with the abdication.[48]

Above all, the Christian Church at worship senses its responsibility for the world outside. Can we truly experience the presence of the cosmic God without being incorporated into his purposes of peace and justice in the world? Each person in the community is essential for God's will to be done on earth.

This challenge is addressed to all in my intended audience for this book. I write not only for worship leaders, pastors, and musicians, but for everyone in the pew. Worship requires the creativity and active participation of everyone in the community, and that can happen only if we all recognize that worship is indeed the work of the people. The participation

---

48. Walter Brueggemann, *The Message of the Psalms: A Theological Commentary,* Augsburg Old Testament Studies (Minneapolis: Augsburg, 1984), p. 67.

of every single member of the congregation is eminently important, but even more important is the gathering of the whole. We must ask not only if we have the courage to sing the faith, but also if we can be selfless enough to be a community. When God is the subject, he invites us to be servants, submitting ourselves to the well-being of the Body and, consequently, of the world. When God is the subject, the community has the courage to sing the faith — and then to live it.

We considered in Part II the nature of the culture to which we want to reach out with our faithful songs and in Part III the particular culture of our faith community. On the basis of these reflections, we can now turn in Part IV to specific questions about the ways in which we sing the faith.

PART IV

The Culture *in* Our Worship

8. *Throwing the Baby Out with the Bath Water or Putting the Baby in Fresh Clothes: Music*

What language shall I borrow to thank thee, dearest friend,
For this thy dying sorrow, thy pity without end?
Oh, make me thine forever, and, should I fainting be,
Lord, let me never, never outlive my love to thee.

Bernard of Clairvaux, 1091-1153

I have heard it too many times — an unfounded assumption that should be rigorously questioned. Last week in a national meeting at a denominational headquarters, a workshop leader adamantly declared, "Baby boomers don't like hymns. They want to hear music like they hear outside the church."

First of all, how can she be so sure? I know *lots* of baby boomers who *love* hymns. I am one of them. Furthermore, many of those who dislike hymns participate in churches that disdain hymns, don't teach them well, and sing them poorly. What would happen if they were exposed to good hymn singing and better education about the Church's musical heritage? What if they came as adults to a parish with a vital musical life

165

including various styles of music sung with vigor and gladness? Furthermore, as this book has already asked, should worship be simply what we want, and should the Church be like the culture surrounding it?

I am not an old-fashioned musical elitist. I enjoy new music, creative worship forms, different approaches. What I am opposed to is dumbing down the Church — and throwing the baby out when we throw out the bath water.

Bad Questions: Scapegoats, Opinions, Musicians

We look at music first among the particulars of worship because so often discussions about worship contain the implicit assumption that if we just use the right popular sounds, people will flock to our services. Samuel Adler, a teacher of composition at the Eastman School of Music, unmasks the deception of this assumption when he complains, "The music of worship has been cast in the role of convenient scapegoat for all maladies afflicting the attendance at, participation in and comprehension of worship services."[1]

Music often becomes the scapegoat after pastors have failed for years to train congregation members to evangelize in their daily lives. As previously noted, most conversions are the result of friendship, not worship style — but if such reaching out has not occurred over the years, sometimes churches suddenly switch music and worship styles in order to "attract" people. The music of the faithful Church is jettisoned to compensate for long-term failure to be the Church, inviting unbelievers by friendship and by active Christian life.

---

1. Quoted in Paul Westermeyer, "Professional Concerns Forum: Chant, Bach, and Popular Culture," *The American Organist* 27, no. 11 (Nov. 1993): 35. Page references to this article in this section are given parenthetically in the text. David Wells (*God in the Wasteland* [Grand Rapids: William B. Eerdmans, 1994) insists that

> the fundamental problem in the evangelical world today is not inadequate technique, insufficient organization, or antiquated music, and those who want to squander the church's resources bandaging these scratches will do nothing to stanch the flow of blood that is spilling from its true wounds. The fundamental problem in the evangelical world today is that God rests too inconsequentially upon the church. His truth is too distant, his grace is too ordinary, his judgment is too benign, his gospel is too easy, and his Christ is too common. (p. 30)

166

Music is also blamed for what might simply be the result of demographics. It is difficult for a congregation to grow if it is located in a dying small town in rural Nebraska. Myriads of other factors affect participation in worship, so we must ask better questions before we throw out hymns — or any other kind of music — for the sake of appealing to the masses.

One advocate of "contemporary" music for worship wrote in a nationally published letter to another pastor, "you mentioned that your contemporary service has 'become your most popular service.' That should surely say something." Shouldn't we look more closely at something that is "popular" to ask if it is being faithful? When Jesus told the truth, some of his disciples left him (see John 6, for example). Is the point of worship to make participants comfortable or to teach them about God? Keeping God as the subject might lead to comfort — or its opposite! What kind of character is being formed by certain styles of worship? Candy is very popular with children, but we wouldn't feed them only candy if we want them to grow strong and healthy.

At this point we must sidetrack to recognize that many terms typically used in worship wars are inaccurate. What is called "contemporary" worship music is often more like the soft rock of the earlier, boomer generation. Truly contemporary music might include acid rock and heavy metal, the esoteric church music of Krzysztof Penderecki, or my new hymn for this year's Pentecost service. At the 1986 "Lectures in Church Music" held at Concordia University in River Forest, Illinois, Thomas Gieschen gave new sacred choral styles the following names so that they could be discussed more intelligently: Contemporary Esoteric, Church Modern, Neo-Romantic, Pop Chord Romantic, A Touch of Broadway, Popular Triumphalism, Holy Pop, Pseudo-Folk, Clever Casual, and Trivial.[2] It does not serve our purposes here to cite his illustrations of these styles since few of us would know all the composers of choral music whom he names, but it is useful simply to note that the term *contemporary* encompasses a wide variety of styles, some more or less fitting for worship.

2. Thomas Gieschen, "Contemporary Christian Music — Problems and Possibilities," unpublished paper prepared for the "Lectures in Church Music" series, Concordia University, River Forest, IL, Nov. 6, 1986, pp. 4-5. All subsequent references to this paper in this chapter are given parenthetically in the text. I owe Dr. Gieschen enormous gratitude for many other insights that cannot be specifically documented but were gained from his course in liturgy, his choral training and organ instruction, and many conversations over the years.

Similarly, the meaning of the term *traditional* is ambiguous when applied to music, for the traditions of parishes vary as much as do those of families. When it is necessary in this book to use a quick name in order to avoid long convoluted explanations, I intend the term *traditional* to signify music in the standard denominational hymnals — that is, music in the memory of a particular faith persuasion. The word *contemporary* indicates attempts to utilize music that will appeal to younger people, who often have not been actively involved in congregations. The noun *hymns* will primarily signify the former and *songs* the latter, though there is considerable crossover of these forms between eras of church music. Any terminology is inadequate to describe the broad range of musical styles represented by these names, but these will have to suffice.

It is terribly naive to think that music is the main thing that attracts people to a worship service. The most well-known marketing specialists admit that personal invitations are the key, for encouragement to participate from a trusted friend "builds upon an established relationship, which means that the recommendation or invitation springs from a credible source."[3]

We should, of course, ask good questions about the kinds of music we use in our services, but we must first end the scapegoating that inhibits proper analysis. Similarly, we should carefully assess popular opinion, especially as it is gathered in such uneven samples as worship surveys. We don't let our children do only what they want; instead, we rely on better judgment, informed by ethical principles and moral standards. Mercurial public opinion should not bear the same weight as the wisdom of talented and well-trained worship leaders, whose duty and delight it is to use their gifts for the glory of God. Nor should we shape the believers' worship and praise of God around the needs of visitors.

Unfortunately, some classically trained church musicians have been elitist and have not related well to the community — such as organists who play to highlight their own performance more than to lead the congregation in worshipful singing. But to use music as the scapegoat or to choose popular music to "sell" the congregation to the masses leads to destructive consequences for worship — and for the gospel, too, if God's converting power becomes subservient to the tools of human beings.

Paul Westermeyer explains how the use of music to sell worship to

3. George Barna, *Marketing the Church* (Colorado Springs: NavPress, 1988), pp. 109-10.

the culture around the Church "puts the musician in a terrible bind." The musician becomes perceived as the one whose task it is

> to market a product whose truth is not the issue. The issue is solely how well the advertising is done and how many customers you can sell on your product. That has never been the role of the church or synagogue musician. It may work to sell carpets or soap, or cars, but it's an impossible contradiction for the church or synagogue musician who by it is set against the people as their manipulator, rather than as one who lives with and for them as the leader of their song. (p. 35)

Many musicians who understand their role and try to offer their best gifts to the congregations they serve get caught in worship wars, with pastors or parish committees demanding changes without adequate discussion, questions, or caring. In a footnote Westermeyer shows the damage done by

> the tyranny and abuse those in authority exercise over musicians, who are almost always in positions of weakness. It accounts for the initial confusion and then the rage among some musicians, like the rage of abused spouses or children. It has nothing to do with perspective and everything to do with abuse and abused. Musicians probably can seldom influence this positively, any more than any victims of abuse can positively influence their abusers. The real puzzle is to find colleagues who are not driven by greed or power or abuse, and who are interested in figuring things out together with church musicians, for the sake of the church and the world. (p. 39, n. 7).

In my freelance work throughout the country I have met far too many musicians who feel this way — that they have not been given the opportunity to express their desire for authentic worship and the reasons for their musical perspectives, but have instead been criticized as elitists who are not concerned for the salvation of lost souls (as was the musician noted in the letter mentioned above). Many pastors and parishes, though with good intentions of appealing to nonbelievers, meanwhile deal in this abusive manner with their musicians.

My goal in this chapter is to provide criteria by which congregation members, pastors, and musicians can analyze music and come to consensus about its suitability for worship. Can we learn together to ask better questions? Our primary questions should concern the place of God, the character of the believer, and the building of the Christian community — the themes of our previous three chapters. (Many of these questions can also apply to our proclamation of the Word and to other aspects of worship that we will discuss in the following two chapters, so we won't need to repeat them there.) After reflecting on these themes, we can consider questions of style and musical worth.

God as the Subject and Object in Worship Music

Thomas Gieschen, in his paper for the "Lectures on Church Music," proposes a "selection grid" by which choral directors could screen repertoire choices and discusses how matters of style fit into the selection process. His guidelines provide an excellent framework for decisions about all the music used in worship, for it utilizes a series of selective stages that analyze the text, style, propriety, and worth of different music pieces. He begins with the text since it is the most objective check and because music that fails this test need not be submitted to the other, more difficult to measure aspects of the grid (pp. 6-7). Since we are concerned for the formation of the character of believers and community, I would add that this stage *must* be first. No matter how musically wonderful, pieces must be rejected if the text is theologically inadequate.

Johann Sebastian Bach, who is often called "the supreme religious composer" and whose compositions are more often performed and studied than the music of any other composer,[4] sets a superb example. In all of Bach's work — even his secular compositions — music, theology, and worship are all intertwined. On many of his compositions he inscribed the letters *I.N.J.* or *S.D.G.,* which stand for "In the name of Jesus" and "Soli Deo Gloria." All music is "for the glory of God alone," according to Bach, and for "the instruction of my neighbors." As Gaddy exclaims, "Certainly Bach described the spirit which should be prompted by and pervasive in the music which is made a part of authentic worship."[5] Elizabeth Achtemeier describes how she learned about God as she was

4. Jane Stuart Smith and Betty Carlson, *A Gift of Music: Great Composers and Their Influence* (Westchester, IL: Cornerstone Books, 1979), pp. 41-52.

5. C. Welton Gaddy, *The Gift of Worship* (Nashville: Broadman Press, 1992), pp. 159-60.

exposed to the excellence of sacred music. The church to which Mother took her children had an astounding choir. . . . From childhood on I heard the finest church music, sung in a spine-tingling manner. I learned theology from Bach as well as from the preacher. I knew Isaiah from Handel long before I knew it from the Bible.[6]

Theological soundness is not restricted, of course, to the music of the old masters. We will see below that many kinds of musical styles should be used for worship, but whatever we use must pass this first critical test.

Thomas Gieschen suggests three ways in which the text of a song might not pass the test for Christian theological quality. The first occurs when a song exclaims something like "God is calling you to turn to Him" or invites worship participants to "believe and be saved." Gieschen objects that he feels "put off" when such words are sung because, as Christians, "the congregation is there to worship and to be edified. They do not need to be evangelized" (p. 7).

Many pastors and music leaders would not agree; they insist that worship should appeal to those, especially the boomer generation, who have rejected or have never been part of the Church. Yet the vast majority of those attending a given worship service are already Christians. Evangelistic appeals should be reserved specifically for occasions designed entirely for that purpose, since the point of *worship* is to worship God.

The second common fault of music texts is synergism, as discussed in the previous chapter. Here we must specifically reject songs that add our efforts to God's saving work. Songs that stress our searching for God or our success at finding him ignore the total inability of our sinful selves to want or to find God and miss the immense searching of God's gracious love.

Gieschen simply mentions the third flaw, which he calls sub-Christian thought, and offers the example of a song that discusses "how pretty the snowflakes were in Bethlehem without getting to the purpose of Christ's Nativity" (p. 8). To Gieschen's subset of songs that are sub-Christian because they do not proclaim any message about God or faith, I would like to add four other subsets within this category that are very common and not commonly noticed.

6. Elizabeth Achtemeier, "An Excellent Woman," *The Christian Century* 110, no. 24 (22 Aug.-1 Sept. 1993): 809.

The first of these additional subsets consists of sub-Christian texts that are theologically correct but shallow. Raymond Gawronski describes the example of a modern religious song

> of the sort one hears endlessly these days. Written, no doubt, within the past 20 years, it is a piece of that resigned sentimentality that is characteristic of "easy listening music." Although pleasant enough, it is spiritual Wonder Bread: It utterly lacks roots, depth, sustenance. It is all right as a starter, to open the heart to prayer. But unless fed by some solid food, . . . serious seekers will turn elsewhere.[7]

Worship service planners dare not include too much of such sub-Christian superficiality if they intend worship to form the character of participants. One fellow visitor, who was not yet a professing Christian, to a congregation that uses much of the "Wonder Bread" kind of music remarked after the service, "If that church is really trying to appeal to young educated people, they're doing everything they can to send them away. This service is an affront to my intelligence. Both the words and the music are demeaning!"

A second additional subset within the sub-Christian category includes pieces characterized by disinformation, a term used by Postman to describe misleading information on television. He insists that such information is not false, but rather is

> misplaced, irrelevant, fragmented or superficial information — information that creates the illusion of knowing something but which in fact leads one away from knowing. In saying this, I do not mean to imply that television news deliberately aims to deprive Americans of a coherent, contextual understanding of their world. I mean to say that when news is packaged as entertainment, that is the inevitable result. And in saying that the television news show entertains but does not inform, I am saying something far more serious than that we are being deprived of authentic information. I am saying we are losing our sense of what it means to be well informed. Ignorance is always correctable. But what shall we do if we take ignorance to be knowledge?[8]

7. Raymond T. Gawronski, "Why Orthodox Catholics Look to Zen," *New Oxford Review* 60, no. 6 (July-Aug. 1993): 14.

8. Neil Postman, *Amusing Ourselves to Death* (New York: Viking Penguin, 1985), pp. 107-8.

The same sort of disinformation happens with worship music that is primarily catchy, that makes us think we are learning something when we are only psychologizing ourselves. An example is the convention song, described in a previous chapter, which reiterates how much "I will praise God," but never actually praises him. This disinformation prevents us from really knowing how to worship God — because we spend too much time focusing on ourselves.

A third additional kind of sub-Christian text muddles Christian doctrine. One example is a favorite song in a parish at which I have taught. The chorus is

> Mighty, mighty Savior, Mighty, mighty Lord,
> Mighty, mighty Savior, You are my God. (repeat)

Then the verses are as follows:

> 1. Father! Father! Father, my Lord.
> Father! Father! Father, my Lord. Let Your praises ring.
> Let Your people sing That you are a . . . CHORUS
>
> 2. Jesus! Jesus! Jesus, my Lord (continue as v. 1)
>
> 3. Spirit! Spirit! Spirit of God (continue as v. 1)

This song's problem (besides not saying much) is that adding the chorus after each verse turns both the Father and the Spirit into a mighty Savior. If we are trying to teach children about the Trinity, this song will bewilder them. We must avoid sub-Christian music that is doctrinally confusing.

A final type of sub-Christian music can best be called camp songs. These are fun to sing and might be thoroughly true in their doctrine, but their message is not carefully expressed in a way that we would call worshipful. The songs are great for campfires at Bible camps or family reunions, but we would not sing them to God or about our relationship with God in the Church's primary worship settings.[9]

The example that immediately comes to mind is a song about "Walking with the Lord." I don't remember the entire text. I only remem-

---

9. I am grateful to Rev. Gary Cockrell, director of Flathead Lutheran Bible Camp in Lakeside, MT, who carefully trains his staff to distinguish between "worship music" and "campfire songs."

ber my horror when all the kids in the sanctuary burst out shouting "One, two, three, four, whaddya got your feet for?" in between verses. Some teenagers commented later on what fun it was jiving. They really were getting into *it* — instead of into God — so we could hardly call it *worship*. Would they shout that to Jesus when he comes back?

As Thomas Gieschen asserts, "The text needs to have a degree of nobility in its mode of expression and lean to the poetic in order to qualify. All of the doggerel, clumsy, inept wording will also not get past this stage" (p. 8) of the assessment grid.

Formation of the Believer's Character

Besides demanding that the text be faithful to the biblical revelation of God, we also ask that any words used for worship nurture in participants a godly character, form us to be God's children and followers of Jesus. As the apostle Paul writes, "All things are lawful, but not all things are profitable. All things are lawful, but not all things edify" (1 Cor. 10:23, NASV).

For the sake of believers' character, we would not continually use evangelistic music in worship, for to be constantly asked to come to faith again is to question the validity of one's relationship with God. Those who worship God already know him and know that he is worthy of their praise. Let us then concentrate on deepening that knowledge and praise.

As we have seen in previous chapters, an overemphasis on subjective feelings is destructive to the formation of character. We learned from Louis Sass's exploration of the connections between insanity and modernity the dangers of the modern emphasis on detached, subjective experience.

As our culture moves into postmodernism, the Church offers great gifts in its recognition of an objective knowledge of God in the scriptural revelation. We do a disservice to worshipers if, by overemphasizing music that only appeals to feelings, we promote the postmodernist attitude, "I can't know anything — there is no Truth unless I make it so." If we do not proclaim objective knowledge of God, we encourage each person to create his or her own faith.

To minister best to the boomer generation, which accentuates choice, we dare not submerge our conviction that Christianity's truths are the best choice. We have seen in previous chapters that many boomers are looking for stability, moral values, deeper relationships, a reference point by which they can get their bearings. Let our music convey the hope and sureness of faith, the virtues of Christian morality, the love of Christian relationships, and — most of all — the conviction that the God known in Jesus Christ is the only reliable reference point.

At the same time, we dare not ignore feelings in our music. As we learned from Richard Keifert's emphasis on "public" worship, however, emotions are not best addressed by focusing on cozy feelings into which all worship participants might not be able to enter. Instead, let us convey glorious and wonderful truths to which we might all respond with genuine emotions of our own. Subjectivities cannot be shared; telling you about my feelings will not bring about the same feelings in you. Only if I tell you what aroused my feelings can you respond to that same stimulus with subjective reactions of your own.

We want our worship music, then, to appeal to the whole person — will, emotions, and intellect. Our goal is that worship practices will form character so that believers respond to God with commitment, love, thought, and virtuous action. The Scriptures make it clear that God wants his people not just to feel good, but to be good.

Shallow music forms shallow people. One congregation in which I taught sponsors both a "traditional" and a "contemporary" service each Sunday. Such a split is destructive to the congregation, as the next section will explain. In this parish the difference in the worshipers was made apparent by the comments the pastor made at the beginning of each service. On that particular day the service involved a very long Scripture reading of the whole Passion story, which had been divided into reading parts for several people. In the traditional service, which regularly utilizes hymns that require sustained attention and intellectual work, the pastor merely mentioned that the readers should come forward at the appropriate time. All of the readers, who were highly committed parish members, were reliably present. In the contemporary service, which that day included some lightweight songs with little theological content, the pastor had to ask if all the readers were there, and before the extended reading he warned the congregation that it was going to be very long and urged them to try to pay attention to its entirety. Participants in the traditional service were already characterized by an adequate attention span. In the traditional service the meditative hymn "Jesus, I Will Ponder Now On Thy Holy Passion" was sung reflectively after the extended reading. In the contemporary service, no time or music was included for any sort of reflection followed the reading.

Does our choice of worship music increase or reduce our capacity to listen or to think theologically? Does superficial music dumb down the faith? Does our music nurture sensitivity to God? As Gaddy observes, "Worship strengthens a person's spiritual muscles. . . . And worship becomes better and better as worshipers become stronger and stronger."[10]

Another important question that we must ask is whether our worship music is true to human experience. Last year when I was very ill from chemotherapy I found it extremely difficult when my freelancing took me to congregations that sang only "happy" songs. I could respond with Joy when we sang about God — those truths encouraged me in my struggles with the constant pile of physical afflictions I'd been facing for several years — but I couldn't enter into songs that spoke only about wonderful feelings. As Walter Brueggemann asserts, "The problem with a hymnody that focuses on equilibrium, coherence, and symmetry . . . is that it may deceive and cover over. Life is not like that. Life is also savagely marked by disequilibrium, incoherence, and unrelieved assymetry."[11]

In general — no matter what styles of music are used — there is a lack of lament in most of the Church's worship. A great percentage of the biblical psalms of lament are not even printed in *The Lutheran Book of Worship*, and they rarely appear in the Sunday lectionaries of the Episcopalians or Roman Catholics.[12]

The use of laments forms the believers' character by providing the means for worshipers "to reflect upon and articulate their sense of God's hiddenness." They give the sufferer words for an urgent appeal to God, without claiming to understand the irrationality of personal circumstances (p. 73).

> Do believers today, however fortunate their circumstances, differ from their forebears in the faith in being spared the anxiety, disappointment, and suffering that call into question the nearness and loving concern — even the existence — of God? Are we so insulated from the tragedies

---

10. Gaddy, *The Gift of Worship*, p. 159.

11. Walter Brueggemann, *The Message of the Psalms: A Theological Commentary*, Augsburg Old Testament Studies (Minneapolis: Augsburg, 1984), p. 51.

12. Lester Meyer, "A Lack of Laments in the Church's Use of the Psalter," *Lutheran Quarterly*, Spring 1993, pp. 67-71. Page references to this article in the following paragraphs are given parenthetically in the text.

that beset our fellow believers, and all human beings, that our faith is less shaken than was theirs? Surely for contemporary Christians, as well as for ancient Israelites, the experience of divine hiddenness "ought not to be treated as if it were merely a footnote to an otherwise optimistic and unshakeable faith" (74-75).

One final comment about music choices is necessary in light of our goal that worship form believers' character. Churches must teach congregants the distinction between music appropriate for private enjoyment and music suitable for public worship. We must learn the difference between individual pleasure or having fun and the corporate effort of worshiping God. For the community's sake, we cannot restrict worship music to personal favorites. Neither side in the worship wars that pit traditional hymns against contemporary songs can be right if the basis for argument is merely a matter of individual taste. To that concern for community life in the music of worship we now turn.

Formation of the Christian Community

It seems unwise to me to create two different Sunday worship services utilizing two different styles of music because almost always that splits the congregation into two camps. Throughout the country I have seen how divisive that can become. Moreover, the split between "traditional" and "contemporary" usually divides the parish also along age lines, and consequently younger and newer believers lose the opportunity to gain from the faith experience and maturity of older members.

The use of two different styles often reflects deeper problems in a congregation. It might indicate a greater concern for "people out there" than for the people in the pew — an attitude that demonstrates an inadequate understanding of what worship is for. Such a split also allows a congregation to escape talking about worship and types of music and precludes genuine communal conversation about the weaknesses and strengths of various styles.

Thus a question we must always ask about our music is whether it unifies the congregation. Correlatively, we must also do a much better job of educating worship participants to value a wider variety of styles. We will look at the need for diversity below when we consider the issue of musical style, but at this point we must remember that community life does not simply happen. It requires constant efforts to teach why we do what we do together.

Paul Westermeyer points out the danger of choosing music to target a certain sector of the society — usually baby boomers. He insists that "this immediately flies in the face of the nature of the church, which by definition crosses lines of generation, race, sex, economic status, likes and dislikes, tastes, etc."[13] Instead, we will want our music to reflect the broad inclusivity outlined at the end of the previous chapter — sharing the concerns of the universal Church, welcoming all races and classes, paying attention to global suffering, and remembering God's grace and power in the midst of it.

Music that shapes community will use many styles to invite greater inclusivity, but when the gospel is heard therein and obeyed it will ultimately prove subversive to the wider culture. This is a good test for all the music we choose: Does its text have the subversive effect of Christian truth? Does it call the culture around the Church into question and strengthen the culture of the Christian community? At the same time, is the music in the vernacular, in language that worshipers will understand? We must think more deeply about the "distinctive talk" of the Christian community and how to educate people to participate in it.

A wonderful example of how the Christian community can be united by means of the Church's distinctive musical talk occurred at the founding of the Lutheran synod of Kazakhstan, a republic of the former atheistic U.S.S.R. I will quote the story at length since it so beautifully illustrates the depth of the Church's heritage. For this first gathering of Lutherans, Heinrich Rathke,

> former bishop in the Evangelical Church of Germany and organizer of the synod, had deliberately rented a big music hall, seat of the Kazakhian Philharmonic Orchestra and home of the only organ in Kazakhstan. He had brought with him a renowned church musician from Germany, Neithard Bethke, to give a public concert with organ music by Bach and Reger. Many delegates had qualms about entering the music hall, a secular building belonging to the government that had persecuted them for so long. Why enter the "seat of the devil"?
>
> Nevertheless, the hall was filled with 500 people: the 80 delegates to

13. Westermeyer, "Professional Concerns Forum," p. 37.

the synod along with Russian and Kazakhian friends of music. Unbe-
known to the delegates, Bethke had planned to intersperse his program
with four hymns cherished by the Lutherans: "Praise to the Lord," "Now
Thank We All Our God," "Jesus Still Lead On" and "Lord, Take My
Hand and Lead Me." He also had planted a few "conspirators" among
the crowd — people who knew that the hymns were coming and were
prepared to start singing at the right time. As Bethke started in with
the first hymn there was a moment of amazement and incredulity. Then
the delegates began to sing, loud and clear, as a single voice. They put
into their singing all the humiliation and suffering of their past lives;
they grasped hold of their new freedom; they were proud to be in the
open, without having to hide any more. Tears came to their eyes but
not only to theirs: many Russians and others in the audience caught
the sentiment of that moment and wept with them.[14]

Recently, in our annual choral festival service, the choir I direct sang
a quodlibet (a musical piece combining sections of two or more melodies
in close succession) composed of the first two hymns that Bethke played,
and before we sang it the worship narrator read this account of the concert
in Kazakhstan. It brought tears to our eyes to think that we were joined
in these wonderful hymns of praise with our fellow Lutherans on the other
side of the world.

My husband and I felt the same global connections when we attended
worship in Madagascar while we were there to teach. As we sang the
Malagasy words in the hymnbook, we knew the content of several of the
hymns because they were translations of familiar Lutheran ones. Recipro-
cally, my choir enjoyed learning a Malagasy tune with its vibrantly rhyth-
mic men's part, and they sang it, too, for the choral festival worship. We
learned from the hymn's words the profound hope that nurtures Lutherans
in Madagascar despite their immense poverty.

Diversity of Style

Because the people who come for worship represent an immense diversity of
ages, emotions, concerns, and spiritual maturity, authentic worship requires

14. Sabine Downey, "Out in the Open," *The Christian Century* 111, no. 13 (20
Apr. 1994): 407.

a variety of musical styles to convey an assortment of moods and convictions. Lutherans especially have traditionally used "a variety of hymns to move the service liturgically from one mood to another."[15] I really love new denominational hymnals that include a diversity of styles — canons, Appalachian folk melodies, traditional chorales, dance rhythms, spirituals, revival tunes, contemporary songs. The 1990 Presbyterian hymnal includes Spanish, Japanese, Hebrew, Latin, Filipino, Mandarin Chinese, and Native American songs. It has Puerto Rican, Huron, and South African tunes — and it has translated old favorites like "What a Friend We Have in Jesus" and "How Great Thou Art" into Korean.

Our churches should use the best of everything for worship — and the key to adding various styles of music is good education. Our recent choral festival involved more than a dozen elementary through college students and several adults playing a set of handbells, two clarinets, three trumpets, two flutes, an oboe, a cello, a Celtic harp, two guitars, and the organ in different combinations. Worshipers sang traditional hymns and new pieces I had composed for the occasion, folk/contemporary songs as well as German chorales. Some of the youngest students told me that they especially liked playing Bach, and one chose the Quodlibet mentioned in the previous section as her favorite. Some older congregation members appreciated the vitality of the Malagasy hymn. Above all else in our planning, we wanted God to be the subject and for the worship service to build up the believers and the community.

Sometimes false statistics are cited to argue that only contemporary music appeals to people in our culture. The letter mentioned above that advocates switching to a new type of worship music asks, "Why does the church continue to use a musical style that is foreign to 98% of the population?" The writer created this question out of the statistic that only 2 percent of Americans listen to classical music — but that doesn't mean that hymns are "foreign" to the other 98 percent! Classical music and hymnody are two different entities. Many people in the United States deeply love meaningful hymns and choose them for important occasions, such as funerals. I would guess that 98 percent of the population are familiar with hymns — at least the Christmas ones, "Amazing Grace," "God Bless America," and so forth. Furthermore, what people listen to

15. Gracia Grindal, "To Translate Is to Betray: Trying to Hand the Lutheran Tradition On," *dialog* 33, no. 3 (Summer 1994): 187.

during the week on their radios does not necessarily dictate what they want in church music. In fact, some people want the music of worship to be different from what they usually hear in order to remind them of the Otherness of God.

The same published letter also sought to buttress its argument by claiming, "Nor did Jesus ever recommend a worship style," and to prove this point the writer mentions the account of Jesus and the disciples singing a hymn before going to the Mount of Olives. The author almost sneers, "I guess the composer's name and the style wasn't [sic] significant enough to be recorded or the Holy Spirit would surely have mentioned it." In fact, we do know what Jesus sang! Almost unilaterally, scholars agree that it was the last hymns of the Hallel, Psalms 113–118, which were used before and after the Passover meal. The Gospel accounts all show that Jesus was faithful to Jewish worship forms, though he certainly criticized any legalism about them. The early church, building on the disciples' experience with Jesus, used psalms (from their Jewish heritage), hymns (like those recorded in Phil. 2:6-11; Col. 1:15-20; and 2 Tim. 2:11-13), and spiritual songs (perhaps new pieces composed at the moment under the inspiration of the Holy Spirit). Why not advocate that our churches do the same in a blending of styles?

Musical style in worship is not a simple matter of taste, what we do or don't like; rather, it involves the appropriateness of a particular sound for the message expressed. If it becomes only an issue of taste, then power wins. As we consider the suitability of musical style or of particular musical instruments, we can ask such questions as whether this music can bear the weight of the gospel and not trivialize it. I'm not crazy about saxophones, for example — but I would suggest that the sound of one might be perfect to express the wailing of lament or to set aptly a black spiritual. The advantage of an organ is that its various stops are appropriate for different moods and messages. Flute pipes produce a more meditative sound than do the trumpet stops, which are more appropriate for majestic hymns. The problem I find with many "contemporary" combos is that the sound is always the same — and frequently sounds like Muzak in a mall, composed to lull us rather than to awaken us to God. I welcome modern music, but I insist that sounds and styles of worship music convey their message in an honest way and with integrity and internal coherence.

Related to my goal of using a variety of styles is the argument over music that has stood the test of time versus modern music. The advantage of the former is that through the winnowing processes of history most of the rotten stuff has been thrown out. That which remains is usually the best of its era and so can usually be counted upon to have value. However, that does not mean that we should not try new music for fear that it might turn out to be disposable. It simply means that we must do a more thorough job of weighing the merits of new pieces according to the themes sounded in Thomas Gieschen's assessment grid.

Both Wesley and Luther wrote new music to supplement the musical heritage they already had, a faith tradition passed on from one generation to another. Most hymnals contain hymns from almost twenty centuries and liturgical pieces that go back to the earliest Church (as well as to Jewish worship and the worship of the angels). Unfortunately, most "contemporary" services seem to slice out only a few recent years and thereby deprive their participants of their rightful place in that larger picture. As Paul Westermeyer insists,

> Over the long haul, people expect from us the larger repertoire because they hold us accountable for the larger story it represents. Their musical appetites and languages are far greater than we give them credit for. To lock them into the sound and context of one time and place is to deprive them of what they will need already tomorrow.[16]

Maintaining the Church's larger repertoire gives us a wider perspective and broader experience by which to judge contemporary music, to discover more easily those new songs and hymns that have great staying power. Robert Benne describes the music of a religious revival in Cambridge, England, as follows:

> Most obvious is the ever-present musical ensemble, generally made up of keyboard, flute, sax, drums and accompanying choir. The music played is definitely not "Christian rock," and the songs are of higher quality than the saccharine ballads one hears on Christian radio stations. Rather, they are "new hymns" written by a bevy of American and British writers. . . . Some of [these] hymns . . . seem to have enduring quality. The young know these new hymns and songs by heart, much as earlier generations knew the classic heritage. Indeed, these churches wisely intersperse their worship with hymns from that heritage —

16. Westermeyer, "Professional Concerns Forum," p. 38.

especially those of the Wesleys — so that young and old alike might share them.[17]

Westermeyer's and Benne's comments come from opposite sides of the spectrum, but both wind up in the middle — looking for music with enduring qualities of substance and musical worth. Considering music by means of our selection grid, which asks first about the text, we might find a variety of styles with suitable texts. No style should be eliminated outright, but we can look for a dialectic of old and new, both in the hymns and in the musical accompaniment.

Before we turn to specific means for judging style, however, we must sidetrack a bit to ask carefully how cultural influences affect music. These concerns do not eliminate any style, but they should caution us to look very seriously at the more subtle aspects of the intertwining of text and form, and they should also warn us against using any one style exclusively.

The Medium and the Message

In many of the worship wars, the advocates of "contemporary" music insist that preference for a certain musical style is simply a matter of taste. On the other hand, those who prefer "traditional" music declare that modern pop music is usually used for advertising and therefore carries the wrong connotations into worship. The criteria for measuring musical worth explicated below will show that music is not simply a matter of taste, but here we must look more closely at the issue of a "medium" and the connotations it carries.

In *All God's Children and Blue Suede Shoes,* Kenneth Myers presents a thorough case "that popular culture's greatest influence is in the way it shapes *how* we think and feel (more than *what* we think and feel) and how we think and feel about thinking and feeling." Based on the biblical thesis that "not everything that is permissible is constructive,"[18] Myers argues that the very triviality of much of popular culture, "while making it seem

17. Robert Benne, "Cambridge Evangelicals," *The Christian Century* 110, no. 30 (27 Oct. 1993): 1037.

18. Kenneth A. Myers, *Al God's Children and Blue Suede Shoes* (Westchester, IL: Crossway Books, 1989), p. xiii. Page references to this book in the rest of this section are given parenthetically in the text.

innocuous, also enables it to be extremely pervasive, and that is its most toxic quality." Since popular culture "specializes in instant gratification . . . , it may spoil your taste for something better" (p. xiv). As Myers summarizes, popular culture "encourages a mood of expecting everything to be immediate, a mood that deters greater depth and breadth in other areas of our lives, including our understanding of Christianity and our experience of obedient faith" (p. xv).

Myers asks whether there are transcendent standards by which to compare different civilizations. The dominant assumption of cultural relativism, which pervades modern society, is a great obstacle to thinking about culture. For example, cultural relativism makes it impossible to say that Thomas Jefferson was a more significant thinker than a headhunter from Borneo (p. 29).

Myers observes that religious faith is transmitted through high, folk, or popular culture. Because high culture "has its roots in antiquity, in an age of conviction about absolutes, about truth, about virtue," it is "capable of maintaining and transmitting more about human experience in creation, and about God's redemptive intervention in history, than its alternatives." Folk culture, in comparison, "while simpler in manner and less communicable from one folk to another, has the virtues of honesty, integrity, commitment to tradition, and perseverance in the face of opposition." Negro/black spirituals are good examples of folk culture "that retains essential religious truths over the long haul." This analysis leads us to question "the *consciousness* of popular culture, the manners and emotional habits it encourages us to take for granted" (p. 59). Myers objects chiefly to popular culture's "constant quest for novelty," which "can be extremely addictive" and thereby "can easily obscure reflection on eternal realities and claims" (p. 67). Moreover, he complains,

> One of the problems with popular culture is that, *by itself,* it does not teach the sort of habits necessary to enjoy it wisely. Unless you had a taste for something better, you would never get tired of eating fast food or frozen dinners all of the time. If you were dissatisfied with such a diet, you wouldn't be able to define your dissatisfaction unless you had something else to compare it with. (p. 72)

The aesthetic capacity to which Myers refers is "not simply a matter of class or taste, but reflects different ways of understanding creation and one's place in it" (p. 73). He asks, "Is something 'beautiful' just because I like it, or does it have some objective quality rooted in creation that allows me to *recognize* that it is beautiful?" (p. 77). Myers claims that in Philippians 4:8 the apostle "Paul does not say that we should reflect on what we *think* is lovely, or whatever we *feel* is admirable. We are to give sustained attention to whatever is *objectively* true and noble and right." Praiseworthiness can be established by objective standards, rather than by the prevailing market (p. 98).

Some of the factors that cause modern society to reject aesthetic judgments are its egalitarian spirit (and the consequent "moral authority of the majority") and our cultural preference for quantitative over qualitative reasoning — no one can argue with statistics (p. 78). Very much like wisdom, aesthetic judgment requires "patience, training, and a willingness to submit to our elders. . . . Its virtues are incompatible with the American penchant for *practical* reason" (p. 79).

In "The Aesthetics of Popular Arts," published in the *Journal of Aesthetics and Art Criticism,* Abraham Kaplan asserts, "To recognize that how much you get out of an art experience depends on how much you put into it is not moralistic but strictly aesthetic." But popular art will not allow too much to be put into the experience; one doesn't have to work too hard at listening to modern popular singers, which is why more people prefer them to the classical composers. As Myers records, "Kaplan argued that popular art cannot bear the sustained attention that high art can, so we remain well-acquainted with it; but the relationship is always superficial, never maturing into intimacy" (p. 83). Of course, there is nothing wrong with frivolous activity if we are not committed to it, if it is not the only kind we know. "There is no harm in superficial pleasures for one who also has a knowledge of the tragic and of the transcendent." Myers claims, however, that "there are many disturbing signs that many contemporary Christians have made the limited and limiting sensibility of popular culture their own" (p. 87).

Myers compares cultures to the three levels of preparation and service of food — high (gourmet), folk (traditional home cooking), and popular (fast food). He insists that most people

> would agree that fast food has deficiencies that the other two categories do not, not simply in nutritional value or in taste, but in the *ethos,* the way the food is served, consumed, and experienced. Most young men

185

of moderate means trying to make a positive impression on a young woman do not treat her to a meal at the nearest Burger King. They realize there is definitely something missing in the meal's social experience. Now, if every meal you ever ate was from a fast-food joint, would that affect your outlook on the meaning of meals? If there was never any elegance or grace, any ritual or decorum as part of your meals, if all the food you ever consumed was delivered to you by a person in a funny-looking hat, and was wrapped in cardboard or styrofoam, would that affect your impressions of the Biblical metaphor of the Marriage Supper of the Lamb? (p. 89)

Thus the problem with popular culture is "not the inadequacies of any one artifact, but the inadequacies of the whole." Myers names it "a cultural *gestalt*, the consciousness created by popular culture when it is unalleviated by values from traditional or high culture and by deliberate attention" (p. 90).

C. S. Lewis once tried, in *An Experiment in Criticism,* to come up with distinctions by which one could judge between a good book and a bad one, and he discovered that they are read in different ways. His four distinctions between "literary" and "unliterary" reading can be applied to music, too. My musical comparisons follow in brackets the differences that Lewis cites.

Unliterary	Literary
1. "I've read it already"	Read the same good book 10-30 times in life

[How many times could we sing the "Mighty God" song cited above compared to a hymn such as "Praise to the Lord, the Almighty, the King of Creation"?]

2. Do not set much store by reading	Always looking for leisure and silence to read — and do so with whole attention

[Someone once told me that she didn't sing in the choir because it took too much effort to breathe and phrase and sing well. She preferred to be in the group leading contemporary songs because she didn't have to work very hard at it.]

186

3. Entertainment only

A book can be a deep, profound experience, "so momentous that only experiences of love, religion, or bereavement can furnish a standard of comparison. Their whole consciousness is changed."

[This criterion is not as applicable to music because songs in all kinds of styles can be life-changing and momentous experiences. For that reason, I am not inherently opposed to any style of music. I only oppose using just one style.]

4. Use a work of art — for a job or for status

Readers constantly think, have prominently favorite passages for life. Receive art.

Lewis explains the last point as follows. To "receive" a work of art, "we exert our senses and imagination and various other powers according to a pattern invented by the artist." When we "use" it, we "treat it as assistance for our own activities." Thus "'using' is inferior to 'reception' because art, if used rather than received, merely facilitates, brightens, relieves or palliates our life, and does not add to it" (quoted in Myers, p. 92). Myers explores the ramifications of this distinction as follows:

> If what we do when we pursue an interest in high art is in some way similar to what we do in loving someone, in showing justice and mercy, and in the pursuit of knowledge, can enjoyment of the arts (as recipient, not as users) cultivate in us certain skills that seep over into these other areas of life? Are there natural virtues of sympathy, of love, of justice, of mercy, of wisdom that can be encouraged by aesthetic experience? According to Lewis, learning to "receive" a work of art does encourage habits of the heart that have effects in other areas of life.
>
> And now, to put popular culture on the spot, does it have the same capacities? No, and few people, even its most ardent fans, would claim that it does. Is a life influenced more by the ethos of popular culture than by that of high culture thereby deprived in some significant way? Probably. (p. 97)

We must ask the same question of worship that is predominantly influenced by the ethos of popular culture. Is it similarly depriving worshipers in significant ways?

The rest of Myers's description is much too thorough for me to outline here, but he includes a chart that summarizes his main points (p. 120). Not all the items on the following list apply to our questions about worship music, but a surprisingly large number of them do. The fact that popular styles of music entail so many of the characteristics listed in the left-hand column raises serious questions about its appropriateness as the *only* vehicle for worship.

popular culture	traditional/folk and high culture
Focuses on the new	Focuses on the timeless
Discourages reflection	Encourages reflection
Pursued casually to "kill time"	Pursued with deliberation
Gives us what we want, tells us what we already know	Offers us what we could not have imagined
Relies on instant accessibility; encourages impatience	Requires training; encourages patience
Emphasizes information and trivia	Emphasizes knowledge and wisdom
Encourages quantitative concerns	Encourages qualitative concerns
Celebrates fame	Celebrates ability
Appeals to sentimentality	Appeals to appropriate, proportioned emotions
Content and form governed by requirements of the market	Content and form governed by requirements of created order
Formulas are the substance	Formulas are the tools
Relies on spectacle, tending to violence and prurience (including language)	Relies on formal dynamics and the power of symbols
Aesthetic power in reminding of something else	Aesthetic power in intrinsic attributes
Individualistic	Communal
Leaves us where it found us	Transforms sensibilities
Incapable of deep or sustained attention	Capable of repeated, careful attention
Lacks ambiguity	Allusive, suggests the transcendent
No discontinuity between life and art	Relies on "Secondary World" conventions
Reflects the desires of the self	Encourages understanding of others
Tends toward relativism	Tends toward submission to standards
Used	Received

In distinguishing between the content and the form of popular culture, Myers complains that, though Christians are critical of some of the former, they have "a virtually uncritical attitude" toward the latter. A congregation might have "adopted those forms without much resistance, in the alleged interest of promoting its message. But the message has thereby suffered, and so have its members." Myers thinks churches are losing the integrity of their message because they compete with popular culture "*on its own terms,* 'on the basis of their ability to titillate the instincts of their worshipers,' turning the shepherds of the sheep into 'entrepreneurs of emotional stimulation.'" Instead, the Church should "provide leadership in encouraging cultural habits that go against the grain of the search for immediate fulfillment" (p. 182) and should be "*in its cultural expressions as well as in its teaching a living testimony to a culture of transcendence, . . .* life rooted in permanent things" (p. 183).

We can see the similarity of Myers's case to that of Postman's concerning television (outlined in Chapter 2). Postman, too, insists that "the form in which ideas are expressed affects what those ideas will be."[19] For that reason I continue to advocate a diversity of forms and styles of music, so that our worship conveys the widest range of emotions and truths.

Questions to Ask of Styles

Martin Luther is supposed to have said, "Why let the devil have all the good tunes?" His comment invites us to bring some of the more "secular" styles into the Church and thereby "sanctify them to a better use" (Myers, p. 9). We can ask a few questions of style, however, to make sure a particular song or form is appropriate in worship.

Janet Hill, a superb church musician in upstate New York, uses the idea of honesty to question musical style as well as use. Is the music honest in the way it expresses a text? We wouldn't use a light and airy melodic style to sing about the suffering of Christ on the cross. We wouldn't use a heavy, plodding hymn tune to capture the ecstasy of the resurrection.

Honesty must also mark the singing or playing of music during worship. I have seen music leaders act happy and tell worshipers to "get

---

19. Postman, *Amusing Ourselves to Death,* p. 31.

excited" simply for excitement's sake. The advantage of texts that focus on objective truths instead of subjective feelings is that we bring to them our own honest emotions.

Related to the criterion of honesty is the requirement that no musical style used in worship foster vanity and show (see below for comments about choirs). We need "a model of the church that is not built around performance theater. We need churches built around people sharing their lives in everyday ways instead of watching speakers and musicians perform."[20]

Those who lead music function only to help the congregation sing better. Organists are not to present concerts; they should play to enable the people to sing, using a variety of settings and stops to give the music vitality and freshness. Music should be led by people who practice their instruments for the sake of others and not to elevate themselves above others or to manipulate others. If music leaders lead from the front of the sanctuary, great care must be exercised to prevent worshipers from becoming passive. Recently, a person who plays guitar for contemporary worship told me how he changed his approach after sitting through a service in a central pew and noticing that nobody was singing except for the leading music team. Both entertaining or manipulative kinds of worship and showy ceremonial or formal styles are inimical to worship that is the work of all the people. These lead to idolatries of the performers and disrupt authentic worship by shifting the focus from God.

Style can best be evaluated by asking whether it disrupts worship. Sometimes feminist efforts to replace masculine language are disruptive of worship. This, of course, involves text rather than music, but it demonstrates the point. Singing the following hymn, I was distracted by word changes from focusing attention on the God I praised:

O worship our God, all glorious above;
O gratefully sing Her power and Her love;
our shield and defender, the Ancient of Days,
pavillioned in splendor, and girded with praise.

O tell of Her might, O sing of Her grace,
whose robe is the light, whose canopy space.

20. John Alexander, "Bleeding Hearts: How Church Communities Can Flourish," *The Other Side* 29, no. 3 (May-June 1993): 61.

Her chariots of fire the deep thunderclouds form,
and dark is Her path on the wings of the Storm.
                          Robert Grant, 1833 (text modified)[21]

We must ask why such modification is necessary. For those who have sung the hymn since childhood and have it memorized, the modified version disrupts worship (and would be rejected in our selection grid). Why not create a new hymn, as Brian Wren does, with new feminine images for God, rather than disrupt a familiar hymn that means so much to many Christians?

In musical style the same disruption can happen when well-known hymn tunes are changed to "liven them up." Some modifications or variations are tastefully done, but some — such as setting "Silent Night" to a rock beat — are more offensive than useful. Any modification of hymn tunes must always be done with care not to disrupt the worship of those who have known and loved the melody in its original form.

We must also ask if certain kinds of musical style should not be used in worship because their associations would be disruptive to worship. Heavy metal or acid rock probably has too many negative associations to be worshipful for most people in the pew.

Many critics, such as Paul Westermeyer, suggest that contemporary music is associated too much with advertising to be appropriate for worship. He objects to music that "becomes a slick and attractive envelope to make the text attractive" — but I think that he overstates his case in identifying "contemporary" music itself with selling. He is certainly right that "churches and synagogues have always assumed the message they have and the texts they sing are true," but I don't believe that composers of pop-style worship music assume any differently. It is true that texts should be sung "out of an inner necessity to be sung," that their "very truth [has] demanded music" — but Westermeyer goes on to claim that "advertising assumptions reverse this whole process" and that when "the music from advertising is applied to worship" troubling questions are raised.[22]

We must nuance this issue more carefully. It is not that the music itself is the advertising agent. Contemporary Christian music (CCM) is

---

21. Hymn text modification by Marchiene Vroon Rienstra in *Swallow's Nest: A Feminine Reading of the Psalms* (Grand Rapids: William B. Eerdmans, 1992).

22. Westermeyer, "Professional Concerns Forum," pp. 35-36.

not usually based on the assumption that music has to sell a text that really isn't true (as in advertising); most CCM stars are believing Christians who express their faith in modern forms. What *is* faulty is churches' assumption that if we choose the right *kind* of music people will be attracted to Christ. It is idolatry to think our work makes the difference. Christ himself draws people to believe in him through the Holy Spirit. Worship music is used to proclaim Christ, not to advertise him. God must be worship's subject, and music is the outgrowth/consequence (not the antecedent) of worship, the response to God's presence.

A final question about style must be whether music is edifying to the worshipers. Most styles, with adequate education, will qualify in this stage of the assessment grid. However, few members have the great degree of aesthetic awareness required for extremely esoteric music that might be sung by choirs. These pieces might be performed wonderfully in Christian choir concerts, but they would probably not aid a congregation in worship.

As Gieschen stresses, the category of style should be left as broad as possible. This screen in our selection grid should be "generous rather than restrictive" (p. 10). Other aspects of the testing process that follow will eliminate specific songs within a style, even as our text considerations weeded out the sub-Christian pieces.

Propriety

Gieschen lists three aspects of the suitability of a piece for a choir, but they all apply as well to the general music planning necessary for a worship service. He asks, "How appropriate [is a piece of music] to the balance of the program? . . . to the choir doing the piece, and . . . to its function in the service?" (p. 11).

The first question relates to the goal of using a wide diversity of styles in worship music. Gieschen is concerned that choirs present a wide range of styles over the course of time. In our congregational planning, we should do the same. In this aspect of the selection grid, planners of contemporary worship services err as much as the traditionalists by limiting themselves to just one style.

Next, in asking how appropriate the music being considered is to the congregation, we recognize that we must look far ahead to what styles we would eventually hope to use, so that in the meanwhile we can intro-

192

duce intervening styles. Just as I wouldn't give my novice choir an intricate Bach piece in a season's first few weeks, so we shouldn't immediately spring on a congregation a style of music for which they are not prepared — and this applies not only to difficult music but also to simple contemporary music. Some churches suddenly start an "alternative" service, composed entirely of contemporary music, and parish members feel instantly robbed of all that is familiar. Besides being opposed to services that utilize such a small slice of the Church's hymnody, I am especially bothered that such nasty jolts are delivered without adequate preparation.

A related issue concerns the preparation necessary if we want the congregation to learn a new, more difficult hymn. A few weeks before the service in which it fits, the organist could play the melody during the offering with an announcement in the bulletin that this melody will be used in the future so that congregants pay special attention. The choir could sing it during communion the next week so that people hear the melody once again before they actually are invited to sing it, too. Then, on the day it is used, an instrumental ensemble (perhaps utilizing elementary school students of the flute or clarinet) can play the melody and then the choir could sing the first verse before the congregation joins in for the rest of the hymn. Other preparatory measures could involve restoring the German position of "cantor" to introduce the melody and lead the singing or offering classes in hymn-singing to teach both how to sing and why.

As always, a key to excellent singing is education. Correlative to training in singing is an honest assessment of the parish's abilities. Some churches, tired of boring traditional hymns, introduce contemporary services that are equally boring. Or, lacking good instrumentalists who are able to play traditional music, they substitute poor instrumentalists in another style. Perhaps if there are no musicians to play, the congregation could do much better singing without accompaniment — or hymns/songs could be chosen that are easier to play well.

I believe we could teach young children much more about music than we do and enable them to appreciate a wide variety of composers and pieces with various degrees of difficulty. Janet Hill introduces her children's choir to a diversity of styles, including the psalm chanting that they lead with bells every Sunday as their gift to the congregation. When they were asked on tour a few years ago which piece they liked best, the children chose their Bach anthem (a difficult three-part piece) because they had worked so hard to learn it and felt such accomplishment in singing it well. My father once wrote an eight-part angels' song for a children's Christmas program and gave one part to each Lutheran-school grade. I can still remember the thrill of singing it. I believe that adults in the parish, too, feel a sense of accomplishment when they learn to sing better and in more than one style. Whatever we do, we want to be sure that our choices are within the range of possibility and not just somebody's favorite piece.

Several traditional hymns in the *Lutheran Book of Worship* are unsing-able, even for well-trained singers! (Probably the same is true in other denominational hymnals.) It is better to leave out of the worship service music that is too tricky or unmelodic or ill conceived. If the text is particularly fitting to the service it could be put to another melody or spoken aloud together. Sometimes contemporary songs are unsingable also. Once the pastor in a congregation I was visiting chided me because I hadn't sung two of the "Praise" songs. I had sung the third because its music was printed — but for the other two the music wasn't provided and the song leaders were not loud enough for the melody to be heard. The worst thing we can do to worshipers musically is to hinder them from singing by not making the music available — either in printed form or by having a cantor or group sing the melody through a few times so that everyone can learn it. In another parish the leader of a contemporary song said (on Easter no less!), "If you are uncomfortable singing the verses, just join in on the chorus," though the music was fully printed and the verses were easier to sing than the chorus. However, no attempt had been made to teach the melody to the congrega-tion. How destructive it is to the community to fail to teach a song and then invite people not to participate (especially on Easter!).

Many church marketers suggest that high art drives people away from the Church, but what about all the artists and others who appreciate good music who are driven away by the Church's toleration of mediocre music or art? One of the "exit interviews" that William Hendricks con-ducted was with a person looking for people she could relate to "intellec-tually, artistically, [and] spiritually." At the end of his description of her situation, Hendricks comments, "it does seem to me tragic that a person with the ability to interpret Bach, Bartok, Mozart, or Mahler should struggle to find her place among God's people."[23]

23. William D. Hendricks, *Exit Interviews* (Chicago: Moody Press, 1993), pp. 84 and 85. Page references to this book in the following paragraphs are given parenthetically in the text.

In another interview Hendricks asks, "Why is it that so many churches — which once were a fountainhead of the arts and culture — now seem to many artists like cultural wastelands?" (p. 194). Later he wonders, "Why is it that the church so often seems impotent at producing people of craft? Walt Whitman said that to have great poets, we must have great audiences. In that light: What kind of audiences do today's churches make?" (p. 195). He concludes,

> It has been said that in ancient Greece, art killed religion; later in Christian Europe, religion killed art. That alone is worth some reflection. But we can add that in modern America, entertainment is killing both art and religion — a situation that leaves very little space for the Christian artist. (p. 196)

All kinds of musical possibilities open up if we carefully plan our educational processes. An organist friend described how his congregation used "Dear Christians One and All Rejoice" (*Lutheran Book of Worship* #299) with commentary from the pastor interspersed among the stanzas as the morning's sermon. He wrote,

> In this case, the hymn was quite unknown to the congregation. The choir sang the first two stanzas, and by then the congregation was able to join in. Afterwards, everybody commented on how meaningful they found it. I believe that our hymnal, and particularly such rich hymns as this, are a resource greatly overlooked. People . . . are hungry for an investigation of the meaning of what they say and sing in the worship service. This could be a gateway into Scriptures and theology for many. And as people increasingly find meaning in hymns, they sing them!

He suggests that this hymn could provide the overall theme for Vacation Bible School curriculum and asks, "What greater treasure could be given the children than to know such a hymn by heart? The whole gospel is there in a nutshell."[24]

A final aspect of appropriateness is the place of a particular piece of music in the whole order of worship for the day and that day's place in the liturgical year. Musical selections must fit the place in which they are used in the entire shape and flow of the service, so that suitable songs are

---

24. Personal correspondence from organist/choir director Dr. David Hendricksen.

sung in connection with the confession of sins or the confession of faith, the theme of the sermon or the Scripture lessons, and the beginning or end of the service. The great treasure of the Order of the Mass as it has been passed down through the centuries is the natural flow of the service as it moves from the assembling of the congregation in the invocation, the opening hymn, the confession of sins, the absolution, and the collect (the prayer gathering our thoughts into the theme for the day) to the first highlight in the Gospel reading and on to the second highlight in the Eucharist. All music should be chosen in keeping with this flow, so that none of it is disruptive to authentic worship.

I mentioned in Chapter 5 the value of the liturgical year as a means for displaying more thoroughly the resplendence of God in the course of worship over time. This is especially reflected in the music of Church seasons. Christmas is much more meaningful if we have really sung the Advent hymns of longing, just as Easter contains so much more Joy when we have lamented in the dirges of Lent. Liturgical themes are wonderfully expressed in hymns and songs written especially for specific days of the Church year.

Though often contemporary services are instituted because people plead for variety in worship, I have found frequently that such services actually lack variety because the new services use the same style of music throughout, musical pieces are selected from only a few years of Church history, and the music and texts contain little seasonal variation. I noticed this particularly one Advent while working in a parish that offered both traditional and contemporary services. Worshipers at the former sang Advent hymns about John the Baptist, the Messiah's coming, and looking forward to Christ's second coming — hymns not usually sung at any other time of the year and played with a lot of variety by the organist. In the contemporary service the songs dealt with the theme of "light" and had been used, I was told, on several other Sundays in the year. As James White emphasizes, "Nothing is a better source for variety and interest in Christian worship than careful following of the Christian year."[25]

One problem with the criterion of appropriateness in our selection grid is that "the aesthetics of popular culture define fittingness solely in terms of the self's desires and the market (which is, after all, a collection of many

---

25. James F. White, *Introduction to Christian Worship*, rev. ed. (Nashville: Abingdon, 1990), p. 77.

desiring selves), not by any objective standards."[26] To give one example, one Good Friday — the day of all days when we want worship to be very meditative so that congregants can think deeply about the profound events we commemorate — the choir sang Bach's setting of "O Sacred Head, Now Wounded." In contrast, later in the service a soloist sang a song that said something like "one Sunday evening I was sitting under a tree thinking about how much God loves me." The melody was appropriate to those words, but neither was suitable for the occasion, yet the song had been chosen because so many people requested it! It could have been fitting for another occasion, but it was entirely too trite for Good Friday. Propriety, not mere popularity, must guide those who plan worship music.

Musical Worth

The final screen through which music must pass on our selection grid is the criterion of musical worth. On the basis of works by music scholars Bennett Reimer and Leonard Meyer, Gieschen divides this worth into two qualities in the music itself — excellence and greatness.[27] In answering the question "Wherein does excellence consist?" for choir repertoire, Gieschen lists these criteria, most of which are applicable to the composition of general music:

> Skillfulness, expertness, competence, aptness, consistency of style, clarity of basic intent, adroitness, inventiveness, and craftsmanship. Pieces which contain these qualities of excellence in sufficient amounts would be accepted for use; those deficient would be rejected. It is on this basis that we exclude music with forced or awkward harmonies; music that is too repetitive and boring; phrases that don't seem to be going anywhere; music that is so predictable and full of cliches; clumsy part-writing; music that lacks any sense of freshness or newness; music whose discourse is so rapid that its experience seems empty; pieces that don't

26. Myers, *All God's Children and Blue Suede Shoes*, p. 99.

27. For further information on these two aspects see Bennett Reimer, *A Philosophy of Music Education* (Englewood Cliffs, NJ: Prentice-Hall, 1977); Reimer, "Leonard Meyer's Theory of Value and Greatness," *Journal of Religious Music Educators* 10, no. 2 (Fall 1962); and Leonard Meyer's *Emotions and Meaning in Music* (Chicago: University of Chicago Press, 1966), all cited in Gieschen, "Contemporary Christian Music," pp. 13-14.

engage your interest so that after playing pages one and two, you're not even curious about the rest of the piece.

If music of excellence can be written in all styles, then all styles can also come up against these criteria and fail. And Pop music, since it has not been screened by history, should be expected to fail rather frequently. (p. 14)

Recently a worship service exploring new music used a song in which each verse began with "Kumbaya, Kumbaya" repeated four times in the same descending scale. Then another phrase was sung three times on the same descending scale, followed by a final line that was the same for all four verses. It was crushingly dull! After the first verse I tried singing creative harmonies to stay interested, but to no avail. The music only used three chords.

Music of excellence makes use of interesting melodies and/or rhythms and accompaniments appropriate to the subject, melody, and rhythm. It is not bland, plodding, inert, or trite. A good test for excellence is whether we can stand to listen to the music (without the words) over and over several times without getting tired of it.

In his discussion of the search for excellence Paul Westermeyer makes overly tart comments in his suggestion that popular music is designed to be listened to in a car.

A car at 65 miles per hour with all its associated road noise and traffic hazards is no place to concentrate on a Palestrina motet, a Bach fugue, a Brahms symphony, slabs of sound by Varèse, or bird song by Messiaen; but it is precisely the place to listen to short pieces with a few chords, much unvaried repetition, sounds that are not clean or pure, a percussive and regular beat, and little dynamic variation — all conceived so as to require little concentration and to be heard above the racket.

If that is so, how does one get from the high decibel level and distractions of a technological culture to waiting in silence before God? Should anybody try? Does the silence that frames a piece have any relevance here? Does the highest art of human conception with nuance and subtlety fit? . . . Are we to be concerned about justice and peace, or do we assume camouflaging them, as in the surrounding advertising culture, is the norm? Is our attraction to technological capability a good thing when we apply it to worship with the perpetual drizzle of Muzak, which dulls our senses, or with canned music, which denies people their own voice? Why are we so afraid to use genuinely contemporary music of our period, which so obviously expresses the issues of our generation?[28]

Though we might not agree with Westermeyer that popular music was designed to be listened to in cars, he is certainly right that much music requires more concentration than one has available while driving, and he raises several points relevant to our discussion of excellence. For example, it seems to me far preferable to use simpler music that congregation members can play on whatever instruments are available than to use canned music that is not the worship gift of the people present. Also, at some points in the worship service the most excellent music we can use is silence. And, indeed, we must ask about technological distraction.

The second aspect of musical worth is greatness. Music is disposable if it is not great enough to be preserved beyond its own time. Gieschen cites some phrases from Reimer that define this quality in terms of how capable a piece is of "producing deep, abiding insights" into the nature of reality as experienced by human beings. Greatness "occurs when the sense of feeling fullness is so striking, so 'true,' so revealing of the subjective human condition, that one who experiences the work's impact feels changed." Leonard Bernstein suggested that a great work of art is great "because it creates a special world of its own. It revives and readapts time and space, and the measure of its success is the extent to which it invites you in and lets you breathe its strange, special air!" (Gieschen, pp. 14-15). We must notice in these definitions the blending of intellect and emotions.

Some people might object that while the music a choir sings should, of course, be great, the congregation's singing need not be so elevated. This profoundly disturbing attitude seems to be prevalent throughout the United States. Why do we settle for less than the best in our offering to God of praise? I should think that congregants as well as special singers would want to strive to give God all that their voice, mind, and heart could give, to worship God with excellence of intent and execution. If we do not work hard to choose great music for congregational singing and to make that singing great, perhaps we have lost sight of the greatness of the God who is the subject and object of our worship.

In Carol Bly's description of bringing artistic productions to people

28. Westermeyer, "Professional Concerns Forum," pp. 34-39.

in small rural communities, she emphasizes that one of the most helpful things was "to work with classic material. If a play is going to be middle-ground producing and middle-ground acting, you are still doing something worth doing if you do real art." She continues,

> The Holst quotation ["if something is worth doing, it's worth doing badly"] does set us free to try our wings, but it presupposes earnestness; that is, the "thing" he mentions must be "worth doing." We can kill our countryside art with wised up "audience-related" non-art, in which the producer promises he is starting "where the people are at." The people are, as they ever were, at the point of starvation for excellence. They want to do art themselves, and to share in the grand and ancient things.[29]

We might say the same for music. If we do not have the capabilities of producing superb music, we should at least work with the best material. We might not be able to praise God like professional singers, but we can praise God by singing to the best of our ability the best music that has been composed.

The greatness of many hymns is outlined by Greg Asimakoupoulos, who suggests using the hymnal for private devotions. He explains,

> My lyrical old friend has taught me how to verbalize my love for God. . . . Inwardly I felt overwhelmed by the majesty and power of my Creator, but I lacked the ability to communicate that adoration in thoughts or words. My hymnal increased my vocabulary of praise. Reading the lyricist's words was like learning a new language.

He cites as examples "Immortal, Invisible God Only Wise," Bernard of Clairvaux's "What language can I borrow to thank You, dearest Friend?" (from "O Sacred Head Now Wounded"), and "Holy, Holy, Holy." He illustrates the value of confession of sin with "Come Thou Fount of Every Blessing."[30]

Next, Asimakoupoulos calls the hymnal "An Encyclopedia of Expe-

---

29. Carol Bly, *Letters from the Country* (New York: Penguin Books, 1981), pp. 29 and 30-31.

30. Greg Asimakoupoulos, "Please Take Out Your Hymnal," *Discipleship Journal* 82 (July/Aug. 1994): 25. Page references to this article in the next paragraph are given parenthetically in the text.

rience" because its composers/lyricists talk about aspects of faith-life such as grace, failure, doubts, amazement, frustration, and discouragement. Describing it also as "A Doctrinal Diary," he cites Luther's "A Mighty Fortress" (p. 26). Having given numerous examples of how he uses the hymnal for personal devotions, he concludes, "As much as I love the refreshing informality of contemporary praise choruses, there is nothing quite like the great hymns of our faith. No matter what is sung on Sunday, the lyrics that lie latent on an unsung page can nourish any believer's life" (p. 27).

This author's concept of greatness involves the words of the hymns he cites, but that is inextricably combined with musical greatness, for a hymn cannot be great if its music is not coherent with its text. Musical greatness does not lie in splash; meditative songs with simple melodies appropriate for flutes and guitars can be as great as majestic hymns accompanied by trumpet descants and fully opened organ. The secret to greatness in music is that the emotions and insights it evokes thoroughly match those roused by the theological content and that both music and text speak fully and honestly of that which really matters.

This final aspect of our selection grid thus drives us back to the first. As we assess the greatness of the music, it invites us to question again the greatness of the companion text. And the text is great in proportion to what we can learn from it. Alan Jacobs rejects modern literary criticism, which sees the past as only oppressive and which complains that what we learn from the past is strictly negative. In contrast, Jacobs offers the model of Wendell Berry, who "thinks the tragedy of literary education today is that 'teachers and students read the great songs and stories to learn *about* them, not learn *from* them.'" If we reject the great music of the Church's past, if we discard it as too oppressive or negative, we lose the opportunity to learn not only from its text but also about its musical form, and thus we will miss the opportunity to gain the sensibilities that great art can teach us.

These "great songs and stories" are called great "because of the weight of truth that they carry," Jacobs suggests. "Whereas [other critics] want us to test literature against our own personal standards, Berry challenges us to test ourselves against the standards of great literature."[31] The same is true of great music. Rather than test it by our standards, let us test our

31. Alan Jacobs, "To Read and to Live," *First Things* 34 (June/July 1993): 28.

vision of God, our character, and the character of our Christian communities against its truth.

We can summarize the whole process through which we have gone in this chapter with several questions that state the subject of each step in our selection grid. If a piece of music does not pass the first test, we need not submit it to the others. Those that pass through the steps the most successfully will be our first choices for music for the worship service we are planning. All the facets of the process interplay, so we might choose a hymn to use before the sermon that is less worthy musically, but more apt textually. At the beginning of the service, we might rank another aspect a bit higher in the process because of our goal to use a variety of musical styles. Basically, however, this grid will enable us to make better choices.

1. Is the text theologically sound? Is it true to God's nature, conducive to the formation of character, inclusive for the whole community? Gieschen asks, "Is it a Christian thought?" "Is it carefully expressed?" (p. 7).

2. Does the style disrupt worship in any way? Is it honest? Does it prevent community singing or promote it? Does it have any negative associations that might preclude its use for worship?

3. How appropriate is the piece with respect to our goal to use music for the diversity of congregation members? How appropriate is it to the musical ability of the congregation and the music leaders? How appropriate is it to its function in the service and the place of the service in the Church year?

4. Is this piece of music characterized by excellence and greatness to a satisfactory degree? Do other matters in the selection grid outweigh the requirements of excellence and greatness to some extent (though never entirely, for we do not want to serve God with less than our best)?

Goals for the Choir

Beyond the limited possibilities of congregational singing, we can enrich our worship immensely through the gifts of a choir. I will suggest some of the opportunities simply by listing my goals in directing a small adult choir. This choir was a typical one for an average-sized congregation — short on tenors and on persons who could read music. But the members chose to be in the choir as their way to serve God and the congregation, and they worked hard to do that with excellence. I gladly pay them tribute in this book because they taught me much about worship through their love for singing.

1. Under the overarching goal of praising God, the main purpose of the choir is to help the congregation sing better. For warm-up music we sang the hymns for the following Sunday. My primary intention was to teach the choir the theological depth of the hymns in the hymnal and the wide variety of musical styles and ages in them. We would do such things as sway to the hymns with dance tune melodies, tune the guitar to play drone chords for the Appalachian folk hymns, clap unusual rhythms, sing hymns in four-part canon, etc. It would be good if the choir could lead a hymn-sing for the congregation to enable more people to enjoy the various styles of hymns.

2. A related goal was for the choir to teach the congregation hymns with which most people were unfamiliar. Besides those in our own hymnal, we learned some from denominational supplements, from other denominational hymnals, and new ones that I had written.

3. My main goal in choosing anthems was to teach the choir the breadth of the repertoire of the Church's choral literature, so that they could become familiar with composers from Pergolesi and Bach through the Romantics to modern composers. Each anthem was first checked for its theological faithfulness and for its appropriateness to the Church year calendar.

4. Related to #3 was the goal to introduce to the choir a wide diversity of styles of music — canons, contrapuntal, chorale elaborations, quodlibets, responsory chants, various kinds of harmonic structures, unaccompanied or accompanied with a variety of instruments, straight text or aria forms, anthems featuring soloists or descants, etc. This involved also teaching why a composer used certain musical forms to convey specific aspects of the text and why particular music is more appropriate to convey different elements of the faith or for various seasons of the Church year.

5. Besides a recognition of the heritage of the Church through time, I was also interested in the global Church, so we sang music from South Africa, Russia, Madagascar, etc.

6. In all of this it was important to teach the singers good vocal techniques — proper voice formation, how to produce the best vocal tones, pronunciation tricks, breathing, and phrasing. This was important not only so that the choir could sing its best when we did anthems but

also so that we could be a model in the midst of the congregation and help everyone to sing better.

7. I also chose pieces as much as possible to involve the children in the congregation — combining the adult choir with midweek school choirs, with the handbell choir, and with one or more instrumentalists.

These goals all point primarily to the education of the singers and instrumentalists themselves so that they have more to give to the congregation. I prefer for the choir to sing from the balcony, from behind the worshipers, so that the focus can remain on God and not on the choir, though I realize the advantage of congregants being able to see the facial expressions of choir members to add visual learning to the auditory. That is a debate we do not need to resolve in this book, but I mention it because too often I see choirs that sing more as performance than as praise. We must always ask how best to keep the focus on God, even as we continue to question how we can offer our best in praise.

As Paul Westermeyer inquires, "Does any of this make any difference?" If most people only know the sounds of rock music and advertising jingles, is it

> even possible to engage them at any other level? Does anybody have the responsibility to try? Is the rich engagement of faith with the deepest and most profound musical expressions of humankind totally off the screen? Are people to be denied this legacy and treated contemptuously?
>
> I can only speak from my own experience, which is that people long for what is worth their time and effort. They look to us to struggle with what that is, to provide them with it as best we are able, and to treat them with the respect they deserve.[32]

Let us reach out in the Church and to the world with the best music we can offer from the Church's entire history, from the distant past to the present. The congregation can "sing a new song" not because we are trying to appeal to the culture, but because God is present in our midst in new ways. As we respond to God, the subject of our worship, our song will reach out to the culture surrounding the Church with the Church's best gifts — without dumbing down the faith.

32. Westermeyer, "Professional Concerns Forum," p. 38.

9. Worship Ought to Kill Us: The Word

O God of earth and altar, in mercy hear our cry;
our earthly rulers falter, our people drift and die;
the walls of gold entomb us, the words of scorn divide;
take not Thy thunder from us, but take away our pride.

From all that terror teaches, from lies of pen and tongue;
from all the easy speeches that satisfy the throng;
from sale and profanation of honor and the word;
from sleep and from damnation, deliver us, good God!

G. K. Chesterton, 1906

I wish this chapter's title could be more startling. As Walter Brueggemann says, "The gospel is too readily heard and taken for granted, as though it contained no unsettling news and no unwelcome threat. What began as news in the gospel is easily assumed, slotted, and conveniently dismissed."[1] In a society doing all it can to make people cozy, somehow we

---

1. Walter Brueggemann, *Finally Comes the Poet: Daring Speech for Proclamation* (Minneapolis: Fortress Press, 1989), p. 1.

must convey the truth that God's Word, rightly read and heard, will shake us up. It will kill us, for God cannot bear our sin and wants to put to death our self-centeredness. The apostle Paul exclaims that he has been "crucified with Christ" and therefore that it is no longer he who lives, but Christ who lives in him (Gal. 2:19-20). Once worship kills us, we are born anew to worship God rightly.

Everything that we do in worship should kill us, but especially the parts of the service in which we hear the Word — the Scripture lessons and the sermon. One reason I especially treasure the Church's historic Mass is that so much of it is composed of direct quotations from the Scriptures, which kill me every time I sing them. I get more comfortable under liturgies composed of human words that make it easier to escape the death blow and remain satisfied with myself.

This chapter focuses specifically on the sermon and the preacher — may God use it to deliver us, as Chesterton prays, "from all the easy speeches that satisfy the throng" and "the profanation . . . of the word." Almost everything discussed already in the previous chapters about music and our three main themes of God, character, and community also applies to the sermon.

God as the Subject and Object of Preaching

We need not try in this book to trace the trajectory by which God as the center of preaching has been lost, but those who care notice that God is lost, and those who don't care are busy doing the things that have caused the loss. An example of the latter is Christine Smith's *Preaching as Weeping, Confession, and Resistance*.[2] The cover announces that readers will learn "Radical Responses to Radical Evil" as they encounter "Handicappism, Ageism, Heterosexism, Sexism, White Racism, Classism." Smith is absolutely right that these "isms" are destructive of the Christian community and must be encountered and counteracted. I don't always agree with her solutions, but her analysis of the problems is astute. My objection is that the first word of the title is *preaching*, but the book does not offer any sense that God is the center of it.

2. Christine Smith, *Preaching as Weeping, Confession, and Resistance: Radical Responses to Radical Evil* (Louisville: Westminster/John Knox Press, 1992). Page references to this book in the following paragraphs are given parenthetically in the text.

The book's sample sermons confirm this. "Unspeakable Loss," on Judges 11:29-40, weeps thoroughly over the pain women suffer. This pain is resisted in a Nigerian health clinic staffed by women (pp. 164-69). But there is no God in whom to hope — and if I only hope in myself and other women, I will be disillusioned time and again.

"Behold Crying Messengers," a sermon based on Mark 1:1-8, loses God more subtly. As it concentrates mostly on the messengers, God becomes virtually identical to the handicapped people who incarnate God's presence (pp. 173-77). While it is indeed the case that God is found incarnated in other people — especially in those who suffer[3] — we dare not *identify* God with human beings. We need the hope of a God who is totally Other as the source of healing for our sufferings.

The loss of God as the center of preaching is poignantly described by H. Benton Lutz, formerly a preacher, who says he is now sitting in the pew

> looking for the gospel. It has been strangely absent. . . . [I]n the church, worn-out preachers too often preach worn-out words from a worn-out tradition to people who no longer expect to be challenged.
>
> What went wrong?
>
> Instead of trying to make visible what to many is invisible, the church has been about creating a fabricated reality, a reality of our own design. It is trying to be a force in society while ignoring the force of God already present and working in society.
>
> These pastors force stale, dry words into our heads rather than telling the stories of Scripture in ways that illuminate our lives. They do not crack the *kerygma* open and let those stories spill over the real events of our daily lives.[4]

Keeping God as the center of preaching involves telling the stories of faith so well that God's invisible presence becomes visible, so that we can catch sight of God's intervention in the past and in the present.

God was lost before in the Church's history; the Church recovered,

---

3. See my book *Joy in Our Weakness: A Gift of Hope from the Book of Revelation* (St. Louis: Concordia, 1994) for a thorough discussion of a theology of weakness and of the special gifts from God that those who suffer can offer the Christian community.

4. H. Benton Lutz, "The Self-Absorbed Masquerade," *The Other Side* 29, no. 4 (July-Aug. 1993): 46.

but it took a Reformation. When Luther fought the problem in 1523, he wrote that "in order to correct these abuses, know first of all that a Christian congregation should never gather together without the preaching of God's Word and prayer." Keeping God's presence central, he used this verse from Psalm 102 to describe what preaching does: " 'When the kings and the people assemble to serve the Lord, they shall declare the name and the praise of God.' "[5]

This chapter need not provide a course in homiletics; many superb books do that well. Our goal instead is to see the ramifications of the previous chapters for the preaching art, to call for preaching that narrates not the steps to personal fulfillment but "the promise of God's ongoing rule in the world."[6] Preaching with God as the subject immerses us in God's sovereign Lordship, and the realization of that rule offers the genuine hope for which our society so desperately yearns. We see it happening in Isaiah when

> through his preaching he offered his community the sights and sounds of their authentic world, a world determined by God's "fear not" instead of by their fears. He knew that the only way to move his people out of despair and into the hope-filled future already initiated by God was to reassert God's promises over and over again, so that finally the language that shaped the life of the community would no longer be "I am afraid" but "do not fear."[7]

God is at work to bring about God's future. Why don't we declare it? Why don't we thoroughly celebrate God's presence in our midst through his Word?

Somewhere I heard that William Willimon tells of pastors who admit that the most terrifying moments in their ministry occurred when God really did show up! What would happen if people in the pew really paid

---

5. Martin Luther, "Concerning the Order of Public Worship" (1523), trans. Paul Zeller Strodach, *Luther's Works,* ed. Helmut T. Lehmann, vol. 53: *Liturgy and Hymns* (Philadelphia: Fortress Press, 1965), p. 11.

6. Richard Lischer, "Preaching as the Church's Language," in *Listening to the Word: Studies in Honor of Fred B. Craddock,* ed. Gail R. O'Day and Thomas G. Long (Nashville: Abingdon, 1993), p. 128.

7. Gail O'Day, "Toward a Biblical Theology of Preaching," in O'Day and Long, eds., *Listening to the Word,* pp. 26-27.

attention to what we preach and it changed their lives? What would we do, for example, if someone greeted us after the service and said that because of God's Word through our preaching she was going to sell her possessions, give the money to the poor, and serve in a Catholic Worker community? How would we respond if the Holy Spirit killed someone right in the pew, and his new life was utterly transformed into a deep discipleship of seeking earnestly to follow Jesus?

It is good, Richard Lischer reminds us, that we cannot predict how the Word and the Holy Spirit will work in people's lives. If we could, we would try to manipulate the Word to accomplish our own purposes instead of being the Word's servants. We would advertise our own successes instead of seeking to be faithful stewards of God's mysteries.[8]

Nurturing Believers' Character

If the Word does not bear its fruit and if the Holy Spirit is not seizing control when pastors preach, it might be because they use the tools of our self-help society instead of introducing the God who changes lives. Previous chapters have underlined that when God is rightly kept as worship's subject and object, participants' character will be formed in response to God's.

However, we live in an age of the "Gospel of Therapy." Preaching often dispenses steps to correct one's life disorders or codependencies. Society's technicization, catalogued by Ellul, invades sermons in the form of directions to become technicians of the inner life for the purpose of self-improvement.

As William H. Willimon summarizes it, the thesis of Sass's book *Madness and Modernism* is that "modernism began a movement out of the world and into detached, subjective experience [which is] . . . the very essence of insanity[,] . . . that condition whereby we become detached from other people and the world and engulfed in ourselves." To this awareness Willimon responds,

> As a preacher who preaches weekly to people who often seem to have no criterion for judgment outside themselves, and as a pastoral counselor

8. Richard Lischer, *A Theology of Preaching: The Dynamics of the Gospel* (Nashville: Abingdon, 1981), p. 84.

209

who counsels those who have no other life-journey than a journey deeper into their own experience, this book caused me trouble. . . . Fass *[sic]* shows how modernism may be a euphemism for a worldview that is, in short, insane. Inductive preachers, . . . theologians of experience, take note![9]

Sermons cannot form the character of believers when sin is treated merely as an addiction and redemption is only therapy. The believer's new life in Christ must be based on Christ's objective work of redemption, not on our experience of it, nor on a process of self-improvement or self-actualization.

All the gimmicks sermons use instead of sustained attention to biblical texts hinder the development of faithful life. It is a shame that churches have to be reminded of their failure to nurture genuine character by a national news magazine, but Jeffrey Sheler reports in an article in *U.S. News and World Report* that many congregations

> have multiplied their membership by going light on theology and offering worshippers a steady diet of sermons and support groups that emphasize personal fulfillment. . . . Yet [Rev. Joan] Campbell and others worry that while it's good for churches to address the personal and emotional needs of their flocks, they may be neglecting other important aspects of faith. Martin Marty . . . warns that in the competition for members, churches may be tempted to "package God in ways that make religion immediately attractive" but that downplay the demands of faith. Anthony Campolo . . . describes a growing "culture of narcissism" in the churches that gives short shrift to the Christian imperative of serving others.[10]

This book has highlighted the necessity for keeping God as the subject and object of worship. Preaching provides the unique opportunity to make clear the meaning of that presence of God — a meaning that escorts believers into new life. The essential goal of preaching is that the listener be transformed. Therefore, the new emphasis in homiletical teach-

---

9. William H. Willimon, "Impressions and Imprints," *The Christian Century* 110, no. 33 (17-24 Nov. 1993): 1149.

10. Jeffrey L. Sheler, "Spiritual America," *U.S. News and World Report* 116, no. 13 (4 April 1993): 53-54.

ing on the hearer as participant in, even shaper of, the sermon[11] must be held in dialectical tension with the biblical imperative to speak the Word so that it can do its transforming work. As Richard Lischer concludes, the "listener isn't king; God is."[12]

Richard Caemmerer insists that "the goal of preaching is always more than to inform, to relay fact. That preaching convey clear ideas and sound fact is important, but only as means to a further end. That end is meaning." He explains the difference between sense and meaning simply: "Sense is the shape of a fact. Meaning is the shaping of the hearer." Sense asks, "'Do you understand this fact?' Meaning asks: 'Is this fact doing to you what it is supposed to do?' Sense informs the hearer. Meaning strikes him."[13]

Sermons should shape hearers by bringing the transforming Word to nurture the development of their character in the pattern of Christ. The sermon gives time for specific theological and ethical instruction, for painting the picture of the Christian life and community so that worshipers can enter into it. However, these overt calls to the life of following Jesus can be counteracted by the entire ambience of the worshiping milieu; therefore, everything else in the service must be cohesive with the message for the day. No matter how much the Scripture readings and sermons stress that God is gracious, congregations won't learn that truth and become gracious if worship is not grace-full.

Leander Keck especially points to the importance of preaching for developing the character of leaders, both for the Church and for the society surrounding it. By "the habits of the community of faith" as they are practiced week by week, leaders are shaped. Particularly, leaders need to hear preaching

> that wrestles with the ambiguities of public affairs; . . . that emphasizes what makes for the common good, especially character marked by integrity, self-control, and respect for all people; . . . that is truly pro-

---

11. See, e.g., these chapters in O'Day and Long, eds., *Listening to the Word:* David Buttrick, "Who Is Listening?" pp. 189-206; Thomas G. Long, "And How Shall They Hear? The Listener in Contemporary Preaching," pp. 167-88; Henry Mitchell, "The Hearer's Experience of the Word," pp. 223-41; and Barbara Brown Taylor, "Preaching the Body," pp. 207-21. See also Richard R. Caemmerer, *Preaching for the Church* (St. Louis: Concordia, 1959), especially pp. 87-18, 125-30, and 275-94.

12. Lischer, *A Theology of Preaching,* p. 93.

13. Caemmerer, *Preaching for the Church,* p. 49.

phetic because it springs more from agony than from alienation; . . . that brings the perspective of eternity to bear on our temporal affairs, whether by revealing the transcendent meaning of the ordinary or by exposing the transient significance of the allegedly momentous; . . . that widens the horizons of love and service because it announces the scope and depth of God's love in Christ; . . . that provokes the pondering of our discipleship and the praising of God's grace. From churches with such habits of hearing, and of the doing that flows from them, can come a cadre of persons who can work effectively for a more just and compassionate society.[14]

Such preaching as Keck describes would be wonderfully invigorating for our society through its equipping of both public leaders and citizens. Preaching should energize all Christians "to ennoble whatever space they occupy."[15]

The Formation of the Christian Community

Perhaps my experience is unusual, but until recently I have not heard many sermons throughout my life that highlighted the Christian community as opposed to the individual life of particular believers. Perhaps I missed it because the English pronoun *you* doesn't reveal plurality, but in many churches our culture's invading narcissism leads to an accent on personal faith. It seems to me a great gift is missed if sermons don't enfold us in the faith community that supports us and nurtures us, both locally and throughout time and space.

It is especially crucial that the sermon enfold us in the community of biblically formed faith. The community itself is destroyed as *Christian* community if preaching does not hold before the people the decisive Word from God that makes those who follow Jesus different from the society around them.

The need for strong biblical preaching is urgent. Alexander Pope's poem shows how easily we slip away from what we know to be the moral truth:

14. Leander E. Keck, *The Church Confident* (Nashville: Abingdon, 1993), p. 94.
15. Keck, *The Church Confident*, p. 95.

Vice is a monster of so frightful mien
As to be hated needs but to be seen,
Yet seen too oft, familiar with her face,
We first endure, then pity, then embrace.

This process can often be witnessed in the dumbing down of worship music or preaching. Christians begin by enduring trivial sermons, feeling that it is not their place to judge the pastor. Then they pity the preacher, offering compassionate explanations for his sloth or cowardice; they understand "where he's coming from." Finally they embrace the triviality. They have become so accustomed to sermons that do not change their lives that they see nothing wrong with them.

Whenever we relativize truth and eviscerate its questioning, we succumb to the process Pope describes. Whenever we let "politically correct" hot topics become the guide for what we do in worship, we have embraced the vice of "blessing" our own agendas "by appeal to symbols of ultimacy" instead of embracing God as the subject of what we do in worship. Ted Peters gives the example of chapel services on a seminary campus and reports that in one discussion plans were made for black history month and for a Hispanic week. One professor "murmured, 'Well, it's Lent. Couldn't we emphasize Lent?' No answer." No longer do worship wars rage over remembering the themes of biblical faith. As Peters mourns, "The mere murmur in behalf of Lent indicates that resistance has all but disappeared, so that instead of a war we have a *coup d'église*."[16]

The question that we must constantly ask in our preaching is whether there is normative truth that has called the community into being. Is there a Word from God by which we can order Christian life? Of course, there are disagreements over the interpretation of that Word — and the resolution of those conflicts is the work of the community over time and space. That brings into play the dialectic of hearer and preacher to some extent. However, pastors have been trained in the distinctive doctrines of the community's life together and bear the authority of the larger community as they speak to the local congregation. It is not their own authority but that of the Word and the Church that has faithfully preserved and transmitted that Word.

---

16. Ted Peters, "Worship Wars," *dialog* 33, no. 3 (Summer 1994): 167.

Roger Van Harn's book entitled *Pew Rights* underscores this continuity and authority. People in the pew have the right to hear the Church's faith as it is proclaimed by the Church, to the Church, and for the world. In the light of God's story, which the Christian community carries, we understand both our culture and the "one, holy, catholic, apostolic Church" that we confess.[17]

We can learn from the prophet Ezra. The story of his reading of the law in Nehemiah 8 includes thirteen references to "all the people." We dare not miss this point: we only preach or teach if we have been explicitly or implicitly asked, called, to do so. The text does not portray Ezra as a hero; rather, it teaches us his humility and the lesson "of interdependence, of the reader and interpreter of the law as part of and responsive to the community of faith." This is good news for interpreters of the Word — "that they are not and could not be alone, that they need not be heroes, that what they do is in and with a community of faith." As Gene Tucker tells us, this story proclaims that

> reading and interpretation and understanding are profoundly corporate enterprises. They always take place within some interpretive community. What one says as a preacher or teacher is what one is in the process of learning with a congregation or community, in this case the broad community of those who want to understand and be faithful to the law, to the will of God.[18]

It is critical that preachers keep that broader community in mind. They will not give in to local politics if they remember their responsibility to the larger Church, the corporate Body of those seeking God's will.

The preacher's words, then, emerge from the Church's life and go forth to nourish that life. If the sermon is not theological — that is, if it does not offer words about God and the life to be found in Christ — "it suffers the same fate as the seed sown on rocky soil. But in this case, its rootlessness derives from the preacher's rather than the hearer's lack of depth."[19]

I am encouraged by the current emphasis on ecclesiology as a major

---

17. Roger E. Van Harn, *Pew Rights* (Grand Rapids: William B. Eerdmans, 1992).

18. Gene M. Tucker, "Reading and Preaching the Old Testament," in O'Day and Long, eds., *Listening to the Word*, p. 49.

19. Lischer, *A Theology of Preaching*, p. 14.

motif in homiletics.[20] Lischer recovers the biblical understanding that it is the community of faith that bridges the gap between the biblical record and the modern listener. He insists, "Not human nature or experience but the *church* is the middle term that connects the text and the present community. The church is not a piece in the hermeneutical puzzle but the means by which it is solved."[21]

Lischer is a thoroughly ecclesiological homiletician and thereby connects many of this book's themes. He argues the necessity for the worship service to be cohesive, to focus on God, and to nurture character, while specifically requiring the sermon to form a community of faith over time. "Preaching does this by consciously aligning itself with its primary scene, which is the worship service. The basic unit of meaning on Sunday morning is not the sermon but the service." The sermon articulates what is expressed in the ritualized behavior, liturgy, and music of the service — the "gathering of the congregation, songs of praise and doxology, recitations of God's mighty acts, reminiscences of Jesus, the celebration of the sacraments, and a blessing and sending of the people into the world." Surely it is incongruous if ministers "insert into this corporate observance a speech that focuses either on individual needs or universal truths but does nothing to reinforce the identity of this community, to train it in mutual love, or to equip it for ministry." The sermon does not simply announce a new standing before God or hold up fuzzy parallels between religion and meaningful events; rather, it directs believers into the implications of their redemption in Christ. Instead of the typical sermon illustration that demonstrates "the likeness of Christian teaching to conventional values, . . . preaching-as-formation explores the differences. In so doing, it becomes the voice of the church as a contrast-society."[22]

My favorite sentence for years has been, "The Christian community is an alternative society." That thesis requires all sermons to ask, How does this text form us to be the people of God? What do we learn from this text that cannot be known apart from the community of faith? How can we offer this alternative understanding to the world? If preachers want

20. See, e.g., Long, "And How Shall They Hear?" p. 188. He asserts, "The doctrine of the church, as the speech community of God, will provide the framework for any truly pertinent homiletic."

21. Lischer, "Preaching as the Church's Language," p. 125.

22. Lischer, "Preaching as the Church's Language," p. 126.

their sermons to reach out to the culture surrounding the Church, they serve the public best, not by dumbing down the faith, but by boldly declaring the "new creation" in Christ (2 Cor. 5:17), in which visitors to worship can find a home.

The Pastor's Motivations and Goals

What visitors really seek in pastors is godliness. In William Hendricks's *Exit Interviews,* a young man commented, "I think the bottom line is that if people analyze why they go to church, they have to believe that the pastor is spiritual. Probably not many members of the church are going to go sit under a guy that they don't respect as a spiritual man."[23] If pastors want the worship services over which they preside to reach out to non-members, the most important thing they can do is nourish their own spiritual life.

Sometimes the goal to bring the gospel to our culture leads to confusion over pastors' identity. Earnest, well-intentioned pastors, influenced by fears of a dying congregation, turn to "marketing strategies, communication techniques and product packaging" to help them become more effective, instead of seeking greater faithfulness to God's will. As Douglas Webster chides, "The means and ends of building the household of faith are distinctively ordained by God and not discovered through sociological analysis or psychological profiles. The latest trends and popular expectations do not change the church's agenda or alter its course."[24]

We easily notice the ignorance of the Scriptures and biblical illiteracy that characterize the present Church, yet many react "to cultural pressure by scaling down serious biblical reflection. They would sooner entertain their audiences than risk being criticized for being too serious, abstract and boring." This leads to sermons that might make people laugh and cry, but don't necessarily enable them to know God better, think more clearly, or act in godly ways.[25]

Just as we asked about believers' character formation, so even more

23. William D. Hendricks, *Exit Interviews* (Chicago: Moody Press, 1993), p. 55.

24. Douglas D. Webster, *Selling Jesus* (Downers Grove, IL: InterVarsity Press, 1992), p. 17.

25. Webster, *Selling Jesus,* p. 85.

we must ask about preachers' character. Are they being formed by their immersion in the Word or by the pressures of marketing analysis? Does the sermon come from the Word's imperative or from what a television age teaches about staging?

Neil Postman's *Amusing Ourselves to Death* heightens our awareness of how powerfully television resonates through the culture — as the source for news of the latest murder, government policy, scientific advances, baseball scores, weather, soap operas, and presidential addresses. As a result, its methods and metaphors prevail in every area of life. It affects how we conduct law, politics, religion, business, education, and other important social matters. People exchange images instead of ideas; they argue not with propositions but with "good looks, celebrities and commercials."[26] As a result worshipers sometimes pay more attention to the pastor's personality than to the sermon's substance and worship's meaning. As Postman protests, our priests, lawyers, presidents, surgeons, educators, and newscasters "need worry less about satisfying the demands of their discipline than the demands of good showmanship."[27]

David Wells makes the same critique of the way the market dominates how pastors "exercise their ministry, often taking precedence over the matter of internal calling and over personal spirituality."[28] He cites Jackson Carroll's dissertation, which studied the professional socialization of ministers. Carroll discovered that "authority and professional status" depend on "interpersonal skills, administrative talents, and ability to organize the community," rather than "character, ability to expound the Word of God, or theological skill in relating that Word to the contemporary world."[29]

My concern for the role of pastors has been heightened by the stories of George MacDonald, the nineteenth-century writer, lecturer, and preacher. Many of his novels feature a minister who serves the Church perfunctorily, doing his pastoral duties for the sake of money or prestige.

26. Neil Postman, *Amusing Ourselves to Death* (New York: Viking Penguin, 1985), pp. 92-93.

27. Postman, *Amusing Ourselves to Death,* p. 98.

28. David F. Wells, *No Place for Truth* (Grand Rapids: William B. Eerdmans, 1993), p. 232.

29. Jackson Carroll, "Seminaries and Seminarians: A Study of the Professional Socialization of Protestant Clergymen" (Ph.D. diss., Princeton Theological Seminary, 1970), p. 306, as cited in Wells, *No Place for Truth,* p. 234.

In vivid contrast, MacDonald presents another character who has both a "pastor's heart," a loving character burdened for the well-being of others, and also theological skill in applying God's Word to the situations of other characters' lives. In *The Curate's Awakening,* the latter role is fulfilled by the dwarf Polwarth, who is not a pastor but a gatekeeper. By his ministrations, the curate himself is brought to an understanding of his call — and in two subsequent novels the curate is the agent, through his sermons and life, of great awakenings in the lives of others.[30]

In *The Prodigal Apprentice* MacDonald offers this picture of a preacher:

> Some people considered Mr. Fuller very silly for believing that he might do good in a church like this, and with a congregation like this, by speaking that which he knew, and testifying to that which he had seen. But he did actually believe it. Because he was so much in the habit of looking up to the Father, the prayers took hold of him every time he read them, and he so delighted in the truths he saw that he rejoiced to set them forth — was actually glad to *talk* about them to anyone who would listen.[31]

In the story, Fuller brings great healing through straightforward exposition of scriptural truths conveyed in humble speech and augmented by his godliness.

How pastors function is defined by their pastoral being; what they do grows out of who they are and their sense of calling. As the New Testament pictures it, pastoral being is composed of "worthy character, a passion for truth, and the kind of wise love that yokes together this character and this passion in the service of others."[32] When Haddon Robinson says, "Regrettably, many preachers fail as Christians before they fail as preachers because they do not think biblically,"[33] the context refers primarily to the lack of biblical content in their actual sermon preparation,

---

30. See George MacDonald, *The Curate's Awakening,* ed. Michael R. Phillips (Minneapolis: Bethany House Publishers, 1985). Originally published in 1876 as *Thomas Wingfold, Curate.*

31. George MacDonald, *The Prodigal Apprentice,* ed. Dan Hamilton (Wheaton, IL: Victor Books, 1984), p. 115. Originally published as *Guild Court* in 1867.

32. Wells, *No Place for Truth,* p. 237.

33. Haddon W. Robinson, *Biblical Preaching: The Development and Delivery of Expository Messages* (Grand Rapids: Baker Book House, 1980), p. 25.

but we can expand his dissatisfaction to include the Christian character of preachers. The greatest weakness of much preaching is that the Word hasn't killed the pastor first.

Henri Nouwen invites pastors to recall that "in order to be fruitful, the vine has to be pruned, to be cut back." He admits to being increasingly aware

> of how much I want to go in many directions, do many things, meet many people, be involved in many situations. But to be fruitful I have to stay close to the source of life and allow myself to be cut back.
>
> This is something I cannot do for myself; it must be done by the Word of God. It's the Word that tells me that the grain of wheat has to die in order to bear fruit. Maybe it's first of all a question of becoming attentive to when and where the cutting is taking place, and recognizing these times and places as times and places of fruitfulness.[34]

Of course, it is easier to say that we must be pruned than to undergo the cutting. In fact, we need some pruning in preparation for every sermon, for the Word must change the life of the preacher before that preacher can speak it forth in all of its life-changing fullness.

Philip Turner, dean of Yale's Berkeley Divinity School, asks what it means to be a student of divinity.[35] Primarily, he asserts, it means to be studying "the divine" — not religion, but God (p. 25) — though the divinity school's purpose "to promote the knowledge and love of God" is "contrary both to the spirit of the age . . . [and] to present theological fashion." What could theological fashion be about if divinity schools no longer nurture the love of God?

Turner insists that the first means for the study of divinity is worship (p. 26). Ever since the publication of my book on Sabbath keeping I have wanted to write a sequel responding to pastors who ask how it is possible for them to worship since Sunday is a work day. The ideal would be for pastors to be set free by their prior study and by the Holy Spirit's presence to enjoy worship even as they lead it, but for many pastors that is difficult.

34. Henri J. M. Nouwen, "Finding a New Way to Get a Glimpse of God," *New Oxford Review* 60, no. 6 (July-Aug. 1993): 11.

35. Philip Turner, "To Students of Divinity: A Convocation Address," *First Things* 26 (Oct. 1992): 25-27. Page references to this article in the rest of this section are given parenthetically in the text.

Of course, one might choose any other day to observe the Sabbath (the Hebrew word *Shabbat* means "to cease" rather than referring to a certain day of the week), but how can one then have some sort of corporate worship? Perhaps clergy can take turns hosting each other for worship; in Lutheran circles, for example, pastors in a circuit meet monthly for study, fellowship, and worship. In some towns, clergy of various denominations gather for worship and add a family potluck meal or a celebrative dinner with spouses. Church conventions, clergy conferences, and local pericope study groups should create the best worship they can in order to feed those who give so much of themselves to enable others to worship on Sundays.

The preacher's personal devotional life should be a top priority — and members of the congregation should honor that time and not disturb the pastor. When I previously worked in a congregation, the secretary would tell callers that I was not available during my "quiet time," the first hour of each day. One of my favorite resources for personal worship is the *Moravian Daily Texts,* first printed in 1731. For each day of the year this book offers a Scripture lesson from each Testament (chosen in Herrnhut, Germany), a hymn verse related to each passage, and a prayer composed by clergy or laypersons in the United States and Canada. The practice of the "Watchword," the biblical text that Count Nicholas von Zinzendorf gave daily, beginning in 1728, to members of the community at his Herrnhut estate, made me so interested in the Moravian heritage that I purchased their hymnal and can now enjoy singing all the verses of the day's wonderfully faithful hymns — a great addition to my worship repertoire.[36] Those who preach especially need devotional materials to take them away from their customary analytical work with the Scriptures and into the presence of God. For me that requires "right-brain" tools such as singing, stories, and art.

Besides worship and devotion, the preacher's study of God involves what Wells calls "reflection," which must "range over the whole of God's disclosure within Scripture." The goal is to connect the various parts of Scripture to envision "God's intent in so revealing his character, acts, and will."[37] We might liken this to Paul's urging the Philippians to "have the

---

36. *Moravian Daily Texts* and the 1969 *Hymnal of the Moravian Church* (from which most of the hymn verses are taken) can be purchased from the Department of Publications and Communications, Moravian Church, P. O. Box 1245, Bethlehem, PA 18016-1245, phone (215) 867-0594, FAX 215-866-9223.

37. Wells, *No Place for Truth,* p. 100.

mind of Christ." As preachers study the divine, God's character is formed in them.

Turner asserts that the second task of divinity study is to master the tradition of the Church, the history of its knowing. He complains that

> American Christians may fairly be characterized as a body suffering from collective amnesia. On the whole, they know less and less about the way in which the tradition handed on by the Apostles has been interpreted and appropriated through the ages, and as their knowledge of that tradition decreases so also does the adequacy of what they have to say about who God is and what God requires. (p. 27)

In the next section of this chapter we will look more closely at the loss of theological tradition. At this point we must see the value of the tradition for forming the pastor's character. As Wells explains, reflection on the past helps preachers "gather from God's working in the Church the ballast that will steady it in the storms of the present."[38] Storing spiritual treasures of the past helps to put the present in proper perspective.

Turner's third component of divinity study is learning the way of life necessitated by liturgical and theological traditions and what they teach us about God. He asks, "Can we know the life of God apart from a struggle to share in it, and can we share in it if we do not seek to imitate it?" (p. 27).

To live and serve in this way — and therefore to be able to preach with power and truth, humility and earnestness — requires certain convictions on the pastor's part. We have been discussing these convictions throughout this book: the conviction that God is the center of worship, that the Scriptures reveal to us who God is, that the Church is an alternative society, that the Christian community and its worship are the locus for the character formation of believers, that the pastor is the steward of the mysteries of God and entrusted with the sacred responsibility to proclaim God's Word in this time and place.[39]

---

38. Wells, *No Place for Truth*, p. 100.

39. John R. W. Stott's classic homiletics text, *Between Two Worlds: The Art of Preaching in the Twentieth Century* (Grand Rapids: William B. Eerdmans, 1982), pp. 92-210, underscores the convictions necessary for preaching — convictions about God, the Scriptures, the Church, the pastorate, and preaching itself — as well as the depth of study necessary for preaching as a bridge between the worlds of the Bible and contemporary society.

The Loss of Our Theological Center

Many pastors tell me that they find it difficult to preach biblical and theological sermons because they learned in seminary so many things that reduce the Scriptures, that question their theology, and that pertain to practical, organizational matters rather than to doctrinal foundations. Many preachers have no experience in explaining the basics of theology in terms laypeople can understand. Others have believed the notion that sermons must appeal to people by meeting their "felt needs" rather than by giving them the Word of God that actually meets their genuine needs.

It is hard to avoid the prevailing notion that the Bible is outdated, that human beings have progressed too far to find value in old things, that we cannot slip back into an ancient worldview. Many think that the biblical witness is characterized by an intellectual simplicity that does not stand up in the present marketplace of religious pluralism. How ironic it is that the multiplicity of worldviews and truth claims that characterizes our environment is so very similar to the world in which the earliest Christians lived.[40]

An article by Jacques Ellul entitled "Notes innocentes sur la 'question herméneutique'" responds profoundly to the question of the Bible's applicability in the modern world, but unfortunately this piece has never been translated from the French. Using linguistic tools that I need not elaborate here, Ellul soundly refutes "secular 'evidence'" that language and conceptual apparati are no longer the same as those in which the revelation of God is recorded.[41] The following clarification of Ellul's ideas is still a bit thick, so please bear with me. His explanation is worth the effort.

The hermeneutical problem — that is, the difficulty of applying ancient Scriptures in the present time — rests on presuppositions that are accepted as certain truths but are never demonstrated or critiqued. The first of these presuppositions asserts that the language in which the biblical authors wrote was the daily language of their times and that their ideas were normal in their culture's intellectual milieu. Ellul reminds us that, though the biblical writers received the revelation of God with their own

---

40. See Wells, *No Place for Truth,* pp. 260-64 and 267-68.

41. Jacques Ellul, "Notes innocentes sur la 'question herméneutique,'" *L'Evangile, hier et aujourd'hui: Melanges offerts au professeur Franz J. Leehardt* (Genève: Editions Labor et fides, 1968), p. 181. Page references to this article in the following paragraphs are given parenthetically in the text. All translations of quotations are mine.

conceptual apparati, the recorded words were *the revelation of God,* a relation that overturns the apparatus. Consequently, the customary language is modified, often profoundly. Though the language might still appear in its historico-cultural structures, it is disconnected by God's utilization and therefore becomes a source of incomprehension and misunderstanding between the carriers of the revelation and the people around them. Thus the contemporaries of Isaiah or Jesus did not easily comprehend them; they were a source of confusion. Their language was not merely the average level of communication in their times.

A second presupposition is antithetical to the first, but both have to be held in tension, for Ellul's refutations of both are dialectically true. This second presupposition insists that the biblical language no longer transmits anything, that modern human beings are too rational for its myths. Ellul responds that Christian language is always current and rational, that the content of words such as *grace, love, hope,* and *faith* are no more misunderstood today than previously.

Furthermore, it is necessary to mistrust the obviousness of the basic claim that biblical thought was mythic and that modern thought is rational. Ellul shows, first of all, that ancient thought was highly rational — as evidenced by such things as the school of Alexandria, from which came Archimedes, or Roman juridical thought, neither of which in their rigorous formulations was an exception. Secondly, Ellul objects that it is audacious to claim that modern people have become rational when tens of thousands consult fortune tellers and horoscopes, desperately gamble, believe all the publicity and propaganda with which society bombards them, accept a thousand new forms of religion with all their myths, and live in a technologized universe as if obsessed by magic. He concludes that there is always a mixture of the rational and the irrational, the mythic and the logical with diverse proportions and forms, but never such that communication and signification would become impossible (pp. 182-84).

If we recognize that biblical language reveals meaning for faith, then we must go further and admit that if God is God, his revelation does not vary essentially over time, since he is the same yesterday, today, and tomorrow. It is a matter, then, of knowing that this permanence gives a certain power or orientation to the meaning of revelation that is rendered perceptible through the language to those who have faith in the revelation. Any inadequacy of language only adds a peripheral but not a decisive difficulty.

Generally one thinks that the language transmitted to us permits us to comprehend what it means, but the dimension of the revelation changes that process, for it is mastered by the Revealed One. That implies, first, that one cannot understand anything unless one receives and believes *le Révélé*. Furthermore, a union between the language and what it signifies is implied, which prevents us from getting rid of it as if it were purely cultural (p. 185).

Ellul insists that while hermeneutics (the science and art of biblical interpretation) might make a text more clear or permit an unbeliever to comprehend it logically, that never makes it true for someone, nor does it enable a person to know the message. The decisive point, Ellul asserts, is that "by faith *I know* that this Bible has a meaning, and that it is true. Faith in Jesus Christ causes me to add faith to this text." There might be problems of interpretation, but they remain radically secondary, for the decisive question is that of faith that perceives truth. Thus Ellul's argument builds this progression: one goes from the meaning to the language, but first one goes from the truth of Jesus Christ to the meaning (p. 186).

The signification received by faith challenges the postmodern crisis of language. Ultimately, either the biblical text carries the revelation or it does not; it is a predecision of faith or of unbelief. Only by faith can we grasp the central object, the goal, the real content, the hidden sense, or the quickening spark of a text. The biblical text itself gives us the method for finding that content. The Word itself shows us that it is not outdated (p. 190).

This summary is too brief to do justice to Ellul's comprehensive and technical-linguistic argument, but it will have to suffice. His emphasis on the Bible as the revelation of God gives us the courage to preach its hope, to grasp its truths, which are never irrelevant. He encourages us to proceed, not from the perceptions of the culture outside the faith, but from inside the community of faith. The faith of that community, however, is being challenged by theological changes that take us away from God as the subject.

As a result of some contemporary currents that we will explore shortly, many churches no longer seriously teach the theological foundations of Christian faith. Worship services fail in their educational mission; pastors evade the responsibility to make their sermons convey the patrimony of our predecessors. Though preaching involves the constant effort to speak God's truth afresh, it should be founded on the Word and the theological insights gained by the Church's response to that Word throughout its history. Massive pressures in modern culture, however, lead preachers away from this foundation.

It seems that this notion has prevailed for some time. In 1969 Dorothy L. Sayers wrote,

> Official Christianity, of late years, has been having what is known as a bad press. We are constantly assured that the churches are empty because preachers insist too much upon doctrine — dull dogma as people call it. The fact is the precise opposite. It is the neglect of dogma that makes for dullness. The Christian faith is the most exciting drama that ever staggered the imagination of man — and the dogma is the drama. . . .
>
> The plot pivots upon a single character, and the whole action is the answer to a single central problem: *What think you of Christ?*[42]

Sayers's question points us back to a fundamental thesis of this book: that worship would reach out more effectively both to Christians and to the culture around us if we kept God as the subject.

Modern theology has lost this focus. Keck outlines four reasons for this, the first of which is that *theology has become anthropology.* The inadequacy of language convinces many theologians, and consequently preachers, that we must be "agnostic about God" — that "there is no way of knowing whether our language about God really describes the Reality of which it speaks because no one can test its accuracy."[43]

We need not trace the whole process Keck outlines — from the triumph of empiricism, beginning with Kant, through the rejection by socioeconomic thought of anything linked with patterns of domination, to current deconstructionism (pp. 48-51) — but his conclusion is very important. He insists that there is no reason to bewail our inability to prove anything about God in an empirically verifiable way, for a god that we could demonstrate is

> a curiosity but not the Creator. Moreover, if one could show that the God-Reality of which we speak corresponds precisely to our language, our relation to it would be no longer one of faith but one of knowledge, and we would become Gnostics. To be sure, faith is not believing what

---

42. Dorothy L. Sayers, *The Whimsical Christian* (Grand Rapids: William B. Eerdmans, 1969), reprinted as "There's Nothing Dull about Dogma," *Discipleship Journal* 80 (March/April 1994): 66.

43. Keck, *The Church Confident*, pp. 47-48. Page references to this book in this section and the next are given parenthetically in the text.

we know isn't so, but it is trusting beyond the demonstrable. It entails believing that our language can speak authentically, though not with descriptive accuracy, about God even if it must at times rely on the *via negativa*, like "immortal" and "invisible," to say what God is not. (p. 49)

Responding to feminism, some theologians "take refuge in the ineffability and unnameability of God"; on the basis of the principle that we cannot know the essence of God, they can thereby avoid using names for God that offend.[44] Rejecting that maneuver, Keck claims that "it is one thing to affirm the goal of real equality of women and men especially in the church (as I do), another to tie that so tightly to our language that the Reality we call 'God' is deprived of its own integrity and freedom to be itself" (p. 51). Keck recognizes that "lurking behind the demand for flawless words is a technological view of language." In the sermon, in contrast, we are dealing with an entirely different Reality, the reality of God, who discloses himself "through our language while at the same time breaking it sufficiently to inhibit our absolutizing it" (p. 54).

We do not have to fear that our language for God is inadequate as long as we keep remembering that it is. What we should avoid is letting our language turn from the truths of God revealed in God's Word to our human adaptations that reduce those truths. Examples of such weakening of theological language abound. Sometimes we change words because we do not want to face up to their truth — for example, when we alter language about our hopelessly desperate sinfulness to make it more palatable. The theological confession that our utterly sinful nature, without Christ, is abhorrent to God is thereby turned into a less disgusting uncomfortableness with our sins.

Will Hoyt points out the difference between "I risk death" (which he calls a "heroic" statement) and "I die daily" (which is creedal). The latter is Pauline logic, a totally different eschatology. This affirmation makes it clear that the real risk is not death but the inability to die. The first sentence keeps us in control; the second invites us to relinquish control and "hand ourselves over to God."[45] Perhaps the accusation of "dumbing

---

44. See Catherine Mowry LaCugna, "Freeing the Christian Imagination," *dialog* 33, no. 3 (Summer 1994): 192.

45. Will Hoyt, "On the Difference Between a Hero and an Apostle," *New Oxford Review* 61, no. 3 (April 1994): 23-24.

down" is too strong here, but we must ask why we often strive to accommodate God and God's Word to our level rather than educating people to understand the theological truth of particular sets of words.

We also reduce theology to anthropology when we engage in what is called "sharing" rather than theological discussion. In Bible classes devoted to sharing, everyone's opinion is equally valid, and all group participants must be equally supported. We are too polite to ask whether something is true, and as a result we eliminate the possibility for genuine theological growth. We cannot teach theological foundations if it is not acceptable to question basic assumptions. Sermons are often thus weakened if they do not use God's Word to disabuse us of some of our pet themes, such as the notion of human progress.

David Wells documents the move in sermons from biblical and theological content to anthropological content by studying 200 sermons, half from *Pulpit Digest* and half from *Preaching* in the years 1981 to 1991. He concludes that in only 24.5 percent were both the content of the sermon and its organization determined by the biblical passage under consideration. Of the model sermons he surveyed, less than half were explicitly biblical; many were not even discernibly Christian. Only 19.5 percent "were grounded in or related in any way to the nature, character, and will of God. . . . The overwhelming proportion of the sermons analyzed — more than 80 percent — were anthropocentric."[46]

The second shift in contemporary theology that Keck sketches is that *gospel becomes law* (p. 55). If preachers allow cultural narcissism to predominate and to turn their sermons into self-help formulas, then the freeing power of Christ's work on our behalf becomes merely an illustration. Keck exclaims,

> But by definition, an illustration is not a revelation; it is a vivid instance of what we know already. It discloses nothing new or decisive about God, the world, sin, goodness, or power. Jesus' death might disclose unforgettably the depth of human sinfulness, but unless that death is somehow God's deed on our behalf, simply understanding sin better gives us a clearer diagnosis but no healing. (pp. 55-56)

When the good news of forgiveness and new life in Jesus is turned into law or into salvation that we have to crank up ourselves, sermons become

46. Wells, *No Place for Truth*, pp. 251-52.

moralisms. Instead of offering the freedom to live differently because Christ dwells in us and the Spirit transforms us, such sermons urge us to live by efforts at self-improvement.

Not only do such sermons place onerous burdens on their hearers, but they are also boring because they are no different from the plethora of self-help manuals on the market. As Richard Lischer remarks, "So much of what has been passing for theology does not draw its life from the gospel and is therefore utterly incapable of transforming lives or teaching and leading the church."[47]

Keck describes the third theological shift as a reversal of Anselm of Canterbury's dictum that theology is faith seeking understanding. This *reversal of faith and understanding* has occurred because "today's theology is propelled and controlled by prior commitments to an agenda for social change." Instead of thinking theologically to understand the faith one already has, now "the question is whether, and perhaps to what extent, the Christian faith is yet compatible with and supportive of those commitments, grounded in a theory and its method of analyzing and explaining human life in society."

Steve Mullet's quip makes the corruption of this way of thinking more apparent: "When a church's theology holds up a vision for swimming upstream — and most of that church's members are floating downstream on yachts — something's got to give. [Usually] it's the theology that gets sold away, not the yachts."[48] Instead of finding resources to illuminate the faith,

> now the task is to ascertain what the faith might contribute to a non-negotiable agenda which is both logically prior to and politically more urgent than the faith itself. Instead of asking, Given my allegiance to the gospel and to the theological structure that supports it, what should my commitments be? current theology asks, Given my commitments, can I still believe the gospel and avow the theology that goes with it? Instead of finding the Christian tradition a way of reading the world, this reversal of Anselm leads today's theology to find in the world a way of reading the Christian tradition in the hope that faith of some sort is

47. Lischer, *A Theology of Preaching*, p. 16.
48. Steve Mullet, "Quick Quote," *Current Thoughts and Trends* 10, no. 3 (March 1994): 20.

yet possible. We recall Hans Frei's observation[49] that whereas the Bible once provided the lens through which reality was made intelligible, now a view of reality is the lens through which the Bible is read, and I might add, assessed and often found wanting. (Keck, p. 57)

Keck concludes that we no longer fight against the "assumptions and assertions deemed contrary to Christian faith but against the Christian heritage itself" (p. 58). An example of this that immediately comes to mind is the furor that arose in 1993 with the publication of the ELCA draft document on human sexuality, with its new affirmation of homosexual unions. Those who protested this document on the basis of the Church's acceptance (until recently) of genital activity only within the framework of heterosexual marriage were immediately labelled homophobic. After almost a year of acrimonious debate, someone on the task force that produced the document admitted in a public setting that the real impetus propelling the sexuality study "was the ordination question" of noncelibate homosexual persons. After reporting this disclosure, seminary professor Marc Kolden chided, "When the conclusion is already in place before the process begins, the process itself becomes a sham."[50]

The same is true for sermons. If political or other ideological agendas have already determined the study process's outcome, then the process will quench life instead of discovering it — and the sermon won't speak the gospel.

The Church has been tempted throughout its history to become captive to other ideologies and spiritualities. Colossians 2:8 warns Christians not to become enamored of any "empty, seductive philosophy according to human tradition, according to the elemental powers of the world and not according to Christ." Theological thinking that issues in preaching is the effort to comprehend afresh the faith that has been passed on to us. Sermon preparation is not a process for novelty, but for deep — and therefore newly insightful — faithfulness. It is to share the attitudes of the early Church, in which

adherence to the witness of those whose unique experience authorized them to set the tradition was of paramount importance. The truth was

---

49. See Hans Frei, *The Eclipse of Biblical Narrative: A Study in Enlightenment and Nineteenth-Century Hermeneutics* (New York: Yale University Press, 1974).

50. Marc Kolden, "Homosexual Ordination: The Real Issue?" *dialog* 33, no. 3 (Summer 1994): 163-64.

what they said it was because they were the authoritative witnesses to the whole drama. It was not a new philosophy up for debate, but a teaching which had to be received.[51]

This teaching that we receive gives life, for it is Christ himself inhabiting the Word. Preachers have the privilege to offer listeners an encounter with God.

The fourth theological shift Keck elaborates is the *movement beyond the hermeneutic of suspicion to a hermeneutic of alienation.* The former is like an investigative reporter in that it "withhold[s] credence as a matter of principle until the reliability of information has been assessed." Its goal is to find truth (p. 59). It tests the tradition "to establish its degree of credibility to an unprejudiced observer." In the hermeneutic of alienation, on the other hand, "the tradition is accused so that the committed righteous can distance themselves from it." Primarily this accusation comes from political agendas. Instead of asking the formerly preeminent question of theology, "Is it true?" the hermeneutic of alienation leads to the question, "Who benefits?" (p. 60).

Two of the results from this hermeneutic that Keck identifies are important for our purposes here. The first is that "almost any idea gains credence today if its advocates claim to be motivated by identification with the poor, the powerless, and the oppressed" (p. 61). My disagreements with the preaching book mentioned at this chapter's beginning stemmed from this. Its sermons induced guilt over our complicity in various "isms" and then advocated stances that reject biblical nuances in favor of a false compassion.

The other result related to our concern for preaching is that the goal of "alienation-driven theology is not developing the capacity for independent thinking grounded in a solid grasp of the tradition, but empowerment. When the goal is power, whether to hold it or to gain it, the quest for truth is an early casualty" (p. 62). Politicization hinders "unprejudiced examination of the issues." An example previously sketched in this book is the assumption on the part of many that the Bible is patriarchal. Having already decided that it is oppressive, those so convinced are unable to see all the ways in which the Bible rejects and overcomes the patriarchy of its times.

51. Bernard D. Green, "Catholicism Confronts New Age Syncretism," *New Oxford Review* 61, no. 3 (April 1994): 21.

The Language of Faith

Instead of such a hermeneutic of alienation, the present Church needs what Keck calls a "hermeneutic of affirmation." Keck insists that such a hermeneutic is "as important for renewal as recovering the praise of God in worship" (p. 63). As Keck envisions it, this hermeneutic works in partnership — sometimes sequentially and sometimes dialectically — with the hermeneutic of suspicion. It questions the past and points out its faults, but it is equally willing to learn from the classical Christian tradition and understands its mission by means of it. Through this stance or disposition (rather than a theory or procedure), "the hermeneutic of affirmation is a persistent but pained loyalty to a heritage, which, though flawed, nonetheless has given us what faith we have" (p. 64).

To adopt this stance is to understand clearly the nature of the Christian community. We acknowledge that this community has struggled with its own faithfulness, but that, by the Holy Spirit's power, it has carried the revelation of the God of Israel as incarnated in Jesus. As we preach we recognize the failures of God's people, but even more we praise God's love and grace that work in spite of those failures. In fact, the persistence of our failing is evidence that the faith we carry is true — for it proves that we need a Savior from outside ourselves, that we are incapable of fixing ourselves by our own self-help procedures. A hermeneutic of affirmation gives us the language of faith — knowing our sin and, much more important, knowing our God.

Preaching requires a careful dialectical balance in order to use the language of faith, but in a way that is accessible to people without falling into the ideological language of political agendas. George Lindbeck and Gail O'Day after him are strong advocates for the first part of the dialectic, for becoming "competent speakers of our own language again." Lindbeck believes that learning or relearning its own faith language is the Church's fundamental challenge. "Instead of continuing to interpret the gospel story through the language and categories of the world, the church must now interpret the world through the language and categories of the gospel." Gail O'Day adds that the Bible "offers much more than the subject matter for preaching." It also provides "the decisive, shaping language of sermons." What she means by this parallels my emphasis on the nurturing of character. It is not simply that the words of Scripture should pepper one's sermons, but that the preacher embrace the entire *language world* of Scripture. That is, faithful sermons are molded by the language of our faith and tradition, so that reality is redescribed for us by Scripture. To preach the gospel, we must know and be shaped by the primary language of our faith.[52]

Those who serve in mission fields or in linguistics/translation work (and Martin Luther!) show us the other side of the dialectic — the requirement to preach in the common language of the people. From the linguistic procedures established by Eugene Nida, Lamin Sanneh amplifies the idea of translation to include the background work of investigating the culture, history, language, religion, economy, anthropology, and physical environment of the people.[53]

Preaching requires the same background work, even though we are usually rooted in the same language as the people in the pew. As part of the community with the people they serve, preachers learn the history of this particular group of people, their economic and environmental concerns, their cultural interests and their false gods. The language of the Scriptures provides the content of sermons, but these background factors provide the compassion, guide the application, and reveal the "felt" needs underneath which we must discover the real needs.

Even as translators recognize the context into which their rendering of the biblical text must be put, so preachers offer, not a self-contained text, but the text in community. In the process, of course, the text will always be subversive of the community and will counteract its pretensions or idolatries.

William Dyrness charts the progression in *How Does America Hear the Gospel?* Faith development can only begin under God's common grace with the shared stresses and hopes of all people; it is stirred by "signs of transcendence" to move beyond them to the special grace of the gospel. Ultimately, the goal is for faith to mature into obedience and prophetic discipleship by the transforming power of the Holy Spirit.[54] Preachers must establish common ground with their hearers in aspects of mutual

---

52. O'Day, "Toward a Biblical Theology of Preaching," p. 18.

53. Lamin Sanneh, *Translating the Message* (Maryknoll, NY: Orbis, 1989), p. 192.

54. William A. Dyrness, *How Does America Hear the Gospel?* (Grand Rapids: William B. Eerdmans, 1989), p. 23; see also pp. 143-53, "A Theological and Evangelistic Method for Americans."

human identity, but their specific role is then to transport the listeners to the throne of God.

The community is the hermeneutical key. It is formed by the distinctive talk of faith and yet uses that conversation in relation to its own people. The preacher constantly asks how particular texts, and the gospel of which they are a part, will form the congregation to be God's people, committed to and actively pursuing God's purposes of salvation and justice in the world.

Moreover, a sermon finds its place in the midst of the community's entire worship, in which God is the subject. As Richard Lischer reminds us, "What else is the liturgy but the recital of God's story — from the song of the angels in the *Gloria in excelsis* to the awesome chant of the cherubim and seraphim in the *Sanctus* — interspersed with kerygmatic interpretation?" Preaching "lives, moves, and has its being" in this worship environment. "When it disregards its liturgical material, preaching becomes the individualistic, virtuoso performance with which many Protestants are familiar, and thereby diminishes both itself and the church."[55]

Walter Brueggemann gathers dialectical factors considered here by reminding us, "We shall not be the community we hope to be if our primary communications are in modes of utilitarian technology and managed, conformed values." We know "another way to speak," an "alternative universe of discourse" that won't reduce the truth we struggle to express. Hear his stirring challenge:

> The task and possibility of preaching is to open out the good news of the gospel with alternative modes of speech — speech that is dramatic, artistic, capable of inviting persons to join in another conversation, free of the reason of technique, unencumbered by ontologies that grow abstract, unembarrassed about concreteness. Such speech, when heard in freedom, assaults imagination and pushes out the presumed world in which most of us are trapped. Reduced speech leads to reduced lives. Sunday morning is the practice of a counter life through counter speech. The church on Sunday morning, or whenever it engages in its odd speech, may be the last place left in our society for imaginative speech that permits people to enter into new worlds of faith and to participate in joyous, obedient life.[56]

55. Lischer, *A Theology of Preaching*, p. 43.
56. Brueggemann, *Finally Comes the Poet*, pp. 2-3.

I have heard so many sermons that have no Joy, no discovery, no life. I don't mean that pastors have to be giddy, flashy, exuberant, or entertaining. But I simply cannot imagine talking about the new creation in Christ without hopeful gladness, however that is evidenced by various personalities. Perhaps an analogy will help to convey what I mean.

Preaching seems to me to be very much like talking about how my life has changed since my marriage. When I married Myron, I entered into a different world. It is a world of beauty, integrity, forgiveness, affirmation, stability. In contrast to my messy desks piled with papers and books, Myron fills the yard and house with flowers in scores of varieties and hues. He lives the values of his faith — caring for the earth and for the children in his classroom with gentleness and simplicity. In spite of my bad habits, my obsessive compulsions, and my very obvious sinfulness, his forgiveness is immediately offered. He supports my writing projects and blesses my teaching. Whenever I am away for a speaking engagement, his voice on the other end of the telephone line will be glad to hear mine and will assure me that I am loved. In emotional brokenness and physical crises, Myron carefully reminds me that he will always be beside me. How can I talk of him and the new life I have with him without great Joy?

The parallels to the faith community are probably obvious. When we come to faith in Christ, we enter a new world. Our eyes are opened to the beauty and wonder of God's creation and the immense gifts of God's grace. We enter into a community trying to live wholly in the character of Jesus and faithfully in the virtues the Scriptures describe. We speak the forgiveness of God and God's total acceptance of us through Christ. In the face of the great sufferings of the world, we know that God is at work to fulfill his purposes of justice and hope and that God is with us as we seek to do his will. How can we preach about this God and this new creation, this life in this community, without the authentic thrill of being overwhelmed by grace, the wonder of being loved, the earnestness of great desire to care for the world's needy?

In a society bored with its own lack of meaning, frightened by chaos in world politics and economics, and groping for roots, preaching bestows great gifts of purpose, hope, and stability. Preaching is the privilege of announcing God's good news, of describing his Joy, of worshiping him with all the best images, metaphors, and models we can find. Keck captures the essence of faithful preaching when he claims that "powerful religious language creates dramatic, language-bending metaphors" (p. 52). What we say in preaching is inadequate, but it is true.

In Walter Brueggemann's image, to preach is to be a poet. In a context of "numbness and ache, alienation and rage, restlessness and greed, conformity and autonomy," preachers "dare to speak what is already believed but so little understood, so little embraced, so little trusted, so little practiced." The Christian community believes that the gospel brings healing, hope, and freedom, but these treasures are often not apprehended. In the midst of incongruity, preachers "must voice an alternative much yearned for and deeply feared." They use language that is "subtle, a voice not assaulting but surprising, speech not predictable but faithful in its daring." Brueggemann concludes,

> Despite the seeming odds against the poem, however, despite the awesome challenge of the task, perhaps better, *because of* the odds and the challenge, the preacher must speak. Our lives wait in the balance, hoping, yearning for the promissory, transforming word of the gospel. In the end, all we have is the word of the gospel. There are evidences and signs all around us, however, in the great brutal confrontations of public power and in the weeping hiddenness of hurt in persons, that this odd speech of the gospel matters decisively. We have only the word, but the word will do. It will do because it is true that the poem shakes the empire, that the poem heals and transforms and rescues . . . and gives new life, fresh from the word and from nowhere else.
>
> There are many pressures to quiet the text, to silence this deposit of dangerous speech, to halt this outrageous practice of speaking alternative possibility. The poems, however, refuse such silence. They will sound. They sound through preachers who risk beyond prose. In the act of such risk, power is released, newness is evoked. God is praised.[57]

Children's Sermons

The children's sermon is a special category of preaching, but the same goals apply — to keep God the subject, to form the children's character, and to nurture the community. The main problem with children's sermons, how-

---

57. Brueggemann, *Finally Comes the Poet*, pp. 142-43.

ever, is that so often, instead of inviting with the gospel, they hit the children with the law by focusing on what they should do rather than on what God has done and does. They offer moralisms instead of the freedom of new life in Christ.

For example, the pastor might tell the story of the importunate widow (Luke 18:1-8), the parable of the woman who continually besieged the judge until finally he gave in and granted her request. Then the pastor concludes, "So we learn from this story that we should keep bugging God until he changes his mind." Of course, the pastor won't actually say such words — but that is the kind of impression given when parables are turned into moralisms.

Preachers give such seriously inaccurate readings of the text in their main sermons, too, but it is usually more noticeable in the children's sermon. The text of this example continually reiterates that the judge was unjust, fearing neither God nor people (vv. 2, 4, 6), so that the widow was forced to pester him. What a great contrast he is to our gracious God, who does care about us, even before we ask! The whole point of the parable is that we can freely come continually to God — not because we have to change his mind, but because we know he is *not* like that judge, because he hears us when we first call. Jesus urges persistence in prayer, not so that we can get our way with God, but so that God can get his way in us. That is why the parable clearly ends with the words, "will not God bring about justice for his chosen ones . . . ? Will he keep putting them off? I tell you, he will see that they get justice, and quickly. However, when the Son of Man comes, will he find faith on the earth?"

This parable teaches that God always hears us, that he is not like unjust human judges. In worship, our specific ethical teaching should come only out of such an attitude about God, so that in daily life parish members become conscious of God's presence and grace and respond with gladness.

Children's sermons and parables illustrate well the importance not only of what we teach in worship but also of how we teach and of how carefully we read the Scriptures. The biblical narratives do not hit us with what we ought to do to be Christians; they kill us so that we can be raised into the new life in Christ made possible by the Spirit's transformation within us.

Children's sermons give a parish opportunity to incorporate its youngest members into the habits of the community. Biblical methods for passing on to children the truths of the faith include creeds, songs, and the instruction of God (Torah). We can tell them stories of faithful people and stir up desire to imitate their virtues. We must carefully accent God's grace as the motivation, however, lest our accounts of biblical figures or Christian saints turn into moralisms to "be like them." A good language guide is to avoid all use of the words *must, ought, should,* or *have to.* (How often we use those words on ourselves, proving how desperately we need to be enfolded in grace again and again!)

Children's sermons can be a vehicle for teaching the whole con-gregation about why we do what we do in worship. In the Appendix is an outline of a series of messages on aspects of liturgical worship that I gave over the course of a few months. Unfortunately, I was out of town for speaking engagements about every other week and so could not reinforce the lessons consistently. If congregations were to use these messages, I would encourage them to make sure that the liturgical actions described are explicitly practiced in ensuing weeks. For example, the children and I talked about bowing at the altar as a special practice that helps us pause and remember the holy presence of God — that God is GOD after all, and we could not even dare enter God's presence except that he forgives and invites us. That same day we went to the altar rail and bowed together and closed with prayer. Because the chil-dren seemed really to understand the idea of reverence, it was disruptive in later weeks when the acolytes did not bow before going up to light the candles and, in fact, seemed to have no awareness that this worship place is any different from a school gymnasium. We will discuss liturgical actions and the ethos of the worship place in the next chapter, but at this point we must recognize the importance of reinforcing whatever we teach in children's sermons. Recognizing the need to immerse chil-dren in the habits of faithful worship forces us to question if we are really practicing them ourselves.

Children also teach us how to read the Scriptures. So often lectors read too rapidly and without any attention to phrasing. In an article on preaching from Romans, Leander Keck notes that "even in a text without fluff, all the words and phrases do not count equally, as is true also of notes and phrases in music," and he complains that "hearing Romans read rapidly, and without change of pace or inflection, is as satisfying as hearing Mozart on a player piano." Even as Dr. Suess taught us to "pay attention to unusual words and phrases," so the texts of Scripture abound "in unexpected phrases deliberately created . . . to convey certain dimensions of the gospel."[58]

Just as the sermon is one of the few remaining times in which people can give sustained attention to significant meaning expressed in words rather than television pictures, so the Scripture lessons in a worship service offer a unique opportunity to read aloud the best stories in the world. How we speak matters enormously. These are the stories by which we are formed.

A Community of Theologians

The sermon cannot be a performance if its goal is to "work oneself out of a job" — which is the best advice ever given me before I began my work in the Church. Sermons should not be judged by how flashy they are, what great oratorical skills they manifest, or how publishable they are. The ultimate test is whether sermons turn the hearers into theologians and activists. Do they grapple with texts and teach the people how to question? Do they wrestle with faith and invite the listeners to know that victory is assured? Do they struggle against the world's pain and challenge believers to create justice? Above all, do they bring us all into God's presence to hear his Word to us?

Do our sermons nourish believers in foundational doctrines of the faith to equip them to resist heresies and idolatries and "folk religion," with its too simplistic formulations of how faith applies to life? William Hendricks, after interviewing people to find out why they left churches, encourages pastors to teach people to think theologically so that they can resist what is "essentially 'McDoctrine' — spiritual fast food of proof-texts and clichés that are filling and fattening, but not particularly nourishing."[59]

The goal of preaching to train listeners to be theologians prohibits the sermon from being mere triviality or entertainment. In discussing the educational (dis)value of television, Neil Postman agrees that people learn best if they are interested in what they are learning, "that reason is best

58. Leander Keck, "Romans in the Pulpit: Form and Formation in Romans 5:1-11," in O'Day and Long, eds., *Listening to the Word,* p. 79.
59. Hendricks, *Exit Interviews,* p. 284.

cultivated when it is rooted in robust emotional ground." However, he declares, "no one has ever said or implied that significant learning is effectively, durably and truthfully achieved when education is entertainment."[60]

The entertainment mentality invades sermons if they follow the television-induced assumption "that any information, story or idea can be made immediately accessible, since the contentment, not the growth, of the learner is paramount" (pp. 146-47). This book is especially concerned for believers' character growth, and that necessitates a criterion of content rather than contentment. Sometimes our sermons will be hard for listeners emotionally — they will afflict the comfortable more than comfort the afflicted. At other times, they might be hard intellectually (though we must be sure this is not because we are failing to express the point clearly) because truths of the faith require deeper reflection than is the habit of many in our culture. At those times we dare not dumb down the sermon to make it appealing. How can we instead make the *process* of learning more appealing? How can we challenge worship participants with the worthy goal of becoming more theologically adept? The Scriptures issue that challenge frequently as they invite us to know God, to be renewed in mind, to meditate on the things of God, to understand with all knowledge and discernment.

Postman reminds us of John Dewey's observation that the content of a lesson is the least important thing about learning. As Dewey wrote in *Experience and Education:* "Collateral learning in the way of formation of enduring attitudes . . . may be and often is more important than the [particular school] lesson. . . . For these attitudes are fundamentally what count in the future." Postman paraphrases the point as "the most important thing one learns is always something about *how* one learns" (p. 144). This is a critical lesson for preachers. The way we model how to unpack biblical texts, to think about God, to ask better questions, to raise theological issues about social ills, to apply texts to life/world situations, to care for the poor and suffering — in all of these we teach attitudes and habits and actions that listeners can apply to their own biblical study and theologizing and lives.

Above all, Dewey's insight is important in stimulating us to offer in

---

60. Postman, *Amusing Ourselves to Death,* p. 146. Page references to this book in the following paragraphs are given parenthetically in the text.

our sermons a world in which the hearers can dwell and practice the faith in the company of the community. Since we learn from what we do, how can sermons invite listeners to try out the Word, to live its truth? Worship ought to kill us — and then enfold us in new life.

Richard Caemmerer describes the goal perfectly in this vignette:

> "Pastor, that was a wonderful sermon," said the parishioner at the door after the service.
>
> "That remains to be seen," said the preacher.[61]

---

61. Caemmerer, *Preaching for the Church*, p. 51.

10. Discovering Our Place in the Story: Ritual and Liturgy and Art

You are God; we praise you. You are the Lord; we acclaim you. You are the eternal Father; all creation worships you. To you all angels, all the powers of heaven, cherubim and seraphim, sing in endless praise: Holy, holy, holy Lord, God of power and might, heaven and earth are full of your glory. The glorious company of apostles praise you. The noble fellowship of prophets praise you. The white-robed army of martyrs praise you. Throughout the world the holy Church acclaims you: Father, of majesty unbounded; your true and only Son, worthy of all worship; and the Holy Spirit, advocate and guide. You, Christ, are the king of glory, the eternal Son of the Father. When you became man to set us free, you did not spurn the virgin's womb. You overcame the sting of death, and opened the kingdom of heaven to all believers. You are seated at God's right hand in glory. We believe that you will come and be our judge. Come, then, Lord, and help your people, bought with the price of your own blood, and bring us with your saints in glory everlasting.

The *Te Deum* of the Church

A long-standing misnomer distinguishes between "liturgical" and "non-liturgical" churches as if these terms correctly separate those who use fixed patterns of sung responses from those whose worship seems to be more informal. However, the term *leitourgia,* composed of the Greek words *ergon* ("work") and *laos* ("people"), actually means "the work of the people" and thus designates every action of the laity. Thus every church is in a sense "liturgical." C. Welton Gaddy adds that the name *liturgy* is used to translate the First Testament word *sharath,* which denotes the idea of ministering on behalf of a community.[1] Thus James White defines liturgy as the work

> performed by the people for the benefit of others. In other words, it is the quintessence of the priesthood of all believers in which the whole priestly community of Christians shares. To call a service "liturgical" is to indicate that it was conceived so that all worshipers take an active part in offering their worship together.[2]

This chapter must address the subject of ritual and liturgy because many churches who want to make their worship reach out to nonbelievers think that to do so they must "throw out the liturgy" — as if that were possible! Even congregations that do not practice specific forms outlined in hymnals or service books usually follow some kind of ordering of worship elements and often repeat the same patterns week after week. Unless the service is entirely a performance by musicians and preacher with no involvement at all by the people, every worship service has a liturgy. The question is whether it is a faithful one.

The term *liturgy* has come to signify the specific, historic ordering of public worship developed in the earliest centuries of the Church and basically retained by Luther, who believed it crucial to translate the Mass into the vernacular so that the liturgy could indeed be the work of the German people. Many people complain that this liturgy and its rituals are not "attractive to outsiders" and want to discard it. Sometimes those who value the Church's historic liturgy defend it in ways that mummify or fossilize it. Both extremes must be questioned as we seek to understand the purpose and practice of liturgy.

1. C. Welton Gaddy, *The Gift of Worship* (Nashville: Broadman Press, 1992), p. 36.
2. James F. White, *Introduction to Christian Worship,* rev. ed. (Nashville: Abingdon, 1990), p. 32.

Like the previous two chapters, this chapter builds on themes discussed in earlier sections of the book — understanding the culture in which the Church dwells at this point in history (Chapters 2-4) and creating a specific culture of worship that keeps God as the subject while it nurtures the character of the participants and builds the community of the faithful (Chapters 5-7). We will not repeat the aspects of these goals that have surfaced in the previous chapters on music and the Word, but bear in mind that they are closely related to the aspects discussed here.

God as the Subject

Because God is the subject of worship, we must back up a step to recall that, before liturgy can involve the work of the people who offer their praise, it begins with the presence of God graciously inviting that response. Patrick Keifert turns to the First Testament to observe that, "though God was free to be present everywhere, God promised to be present in Israel's worship. . . . Liturgy was not, then, a human device to hold God on reserve, but a gift from God of God's self."[3]

It seems to me that some of the worship wars over liturgy could be easily resolved if we remembered that we worship by God's invitation and not by our own concoction. Using God's own words in liturgical responses helps to remind us that worship is God's gift to us before it can be our gift to God. Liturgical pieces that highlight the reading of the Scriptures and the Eucharist as the central moments of the worship service also reinforce the awareness that God is the subject and object of what we are doing.

Losing God as the subject can turn liturgy into performance rather than sacrament. This results in a modern form of a medieval notion against which Martin Luther fought — the notion that liturgy's power and effectiveness depend upon the priest's worthiness. The modern version insists that liturgy must be performed well in order to be effective, and its potency is determined according to the criterion that every participant must have had some sort of emotionally satisfying experience.

Luther insisted that effectiveness is independent of the feelings or actions of either the clergy or the lay recipient of the Word or the Lord's

3. Patrick R. Keifert, *Welcoming the Stranger* (Minneapolis: Fortress, 1992), p. 60.

Supper. The risen Christ is present in both. To those who come to worship in faith, even a poorly celebrated Eucharist can be a profound encounter with God. As Gaddy observes, God's grace is not dependent upon "the charismatic presence of the priest, the level of emotional participation of the congregation, or the musical creativity and choreographic expertise of liturgical planners."[4]

Worship wars over historic patterns versus new liturgy forms do not begin with the right question. We must first ask the deeper question of how we relate to Christ's cross and resurrection. What drives our worship is what God has done in Christ, so we cannot collapse worship into one or another element of the faith life — admonitions against social injustice, pleas for financial stewardship, evangelistic solicitation, or campaigns to be "politically correct."

Even as the form of a biblical text influences the form in which it is preached, so God's action in Christ influences our worship forms. The fact that the Word became flesh continued the dialectic of the new and the historical that characterized Israel and separated God's people from the religions around them. Israel remembered and celebrated God's interventions in the past and also observed and longed for God's actions in the present. Still today Jews are reminded of this when they light two Sabbath candles (or two wicks on one candle) to commemorate the commands, to *remember* and *observe*, in the versions of the Sabbath command found in Exodus 20:8 and Deuteronomy 5:12. In our worship, too, we experience the Word in its continuities and also in its startling newness. Our forms must match their content and convey the simplicity of grace in the complex story of past and future. The diversity of grace demands that liturgy never be boring.

Patrick Keifert emphasizes the truth of God as "self-giving," and he claims that thinking in this way enables us to avoid

> some of the liturgical pitfalls that the more traditional language of grace creates. If God's gift of self-presence is understood as substance, it is easy to imagine God presenting grace wrapped in a box — the liturgy — with our job to pry the box open in order to get the gift. Once the box and the object have become separated, it is easy to focus our attention either on the box or on the object. Those who reject ritual believe they can throw away the

4. Gaddy, *The Gift of Worship*, p. 14.

box (liturgy) in which the gift comes and concentrate solely on the gift. By contrast, those who value ritual tend to focus too much of their attention on the box; they worry too much about getting the ritual right, and worship becomes mechanistic. In either case, the basic ritual logic of the self-giving God is lost.

The emphasis on God as host in ritual, as giving of God's self, reminds us that grace is indeed a relationship that is initiated by God's promise and sustained in its fulfillment of the promise. If believers are conscious of the liturgy, they have missed the presence of God. Ritual behavior works precisely because it draws attention away from the self and allows people an opportunity to greet God.[5]

C. S. Lewis made the same point about consciousness of liturgy in his *Letters to Malcolm, Chiefly on Prayer.* Complaining about "the Liturgical Fidget," Lewis objected to innovations that interfered with his focusing on God. He protested, "It looks as if [the Anglican clergy] believed people can be lured to go to church by incessant brightenings, lightenings, lengthenings, abridgements, simplifications, and complications of the service." Lewis insisted that, as a result, "many give up churchgoing altogether" and the others "merely endure." He explained the "good reason" for his conservatism thus:

Novelty, simply as such, can have only an entertainment value. And [believers] don't go to church to be entertained. They go to *use* the service, or, if you prefer, to *enact* it. Every service is a structure of acts and words through which we receive a sacrament, or repent, or supplicate, or adore. And it enables us to do these things best — if you like, it "works" best — when, through long familiarity, we don't have to think about it. As long as you notice, and have to count, the steps, you are not yet dancing but only learning to dance. A good shoe is a shoe you don't notice. Good reading becomes possible when you need not consciously think about eyes, or light, or print, or spelling. The perfect church service would be one we were almost unaware of; our attention would have been on God.

But every novelty prevents this. It fixes our attention on the service itself; and thinking about worship is a different thing from worshipping. . . . A still worse thing may happen. Novelty may fix our attention

5. Keifert, *Welcoming the Stranger,* p. 61.

245

not even on the service but on the celebrant. . . . It lays one's devotion waste. There is really some excuse for the man who said, "I wish they'd remember that the charge to Peter was Feed my sheep, not Try experiments on my rats, or even, Teach my performing dogs new tricks."

Thus my whole liturgiological position really boils down to an entreaty for permanence and uniformity. . . . But if each form is snatched away just when I am beginning to feel at home in it, then I can never make any progress in the art of worship. You give me no chance to acquire the trained habit — *habito dell'arte*.[6]

Against Lewis's analogy of dancing and Keifert's of the wrapped gift, many argue that worship gets too boring if the same liturgical forms are used week after week. This accusation is justified in churches that stiffly follow a hymnbook order of worship without any variation whatsoever. However, most denominational service books include all kinds of options for worship parts, and the seasons of the liturgical year necessitate the weekly changing of the "propers" (the Collect, Versicals, and Scripture lessons). Thus, "it is a wrong kind of variety, not variety itself, which ought to be criticized."[7] A dialectical tension is required that must be carefully maintained by worship planners — to maintain a liturgical form, whatever style that might involve, that actually frees worship participants to focus on God without being distracted by either novelty or monotony. The goal, in Lewis's image, is to be able truly to dance, without having to count steps — that is, freely to experience the self-giving presence of God, without becoming either distracted or mechanistic.

After a long time searching for a parish home, I experienced such dancing one Sunday as a great gift of ecstasy. After too many worship services that jarred me with sub-Christian songs, hodge-podge or monotonous liturgy, boring accompaniments, or lifeless singers, I became weary of not being able fully to enter into God's presence. (I admit that part of the fault was mine for letting the jolts distract me so much.) What a privilege it was then to "enact" the liturgy in a congregation where the pastor spoke it with freshness, an assisting minister sang it with wonder, and the organist was sensitive enough to play the "Agnus Dei" ("Lamb of

6. C. S. Lewis, *Letters to Malcolm: Chiefly on Prayer* (New York: Harcourt, Brace and World, 1963), pp. 4-5.

7. Kurt Marquardt, "Liturgy and Evangelism," *Lutheran Worship: History and Practice,* ed. Fred L. Precht (St. Louis: Concordia, 1993), p. 65.

God") meditatively and the Post-Communion Canticle ("Thank the Lord and Sing His Praise") joyously. All the worship leaders set me free to let my trained habits usher me into God's presence.

Many believe that a liturgical form is more of an obstruction than an asset to encountering God. In private devotions that might be the case, but if we want *public* worship, there must be a vehicle. As Keifert puts it, "To presume that there can be an immediate relationship with God, . . . without such 'outward' things as ritual, is simply to ignore the logic of giving oneself." He cites liturgical scholar James White's emphasis that "to understand the critical role of ritual as creating Christian public worship, we must understand the three conditions for the giving of self: a self that is capable of giving, a recipient, and a means of giving."[8]

Many worship wars miss this essential trio. The point of liturgical form is to receive God's self. The recipients are not private individuals relating to God in their own cozy way; they are the corporate Body of the Church that experiences God's presence through public worship, the means by which God gives God's self. The most basic and most important question that we must ask, then, as we plan whatever liturgy or rituals we use, must be whether the worship elements are vehicles for God's self-giving presence in the community.

Sometimes the original theocentric reasons for particular liturgical elements are forgotten, and then those elements cannot convey their intended meaning. Previous chapters have shown how worship music and sermons can lose their focus on God. At this point let us look at one small liturgical element that is especially being robbed of its focus on God in many parishes — mainly because of a lack of education of laypeople and clergy in the meaning of the tradition.

In many (if not most) congregations in various denominations, the liturgical "passing of the peace" has been turned into a time for friendly greetings and casual chatter. Of course, worship participants need such conversation with each other as part of the community fellowship, but this should take place before or after the actual worship of God. In the historic Mass, the passing of the peace refers to Matthew 5:23-24, 1 Corinthians 11, and the early Church's custom of the kiss of peace. The choice of gesture can be left to the people — to shake hands, hug, or give a kiss of reconciliation — but the point of the liturgical element is that God, the subject, gives peace.

8. Keifert, *Welcoming the Stranger,* p. 61.

247

As pastors say, "The peace of the Lord be with you always," they bestow upon the people the worship service's greatest gift — reconciliation with God through the blood of Jesus Christ. When congregants respond, "And also with you," they affirm their care for the pastors and give them in return the rich gift of that reconciliation. In passing the peace to each other, parish members symbolize that there are no barriers in the community — neither of gender, race, or social class nor from sins against each other. God's peace flows freely among us all.

The passing of the peace takes place at a strategic point in the liturgy. Because Matthew 5 warns that if we are at odds with another community member we should first be reconciled before we bring our gifts to the altar, we pass God's peace to each other before the offering is taken. Moreover, we do this just prior to celebrating the Eucharist, for if we do not intend to live in such unity, then our participation in the sacrament is a mockery. Thus the passing of the peace is not a time for conviviality, but a time to repent, to ask another's pardon for creating barriers, to receive the gift of another's forgiveness and forbearance. The old custom of not taking part in the sacrament if one is at odds with a fellow member of the Body is a good one if it is not taken to a false extreme. We need to recognize seriously the possibility of eating the bread and drinking the wine unworthily (1 Cor. 11).

Wouldn't it be a wonderful surprise if two church members who have been fighting each other actually became reconciled during the passing of the peace? Only once have I ever witnessed someone walking to another part of the sanctuary to seek such reconciliation. Observing that repentance and forgiveness filled all the rest of us who worshiped that day with a profound sense of God's presence in the invitation to, and the promise of, God's peace.

When we train congregation members in the habit of that liturgical element, it can be a vehicle for God's self-giving. Then turning to the person next to us in the pew to say, "The peace of the Lord be with you always" represents for us God's reconciling presence in all of our relationships.

The Formation of Believers' Character

As previous chapters have shown with regard to music and sermons, keeping God as the focus of liturgy and ritual will undoubtedly nurture believers' character. Commenting on the *Book of Common Prayer,* Bernhard Christensen points out that its forms for public worship are "beautiful, thought-stirring, and edifying" and that "a common note of humility, awe, thanksgiving, and petition pervades all the forms of true worship."[9] These seven elements are a good summary of the process and the virtues that good liturgy will entail with respect to character formation.

Good liturgy will certainly be beautiful; the Scriptures are filled with exultant praise over the beauty of God's presence. Our increasingly ugly world makes it all the more imperative for worship to remind us of God's beauty. Psychologists and sociologists (and even architects) comment on the fact that fewer and fewer people are able to enjoy the beauties of creation. Poverty leads to city squalor and overcrowding; busyness prevents many from taking time for the beautiful; and modern art often turns to grotesque and violent forms. Beautiful worship will foster in our character genuine humility in the recognition of our sinful ugliness, a sense of wonder and awe at the beauty of forgiveness, and profound thanksgiving that God invites us to share in the heavenly beauty of which we get glimpses while here on earth.

We will also want liturgy to be thought-provoking and edifying. It should stir new thoughts about God — new insights into God's character, which will result in a transformation of our own character. Liturgy that keeps God as the subject will build us up spiritually and morally; it will establish us in the faith and root us in sound doctrine. The result will be new attitudes, new petitions and intercessions, new behaviors.

Out of concern for character formation, churches must think very carefully in planning the liturgy. We must not ask, Is this liturgy attractive? but always, What kind of character does this nurture? Does our liturgy focus on feelings rather than on God's character, which evokes those feelings? If so, it will nurture a faith that depends on emotions rather than a faith that can cling to who God is in spite of human experiences of sorrow or estrangement. Does liturgy focus on the self and lead to pride, or does it focus on God and lead to humility, awe, thanksgiving, and petition? In a previous parish job before my years of freelancing, I wrote a new liturgy once a month, and I learned how difficult it is in modern society to keep God as the subject and to nurture godly character in

9. Bernhard Christensen, *The Inward Pilgrimage* (Minneapolis: Augsburg, 1976), p. 71.

worship participants. We must ask very careful questions and write with humility.

Less than ten years after the beginning of the Reformation, Luther responded to questions about liturgical form. He admitted that he did not make any innovations because of his concern to care for "the weak in faith . . . and more so because of the fickle and fastidious spirits who rush in . . . without faith or reason, and who delight only in novelty and tire of it as quickly, when it has worn off." He wanted to detach himself from "frivolous faddism."[10] As Ulrich Leupold attests, he "avoided liturgical sensationalism because he had a pastor's concern for the faith and piety of the common people."[11] Leupold, editor of an English volume of Luther's works on liturgy and hymns, summarizes Luther's liturgical reform thus:

> In this spirit of liberty and with this concern for the [person] in the pew, Luther planned the reformation of the cultus. Like a good doctor who is as careful in protecting and building up the healthy organs in his patient as he is ruthless in removing the diseased, Luther preserved and strengthened every vital feature in the traditional liturgy and deleted all corrupt intrusions.[12]

May this book encourage similar caution and care. The long-term resilience of faith is at stake whenever we plan worship. In any liturgical reform, moreover, we must always remember that one of the most important ways in which liturgy nurtures depth of character is by incorporating believers into the ongoing faith community.

Belonging to, and Nurturing, the Christian Community

Besides influencing profoundly the development of Christian character, liturgical forms — even the smallest liturgical elements — promote the

---

10. Martin Luther, "An Order of Mass and Communion for the Church at Wittenberg" (1523), trans. Paul Zeller Strodach, *Liturgy and Hymns*, ed. Ulrich S. Leupold, vol. 53 in *Luther's Works*, gen. ed. Helmut T. Lehmann (Philadelphia: Fortress, 1965), p. 19.

11. Ulrich S. Leupold, "Introduction to Volume 53," *Liturgy and Hymns*, p. xiv.

12. Leupold, "Introduction to Volume 53," p. xvi.

sense that we who worship are a whole community, belonging to our Head, Jesus Christ, and to each other. Liturgy serves its purposes best when it enfolds worship participants in the *life* of God's people. Faith is not the work of an isolated self but God's gift, passed on by the community or "household of faith." For that reason, in repudiation of a common modern assumption that corporate worship is not necessary for faith, we must insist on the importance of the gathering of the saints for services that are genuinely public. Tragically, many contemporary congregations do not convey the sense of the global and universally timeless Church. We have forgotten, as Hebrews 12:1 reminds us, that we "are surrounded by so great a cloud of witnesses" (NRSV).

We isolate ourselves from that surrounding cloud of witnesses because of the false "ideology of intimacy" that Patrick Keifert describes. Requiring worship to be "spontaneous and wide open, without false barriers and formality," this ideology demands that we "be vulnerable to everyone and willing always to express our true feelings of the moment." Keifert recognizes, however, that this ideology destroys, rather than contributes to, community. Like secretaries and others whose desks are placed out in the open spaces of modern office buildings, exposed to the scrutiny of all who pass by, most people

> feel very self-conscious when they are asked to expose themselves to strangers. In response, they effectively remove themselves from active participation in worship and instead passively observe the few "personalities" in the congregation, or those who have a public role to play. These public personalities on whom most of the attention is centered really function as the executives of the worship service. Although they may attempt to cover their status by using humble-sounding words, they remain the privileged few, centers of the show.
>
> The silent observers are less likely to participate in a communal expression of deep emotion in these wide-open worship services than they would be to risk contributing in a more traditional ritual setting. Ritual builds the social barriers necessary for effective interaction. It provides the sense of cover that allows most people to feel safe enough to participate in expressions of religious value. Despite how things may seem when a visitor comes to church for the first time, ritual can in fact be most hospitable to the congregational stranger.[13]

13. Keifert, *Welcoming the Stranger,* p. 110.

Because this book is especially concerned with creating worship that does genuinely reach out to strangers without dumbing down the faith, Keifert's pleas for public ritual are particularly urgent. He warns that

> the pressure to increase intimate contact in Christian public worship will only decrease sociability. Even though the need for intimacy may be great, precisely because so many of the parishioners may be living without such intimacy, the attempts to turn public worship into intimate space will only intensify the problem. Provide no tangible barriers for the strangers gathered on Sunday morning, and the majority will retreat into their silent, private passivity. . . . We need to give up the expectations and the pretensions of intimacy both to foster public life and to clarify the means and the locations and times where legitimate intimate needs can be met.[14]

The need for intimacy can indeed be met by members of the community in their interactions with each other during fellowship times and throughout the week. Worship, on the other hand, is for God and God's gifts — which will form in participants a character of caring so that they do seek to meet community members' and strangers' needs at other times. Our liturgies should not attempt to meet these needs; if they do try to do so, their attempts fail, and they thereby neglect their true purposes of ushering worship participants into the presence of God and incorporating them into the Body of those responding to God with public declarations and lives of faith and love.

One especially valuable refrain in the Church's historic liturgy that increases our sense of the community and its mutual ministry is the pastor's blessing, "The Lord be with you," and the congregational response, "And also with you." Here ritual gesture is extremely important. Pastors extend their hands to the people as they remind them of the Lord's presence; the people greet their leaders with a prayer for a sense of God's presence as they serve the assembly. Three times the traditional liturgy gives congregants this opportunity to express their gratitude to the pastor for serving as the host at the Lord's Table and for giving them the Word of God and their prayer for the pastor to be filled with the Spirit's presence as he fulfills these tasks. Do the people look directly at the priest and extend their hands to him when they say these words? Does he look at them and receive their blessing?

14. Keifert, *Welcoming the Stranger,* pp. 110-11.

I remember vividly the exuberance of these lines on one occasion when I led an explained-liturgy worship service for about two hundred high school students. Saying the refrains after my explanation, the pastor extended his hands to bless the youth, and they sang their response with all their might. He received it by putting his hands to his heart and grinning from ear to ear. What a profound picture of mutual ministry in the Body of Christ! The youth felt that they truly belonged to the Church.

The importance of this liturgical element for a sense of community was underscored when an acquaintance told me the story of her friend's visit to a shopping mall. While her friend waited at a concession shop, an older woman in line in front of her dropped a coin purse, and the money rolled all over the mall corridor. Seeing that the woman was unable to bend down and retrieve the coins, the friend gathered them and brought them to the flustered lady. She looked at the younger woman with immense gratitude and from her lips burst the phrase, "The Lord be with you." When her helper responded, "And also with you," they both broke into grins and hugged each other — a worshipful moment of community, made possible in a shopping mall by mutual knowledge of liturgy.

This tiny part of the liturgy is easy for children to memorize, and thus it gives them the opportunity at three places in the liturgy to be a part of the community. Because of this, I explained the meaning of the words and gestures in a children's message and taught the kids to extend their hands to the pastor during their response, to reach out to him and enfold him in their care. They loved doing it, and their parents learned why the refrain was important in the service. Unfortunately, because that parish rarely uses the responses, they have probably forgotten it by now. It is necessary not only to teach both children and adults often about our worship rituals but also to follow teaching with regular practice — to imbue their memories with corporate meanings and endow their habits with gestures of community.

Besides enfolding worship participants in Christ's Body, the liturgy also reminds us that we who are God's people are an alternative society. Leander Keck quotes Richard John Neuhaus's declaration that Christian liturgy should "intensify the 'cognitive dissonance' between the community of faith and the world surrounding it."[15]

Liturgy should be accessible and understandable to worship participants — that is, it should be translated into the vernacular — but in that

---

15. Leander E. Keck, *The Church Confident* (Nashville: Abingdon, 1993), p. 23.

translation process we dare not lose liturgy's subversive effect. As Arthur Just insists,

> The goal of good liturgy is always to transform the lives of people (the transforming of culture) by the Gospel of Jesus Christ. This is hardly accomplished if the liturgy is subjected to the whimsies of culture. Culture, untransformed by liturgy, in effect destroys that liturgy. The church becomes indistinguishable from the culture and the Gospel is lost. This is the real secularization and destruction of the Gospel.[16]

I. N. Mitchell also emphasizes the theological problem undergirding many liturgical questions. He proposes that we ask not "What's wrong with the liturgy?" but "What's wrong with the culture?" and that we aim to transform culture through liturgy rather than the reverse, to conform the world to the gospel and not the gospel to the world.[17] Liturgy and the people who enact it show the culture around us what it means to live under the cross and with the risen Christ present in our midst in the Word and sacrament around which we gather.

Our Place in the Story

If we want to incorporate congregants — and visitors — into the ongoing faith community, we will want to notice how the Church has worshiped through the ages. Looking back to our Jewish roots, we discern from descriptions in the First Testament that worship practices were liturgical — that is, they involved participation by the people in addition to oracles from God through priests and prophets. For example, some psalms contain choruses that were spoken or sung by the people (see especially Psalm 136); specific psalm sets were chanted by pilgrims on their way to the Temple (see Psalms 120-134). Similarly, as Gaddy points out, patterns of corporate worship developed within the early Church were liturgical. New Testament scholars have discovered evidence of several common liturgies undergirding the worship of the earliest believers.[18]

16. Arthur A. Just, "Liturgical Renewal in the Parish," in Precht, ed., *Lutheran Worship*, p. 22.

17. I. N. Mitchell, "Liturgy and Culture," *Worship* 65, no. 4 (July 1991): 364.

18. Gaddy, *The Gift of Worship*, p. 37.

The Church into which worship enfolds believers is a community of people who have, throughout the ages, *participated*. How dare we invite people not to sing? Instead, we must do the best job of education we can so that, ideally, everyone can be included in what we do in worship. We will train children and untutored adults in the actions and habits of worship and in the meanings of those actions and habits.

Our liturgy's style may vary — we may speak or sing it, using old or new tunes. What is important is that the liturgy give a sense that the whole Church is present in it. We never worship alone in just this locality, age, or language. As Arthur Just asserts, "For liturgy to become associated with a particular culture in a particular time or place would seriously hinder the church's expression of the eschatological character of its worship. In every age, liturgy bespeaks a trans-cultural and trans-temporal message." The advantage of using the historic forms of the Church is that they enable us to worship "with a liturgy [we] did not invent but which [we] have made [our] own" — a liturgy that our forebears used and that incorporates the song of the angels (the Sanctus from Isaiah 6), as well as psalms which Jesus used.[19]

I disagree with Just's outright rejection of contemporary liturgies, but I do believe that new liturgies should be used along with traditional ones so that their newness is balanced by historical witness. Without that dialectical tension, liturgies "risk becoming sectarian, isolationist, and incapable of communicating the Gospel that knows no cultural boundaries. The liturgy, bound to one locale and one people, ceases to proclaim Christ for all people in all times and at all places."[20] As two denominational leaders stressed in response to controversial liturgies at the 1993 "Re-Imagining" conference, "When various groups reshape the church's theology and worship according to their own viewpoints or purposes, they splinter the church's life. . . . Without shared standards, the church has no common life of service and proclamation."[21]

The story of God's gracious relationship with God's people is a very complex one, reaching from the past to the future. The Church must

19. Arthur A. Just, "Liturgy and Culture," *Lutheran Worship Notes* 27 (Autumn 1993): 1-2.

20. Just, "Liturgy and Culture," p. 2.

21. Joseph D. Small and John P. Burgess, "Evaluating 'Re-Imagining,'" *The Christian Century* 111, no. 11 (6 April 1994): 344.

convey that story's fullness. Consequently, when we plan worship, we need checks to protect us from our own biases — just as our selection process for worship music involved a series of grids. An advantage of liturgies passed down through the Church's history is that testing over time has incorporated those necessary checks. Though we must still be vigilant against perversions of form, using the Church's traditional liturgy frees us from perpetual experimentation. When Luther first described his theology of worship for people of the Reformation, he insisted that "the service now in common use everywhere goes back to genuine Christian beginnings."[22] He hoped to preserve traditions with roots in the earliest followers of Jesus by cutting away accretions that violated Christianity's fundamental principles.

Many complain that old liturgies are dead, and they're often right. In many places they are dead, for churches have turned them into mere traditionalism, which Jaroslav Pelikan calls "the dead faith of the living." Those who advocate using the Church's historic liturgies are searching instead for what Pelikan calls "the living faith of the dead" — that is, worship within a tradition that enables us to be actively conscious of the Church's past as well as of its eschatological future in Christ. As Pelikan insists, tradition has the capacity to develop while still maintaining its identity and continuity. The tradition serves as a mode for relating to the present through contact with both the practices of the past and our collective hope for the future. It places us into the story of God's people and stirs our sense of belonging to a continuing fellowship that stretches throughout time and space.[23]

Those who want to discard the past, as represented by traditional worship forms, must learn the price of modernity's thoroughgoing rejection of history. Leander Keck quotes sociologist Benton Johnson's observation that parish "leaders 'tried to build a fire under the laity by depriving them of the remaining landmarks of church life. In the process . . . they conveyed the impression that the churches are irrelevant to anything that matters in the world.' "[24]

Not only is the Church seen as irrelevant, but, more profoundly, we

22. Martin Luther, "Concerning the Order of Public Worship," in *Liturgy and Hymns,* p. 11.

23. Jaroslav Pelikan, *The Vindication of Tradition* (New Haven: Yale University Press, 1984), p. 65.

24. Keck, *The Church Confident,* p. 17.

lose its essential meaning. As Graeme Hunter observes, "To repudiate one's past has consequences in the search for meaning in life. To find meaning in our lives is to see them as fitting into a larger story, which implies projecting them against the background of some culture."[25] Especially as the Church seeks to convey to its members the meaning of following Jesus and to incorporate them into the community of those who live in that discipleship, our liturgies must bear that larger story by sustaining the culture of worship.

Citing several others, Neil Postman protests vigorously the rejection of the past that has been amplified in our television age. Should not the Church as an alternative society resist this? Postman records the following:

> Czeslaw Milosz, winner of the 1980 Nobel Prize for Literature, remarked in his acceptance speech in Stockholm that our age is characterized by a "refusal to remember." . . . The historian Carl Schorske has, in my opinion, circled closer to the truth by noting that the modern mind has grown indifferent to history because history has become useless to it; in other words, it is not obstinacy or ignorance but a sense of irrelevance that leads to the diminution of history. Television's Bill Moyers inches still closer when he says, "I worry that my own business . . . helps to make this an anxious age of agitated amnesiacs. . . . We Americans seem to know everything about the last twenty-four hours but very little of the last sixty centuries or the last sixty years." Terence Moran, I believe, lands on the target in saying that with media whose structure is biased toward furnishing images and fragments, we are deprived of access to an historical perspective. In the absence of continuity and context, he says, "bits of information cannot be integrated into an intelligent and consistent whole." We do not refuse to remember; neither do we find it exactly useless to remember. Rather, we are being rendered unfit to remember, for if remembering is to be something more than nostalgia, it requires a contextual basis — a theory, a vision, a metaphor — *something* within which facts can be organized and patterns discerned.[26]

I quote Postman at length because much of the impetus to throw away the Church's historic practices arises from the fact that the television culture

---

25. Graeme Hunter, "Evil: Back in Bad Company," *First Things* 41 (March 1994): 38-39.

26. Neil Postman, *Amusing Ourselves to Death* (New York: Viking Penguin, 1985), pp. 136-37.

in which we are immersed is rendering us unfit to remember. We have lost the vision — the theology of worship — that enables us to place ourselves into the story of God's Church.

We need a stronger vision of why we do what we do in worship. Let us be sure that God is still the subject, that Christian character and community are being formed. If the three keys at the core of this book are faithfully maintained, Christian communities will nurture believers who are fit to remember.

In between our culture's refusal to remember and churches seeking to be faithful, however, are marketing gurus who foster the notion that worship must become more like the culture. Martin Marty responds to this growing conflict between market and worship in an article in a *Context* issue about trends. He reports,

> All serious church bodies are concerned that their traditional forms of worship — no matter how integrally connected to the message, the memory, and the theology of their group — may not reach a generation whose sensibilities are shaped by supermarkets and television, where the attention span of a gnat is too long to use as a measure, immediate sensation is needed, and aesthetic mediocrity is demanded. To do nothing to adapt means stultification and, we are told, dwindling congregations. To give the whole store away to match what this year's market says the unchurched want is to have the people who know least about the faith determine most about its expression.
>
> This writer fears that we are on the verge of seeing happen what happened in the 1950s to mainstream Protestant churches: they retooled for people who were casually attracted and liked big parking lots, spectacle, and low demands; and the people left as easily as they came. You can see that I lean toward the search for the dynamisms in the longer-pull worship traditions and against the emerging market orientation. But I am never cocksure about this and try to listen.[27]

We must always listen, always be aware as Marty is that new generations are "far from the meanings of the Mass, . . . the celebration of Eucharist, and the language of Zion."[28] But do we serve them best by discarding the

---

27. Martin E. Marty, "Build a Parking Lot, and the People Will Come (and Go)," *Context* 25, no. 4 (15 Feb. 1993): 3-4.

28. Marty, "Build a Parking Lot," p. 4.

whole story or by working harder to incorporate them into it? Bernhard Christensen insists that even those far away from the meanings can appreciate the worship practices of past centuries. Participating in "these 'common prayers[,]' even the most unconventional and informal of Christians scarcely fail to experience as did the psalmist of old that '*strength* and *beauty* are in thy sanctuary.'"[29]

Instead of throwing away the past, we can update, renew, reform, revive it. We can use new melodies, fresh instruction, thorough education, gentle reminders of what we are doing and why. In an age in which many participants in worship have not been schooled in its habits, to incorporate them all in the ongoing community of saints requires constant attention and diligent care.

As Burgess and Small stress, "The language of worship must be shaped with theological and pastoral discernment." In the dialectical tension of old and new, we must let the past inform any development of contemporary materials, for "liturgy does far more than ask individuals to consider new possibilities; it engages them in confessional acts and communal practice."[30]

The Use of Psalms and Prayers and Creeds

Communal confessional acts are vital for sustaining individual believers. A friend of mine, who has battled cancer twice, recently confided that she is worried because her daughter is not learning any of the liturgical pieces she had memorized as a child while attending worship. Especially she objected that her congregation did not repeat the Apostles' Creed, since she had found the creed to be a wonderful summary of faith to reflect upon in times of illness. "My daughter doesn't know the creed," she mourned, "and that is *so* important."

Though we have already discussed the value of memorized tradition in Chapter 6, I think we cannot overstress its importance in this age of transitoriness. Here we are specially concerned for the memory bank of images, theological truths, and doctrinal statements — food for the heart, soul, and mind — that we need to sustain us. If our liturgies incorporate

29. Christensen, *The Inward Pilgrimage*, p. 71.
30. Small and Burgess, "Evaluating 'Re-Imagining,'" p. 342.

these gifts in such pieces as creeds, psalms, and responses, they provide us with resources for all of life.

We also need memories because we must continue to tell the stories of faith to protect us from modernity's consumerism. As Walter Brueggemann bemoans,

> In a stupor of amnesia, a community may think there is only "now," and there is only "us." . . . [P]eople with amnesia are enormously open to suggestion, blind obedience, and easy administration. These memories [instead] make one angular, odd, and incapable of assimilation. It is clear that consumerism depends upon amnesia, in which "products" are substituted for social reference points, and in time, such "consumer values" lead to a shameless kind of brutality. The Psalm [78] intends that the young should have a heart richly peopled by an energizing past.[31]

We need the memories of being an alternative society in order for the Church to continue to resist the rabid consumerism of contemporary culture.

David Bartlett cites Robert Alter's insight that for pilgrims chanting on their way to the Temple or for such rituals as the thanksgiving sacrifice "you don't want a lot of fancy footwork in the imagery and syntax." Instead, you yearn for "an eloquent rehearsal of traditional materials and even traditional ways of ordering those materials in a certain sequence." Bartlett draws the conclusion that from the very beginning the psalms have functioned

> as they often function for us now, as a kind of memory bank of images that have illumined and strengthened us in the past and that therefore can illumine and strengthen us today. Not surprisingly when crisis comes, people of active or latent faith find themselves humming familiar hymns. Not surprisingly at the great "conventional" moments of our lives, moments when custom and ceremony meet — like baptism, marriage, funeral — we turn again and again to the psalms, not because they provide a brand new word from the Lord but because they revive the words that have sustained us in the past.[32]

---

31. Walter Brueggemann, *Biblical Perspectives on Evangelism: Living in a Three-Storied Universe* (Nashville: Abingdon, 1993), p. 121.

32. David L. Bartlett, "Texts Shaping Sermons," in *Listening to the Word: Studies in*

Though many argue that the churches should throw out traditional materials because they do not appeal to new generations, the speciousness of this argument is exposed by Bartlett's recognition that at conventional moments many people turn to these very materials. What a great gift it is to the culture around the Church that we can offer such sustaining language — words of hope and strength and light!

Recognizing this gift's great breadth, Walter Brueggemann cites Elie Wiesel's remarkable statement, "Poets exist so that the dead may vote," and comments that in the psalms "they vote for faith. But in voting for faith they vote for candor, for pain, for passion — and finally for joy. Their persistent voting gives us a word that turns out to be the word of life."[33] Using psalms in our worship gives us words for all our emotions, oracles from God that invite us to trust, the Word that endures even when human words fail.

Liturgy is a powerful teacher, and constantly repeating the liturgical pieces plants their comfort firmly in the minds of those who participate. In describing her spiritual and bodily care for hospice patients, Eva Cavanagh observes, "In the presence of the dying, I have discovered powerful, transformative prayer." She has found that "the dying do not care for 'creative prayer.' They are probably too tired and weak. They depend on old, familiar prayers that they have been saying for years: the Lord's Prayer, the Twenty-third Psalm." If they are "still strong enough, they like some ritual prayers or services — . . . administration of communion, Scripture services around comforting biblical passages — which they share with family and friends, often with great joy."[34]

Such testimonies should weigh in heavily when worship leaders plan the liturgies for their congregations. If our worship services do not teach these ritual prayers and psalms, who or what will? Many in our culture have not experienced the privilege of growing up in Christian homes with faithful parents who train their children in devotional habits and offer them faith resources.

Honor of Fred B. Craddock, ed. Gail R. O'Day and Thomas G. Long (Nashville: Abingdon Press, 1993), p. 155.

33. Walter Brueggemann, *The Message of the Psalms: A Theological Commentary,* Augsburg Old Testament Studies (Minneapolis: Augsburg, 1984), p. 12.

34. Eva Kavanagh, "Prayer of the Flesh," *The Other Side* 29, no. 3 (May-June 1993): 56, 58.

It seems to me that most of the worship wars over liturgy arise because we have failed for years to teach the habits and meaning of worship. It takes a great deal of energy to educate the ritually illiterate, to interest people in the meanings of traditions. It is far easier to fall into ruts in our planning than to screen carefully what we do. However, good worship should be our top priority since it is the only thing the Church does that no one else can do. Moreover, good worship is worth the effort — not only to praise God, but also to form the character of the believers and to nourish the Christian community.

The Church's Sacramental Life

The point of liturgy is to give the service its shape and flow. Most denominational hymnals are a record of the Church's lore, so that worship is not a string of unrelated items. The services outlined in them fundamentally respond to three different rhythms in Christian life with basic formats and many variations. The rhythm of the week breaks out of time with Sabbath/Sunday worship involving the Word and Supper, lessons, sermons, hymns, offering, and blessings. The rhythm of the day is observed with morning and evening prayer and the eight offices in between. Worship liturgies for the rhythm of life celebrate baptisms, confirmations, weddings, commissions, and burials.

I need not comment on all of the elements in the usual liturgical order. Instead, I will simply highlight areas in which I frequently see abuses as I work in various congregations and denominations in my freelancing. This section is titled as it is because many liturgical weaknesses stem from a failure to accentuate the chief components of the worship service or from disruption of the flow to and from these high points. Congregations need a healthy sacramental life. The Lord's Supper should be offered in all its fullness; baptism should be celebrated as the initiation into an entire life in the believing community. Above all, the point of our sacramental life is to show forth the Christ.

Some churches debate how frequently to offer the Lord's Supper. (This must sound silly to Roman Catholics, whose liturgical life is centered on the Mass.) Certainly we want to commemorate our Savior's death as he commanded us as often as possible, but my main point here is that if a service does not include the Eucharist, the liturgy should possess an entirely different structure. Otherwise, all the service parts build to a climax that never happens. Parishes could use an order for morning or evening prayer, a service of the Word or of prayer and preaching, or another form if Communion is not offered.

Some people object to celebrating the Eucharist every Sunday because they think it becomes boring. If that is the case, then the congregation is not commemorating the Lord's Supper in all its fullness, for this gift has multiple meanings and moods. The Church year's seasons help to establish some of these moods. In Lent, the Supper is more mournful (sharing the grief of the apostles at its institution), humble (to think that our sins sent Christ to the cross), and focused upon the past. In the Easter season, the Eucharist is more joyous (Christ is risen indeed!) and looks to the future and the heavenly feast after we arise. Pentecost concentrates more on the present through discerning the Body of Christ, who, in our midst, calls us by the Spirit's power to be a community without barriers. The best understanding of this spirit I've ever witnessed was at a parish in the poor section of a small city, where communicants drop money over the altar rail as they participate in the Eucharist, and the money is used for a community-wide dinner after the worship service.

How we prepare for the Supper is critically important. No matter what we do or what forms of liturgy we use, all things must bear Christ and usher us into his presence to receive his gift of himself. I particularly love the turn from the service's first focus on the Word by means of the passing of the peace and the offering (as described above) into the great thanksgiving that dramatically anticipates the Feast we are about to enjoy. The liturgical pieces after the Supper serve, then, as the denouement of a story in working out the details of our going back into the world through prayers and hymns and benediction. My point is that the ordering of the service in the historical Mass has such dramatic flow; it cannot help but stir in us a great wonder that we can actually taste of the goodness of God in this marvelous feast.

Liturgy elements surrounding the focus on the Word are equally dramatic. These gathering pieces prepare us for the Word: confession and absolution remove all barriers between us and God, for when pastors announce God's forgiveness they stand under orders from Christ and the Church; the invocation places us under the sign of the cross; an opening hymn sets the tone for the day; the *Kyrie* asks for mercy for all the congregation's needs; the *Gloria in Excelsis* or the new "This is the Feast" both join in the angels' praises; the collect prays about themes to be sounded in the Scripture lessons. Then the lessons are introduced or summarized with psalms, choir anthems, or versicles; the Gospel is spotlighted by responses as the service's first high point; and the hymn of the day prepares for, or responds to, the sermon. The creed joins all the worshipers together in declaring the whole substance of this faith community, and the prayers unite us in concerns for God's will to be done.

After a college liturgics class, subsequent graduate training in English literature revealed to me what an exquisite telling of the story this heritage of the Church is. Our forebears who gradually pieced together the historic Mass passed down through the ages quite brilliantly orchestrated this stunning narrative. I can hardly resist elaborating on all the magnificent liturgical pieces, but I will refrain because there are plenty of fine books describing them.[35] It makes me sad that so few worshipers seem to appreciate these worship elements, savor their flow, and cherish the adventure they present. What is worse is that even many who lead the liturgy do not perceive how luminous it is.

How is it that congregations have failed so miserably to teach the beauty of liturgy, to incorporate new believers into its splendors? Why have we not instructed children so that they may gain from its insights a deeper understanding of their place in the story of the faith community? Couldn't we teach in Sunday school the biblical roots of the liturgy so that children know when they are participating in it that the salutation comes from the story of Ruth and Boaz, the *Agnus Dei* from John the Baptist, the *Sanctus* from Isaiah, the *Magnificat* from Mary, and the *Nunc Dimittis* from Simeon? What a rich web of witnesses we call to mind when we enact the liturgy! As a friend wrote about this timeless community, "The liturgy becomes no longer words, but a testament for real people of faith lived out by real people. We strengthen our ties not only with the faithful of the past, but with all others alive now, and those yet to come."[36]

The purpose of any liturgy, no matter what we use, must be to carry God's presence and the faith of the community. Consequently, political agendas should not be evident in the prayers; announcements should not interrupt the flow of worship; rituals should not engage in ceremonial

---

35. See, e.g., White's *Introduction to Worship* and Carl Schalk's "Music and the Liturgy: The Lutheran Tradition," in Precht, ed., *Lutheran Worship*, pp. 243-61.

36. Personal correspondence from organist Dr. David Hendricksen.

show or be marred by casual flippancy; music should correspond to the message; liturgy elements ought not to be eliminated for the sake of time, nor should extraneous elements be added without reason; the liturgy ought not to be enacted mindlessly. The worship service is a vehicle. Whether worship really happens depends upon the participants.

Henri Nouwen captures the poignancy of shared liturgy, the global unity that is encompassed in it, in this vignette from his trip to Ukraine:

> When we parked the van we saw a few hundred people standing outside the chapel looking in. The first words I heard were: *"Hospody pomyluy,"* "Lord have mercy." It's the *Kyrie Eleison,* the heart of the Jesus Prayer, the most used words in the Eastern liturgy. It was so moving to hear them. It seemed that they introduced me to this new country in the best way: "Lord, have mercy," the prayer of God's people, the prayer that has sounded through centuries of struggle, wars, persecution, and oppression. They are words of the liturgy, but also words belonging to the most intimate prayer of the heart.[37]

Silence

In the hundreds of congregations I have visited in my freelancing, there have been fewer than a handful who actually spend time in silence in their worship services. The angels know better. The heavenly worship described in the Book of Revelation includes a mysterious half hour of silence.[38]

The *Lutheran Book of Worship* includes instructions for silence at three strategic places in the liturgy, but rarely do churches actually observe them. Many contemporary alternative worship services not only neglect silence but also seem to bury any opportunities for meditation and reflection.

The human body and mind need silence, as the monks recognized when they ordered their prayer lives. It is impossible for our inner selves to be prepared to be open to God and receptive to God's Word until we silence our sinful selves — our efforts to be in control, to manipulate

37. Henri J. M. Nouwen, "Pilgrimage to the Christian East," *New Oxford Review* 61, no. 3 (April 1994): 15.

38. See Rev. 8:1 and also chapter 20 of my book *Joy in Our Weakness: A Gift of Hope from the Book of Revelation* (St. Louis: Concordia, 1994).

everything and everyone to accomplish our own purposes. How can we release ourselves totally to God's Spirit? How can we relinquish our desires to God's better purposes? We need the channel of silence to transport us from the busy harbors of our own tensions out to the ocean of God's infinite being.

Some people would insist that only monks and other contemplatives need silence, but such protestations perhaps arise because of our modern inability to endure it. In the silence we have to face ourselves, our terrors, our uglinesses, our emptiness. Most difficult of all, we might encounter God! The Church has the opportunity to offer a great gift — to teach her members and visitors to listen in the silence and learn that God's voice is gracious and merciful.

Writing about her artistic work with rural Minnesotans, Carol Bly muses, "We have finally got it through our heads, too, that what one class of people needs, all the classes of people have a right to. It isn't just Beethoven who needs silence and gravity: it's all of us."[39] Churches, of all places, could be offering this gift — yet they seem to be running away from it the fastest.

Raymond Gawronski invites us to enjoy silence because our faith is in the

> Word who is eternal and personal: a dialogical Word. We are silent in order to hear what the Christmas hymn calls the "silent Word." American fundamentalist religiosity notwithstanding, the Word of God is not like a used-car ad that comes blaring over the radio. The Word of God comes to us like a deer that emerges from the mist in the forest where you have been sitting without moving a muscle. If you are still and gentle enough, you will not scare the deer away. Of course, our deer is also the Hound of Heaven who relentlessly pursues us. But we approach God in paradox, and so He is both Word and Silence, the One who will not be silenced, and yet the One who does not shout or raise His voice.[40]

39. Carol Bly, *Letters from the Country* (New York: Penguin Books, 1981), p. 49.
40. Raymond T. Gawronski, "Why Orthodox Catholics Look to Zen," *New Oxford Review* 60, no. 6 (July-Aug. 1993): 15.

Ritual Gesture and Posture

The three basic worship themes that this book stresses — to keep God the focus and to nourish our Christian character as individuals and as members of a communal Body — are indirectly stated also by gestures and postures. For example, the gesture of bowing at the altar reminds the acolytes, the altar guild as they prepare the Lord's Table, and anyone who enters the chancel that a special reverence is called for in this place because of the presence of Christ in his Word and Supper. Our forebears perhaps took this reverence to an inordinate extreme in their austere rigidity or unwarranted terror, but now sometimes the pendulum swings too far in the opposite direction, with the result that we turn Christ into merely a buddy and not the King of kings and Lord of lords.

Again, as this book frequently stresses, we must balance a careful dialectic. God is immanent, close to us, and accessible, to be loved in an intimate way — but he is also transcendent, beyond us in his perfect holiness, to be adored by creatures who owe their entire existence to him. We can nurture this paradoxical sense of God by our worship gestures and postures.

For a children's sermon at the beginning of a worship service, I invited the children forward to watch the acolytes do their job. We noticed together how they bowed as they approached the altar and again as they left it. We talked together about how God is everywhere, but we especially honor him in this place to remember that he is God after all, and we are wee. We reminded each other that our outside noises are not appropriate in this worship place, which is especially set apart to portray God's character. It is a place for laughter and joyfulness, for tears of repentance or sadness, for silence and meditation, for the Word proclaimed — but not a place for rudeness, noises that disrupt others, or irreverence for the special moments with God that occur here. Then the children and I walked to the altar and bowed together. It was a very holy moment, and the children stood in awe and childlike reverence.

In our irreverent, noisy society, how important it is to instill a sense of the holy, a yearning for a quiet place and the gathering of the community in which we can meet God and be formed to be more like him. Because our children are assailed constantly by the bustle and bombast of television and Walkmans and other technological distractions, how vital it is to offer alternatives — movements of adoration, gestures of sacredness, postures of virtue.

Worship gestures might include lifting hands in praise, holding hands across the rows for community prayer, opening up the hands to receive absolution. The positions of body and face also undergird the themes of various worship segments. Significantly, pastors face the altar when they pray and the people when they speak God's Word to them (and, therefore, they look away from the congregants to the altar or cross in the last dialogue of the *Kyrie* as it turns from addressing the people to praying to God). Worshipers should look at one another when they say the Creed — and not to God, the inside of a hymnbook, or the floor — for this is our declaration of faith to each other.

When we are careful not to let them become mindless habits, these worship postures subtly but powerfully over time affect the development of our character; consequently, a sense of who we are together as a worshiping Body with Christ as the Head is then carried into our daily lives. Our bowing at the altar can influence us to bow to God's will in our daily choices; our telling the creed to each other in worship invites us to share our faith more easily with our neighbors and work colleagues and family. Those who discard ritual as outmoded tradition do not understand the profound effects on character formation of body language and sensory experience.

Art and Architecture, Symbols and Icons

Superb books on the Church's art and worship spaces abound.[41] I bring up the subject here because the television age, which so destructively impacts our society (as we saw in Chapter 2), has also had an enormous influence on art and symbolism that we rarely recognize if we also are too immersed in it.

Other cultures in which television is not so dominant still retain a greater appreciation for the spiritual workings of liturgical art, especially as symbols are combined with gesture and sound. In his diary of his visit to Ukraine, Henri Nouwen comments on the profoundly spiritual experience aroused by "the richly decorated church, the colorful, embroidered vestments of the priests, the hymns, antiphons, and prayers (all sung in

41. For short introductions to the subject see White's *Introduction to Worship*, pp. 88-121, and Wayne E. Schmidt's "The Place of Worship," in Precht, ed., *Lutheran Worship*, pp. 175-218.

rich harmony), the devout attention of the people, the solemn gestures of the priests," and the welcoming hospitality of fellow Christians in the Ukrainian community.[42]

Is such an interweaving of symbol, art, sound, gesture, and solemn devotion possible in U.S. society at the turn of the century? Neil Postman is doubtful because of the change in understanding of religious aesthetics. Writing specifically about the religion that is broadcast on television, he contends,

> there are, of course, counterarguments to the claim that television degrades religion. Among them is that spectacle is hardly a stranger to religion. If one puts aside the Quakers and a few other austere sects, every religion tries to make itself appealing through art, music, icons and awe-inspiring ritual. The aesthetic dimension to religion is the source of its attraction to many people. This is especially true of Roman Catholicism and Judaism, which supply their congregants with haunting chants; magnificent robes and shawls; magical hats, wafers and wine; stained-glass windows; and the mysterious cadences of ancient languages. The difference between these accoutrements of religion and the floral displays, fountains and elaborate sets we see on television is that the former are not, in fact, accoutrements but integral parts of the history and doctrines of the religion itself; they require congregants to respond to them with suitable reverence. . . . The spectacle we find in true religions has as its purpose enchantment, not entertainment. The distinction is critical. By endowing things with magic, enchantment is the means through which we may gain access to sacredness. Entertainment is the means through which we distance ourselves from it.[43]

I have quoted Postman at some length because, though many would protest that his comments apply only to televised religion, his basic point about accoutrements pertains to this book's entire discerning process. As we ask questions about worship, the best questions to ponder about art and symbol are whether they are integral to the history of the Christian faith itself. Do our music, sermon, worship place, and liturgy distance us

---

42. Henri J. M. Nouwen, "The Gulf Between East and West," *New Oxford Review* 61, no. 4 (May 1994): 12.

43. Postman, *Amusing Ourselves to Death,* pp. 121-22. Page references to this book in the following paragraphs are given parenthetically in the text.

from the sacred or draw us to it? Postman raises for us issues of coherence and propriety. Our answers will reveal whether what we do and how we do it is idolatry or genuine worship.

Postman claims that "there are several characteristics of television and its surroundings that converge to make authentic religious experience impossible" in televised services (p. 118). We may disagree with that claim, but the grounds he gives for it engender good questions for worship in our churches. His first consideration has to do with the consecration of space. It is essential for a worship service "that the space in which it is conducted must be invested with some measure of sacrality." If the congregation "is not immersed in an aura of mystery and symbolic otherworldliness, then it is unlikely that it can call forth the state of mind required for a nontrivial religious experience" (p. 119). Do our worship services and the places in which we hold them give the sense of God's presence in all of God's infinite Otherness? Do our church buildings, as the house of God, symbolize the homeland of the soul?

The value of symbols in the worship space is that they hint at more that can be seen. A symbol of the Trinity on an altar cloth, for example, invites viewers to contemplate the mystery of the one God's being in three persons. What symbols denote, however, must be taught, and churches must find new ways to involve the uninitiated in the delight and mystery of their meaning.

Postman's other major criticism of televised worship in *Amusing Ourselves to Death* cautions us against letting worship in churches become too lightweight. He asserts, "I believe I am not mistaken in saying that Christianity is a demanding and serious religion. When it is delivered as easy and amusing, it is another kind of religion altogether" (p. 121). We must always ask if what we do and see in worship reveals the truth about discipleship. Perhaps our crosses are too beautiful — we forget that they are meant to die on.

In a later book, Postman intensifies his concern by decrying the way in which our technopolized world destroys symbols of the faith. He imagines the example of using Jesus to sell California Chardonnay and cites a Hebrew National frankfurter commercial that refers to God ("We have to answer to a Higher Authority"), and explains that these are not examples of blasphemy, but much worse. "Blasphemy is, after all, among the highest tributes that can be paid to the power of a symbol. The blasphemer takes symbols as seriously as the idolater."[44] Rather, these are examples of trivialization.

Postman avers that the trivialization of significant cultural symbols in technopoly occurs "because the adoration of technology pre-empts the adoration of anything else." Consequently, religious symbols must "be made impotent as quickly as possible — that is, drained of sacred or even serious connotations. The elevation of one god requires the demotion of another" (p. 165).

Religious symbols in our culture have "become commonplaces, breeding indifference if not necessarily contempt" (p. 166). One prominent example is the way television so frequently projects the image of corrupt or stupid clergy, which contributes to a cultural loss of the symbol of the clergy collar as a denotation of someone who can be trusted to help in times of illness, sorrow, or confusion. The second reason for "the journey to meaninglessness of symbols is a function not only of the frequency with which they are invoked but of the indiscriminate contexts in which they are used" (p. 167). If rock singers whose lyrics are violent or sexist or nihilistic wear crosses, then what power remains to the cross as the focal point of a worship space?

The evacuation of meaning for symbols in contemporary society has dire consequences for the community and its narrative of faith. Postman explains,

> There can, of course, be no functioning sense of tradition without a measure of respect for symbols. Tradition is, in fact, nothing but the acknowledgment of the authority of symbols and the relevance of the narratives that gave birth to them. With the erosion of symbols there follows a loss of narrative, which is one of the most debilitating consequences of Technopoly's power. (p. 171).

Cultures must have narratives, Postman warns us,

> and will find them where they will, even if they lead to catastrophe. The alternative is to live without meaning, the ultimate negation of life itself. It is also to the point to say that each narrative is given its form and its emotional texture through a cluster of symbols that call for

---

44. Neil Postman, *Technopoloy* (New York: Alfred A. Knopf, 1992), p. 165. Pages references to this book in the following paragraphs are given parenthetically in the text.

respect and allegiance, even devotion. . . . There are, of course, several reasons why such stories lose their force. . . . [O]ne of them . . . [is] how the growth of Technopoly has overwhelmed earlier, more meaningful stories. But in all cases, the trivialization of the symbols that express, support, and dramatize the story will accompany the decline. Symbol drain is both a symptom and a cause of a loss of narrative. (p. 173)

Jacques Ellul issued similar warnings about the dangers of technicization almost fifty years ago, and sociologists dismissed him as a pessimistic crank. However, in recent years more and more scholars are recognizing the accuracy of his predictions.[45] The Church's culture owns the narrative of Christ's gospel and of itself as a community of believers. If the worship symbols of this narrative are trivialized — by other idolatries as well as technopoly — then the narratives themselves are seen as irrelevant. The Church must take great care lest the loss of its symbols (including not only art but also liturgies and worship tools) accelerates the loss of a viable faith.

John Westerhoff criticizes the lack of excellence in the art of contemporary churches. He insists that the architecture is "generally unimaginative" and "few great paintings or pieces of sculpture adorn the church." He laments the "sentimental pictures of Jesus and trivial pieces of music" that "combine to further alienate the artist from the church."[46]

Just as the final grid in our selection process for determining musical worth demanded excellence and greatness, so the Church needs visual arts — symbols on banners or furniture or stained glass, paintings, sculpture, architecture, and icons — that lift us to higher realms beyond the merely human. Westerhoff affirms, "The arts incarnate our experience of mystery, wonder, and awe and thereby aid us to encounter the holy or sacred. Without the arts we are cut off from most of the means by which we perceive life's ultimate meaning (p. 41).

By asking the Church to make use of the best worship art it can find, Westerhoff seeks to counteract some of the idolatries we explored in Chapter 3. He complains, "All too many people have been victimized by

---

45. See my dissertation, "The Concept of 'the Principalities and Powers' in the Works of Jacques Ellul" (University of Notre Dame, 1992).

46. John H. Westerhoff III and John D. Eusden, *The Spiritual Life: Learning East and West* (New York: Seabury, 1982), p. 47. Page references to this book in the following paragraphs are given parenthetically in the text.

a false religion of subjective emotionalism devoid of both thinking and imagination" (p. 44). Good art stirs each person, no matter what their level of maturity, to new insights and visions. At the same time, Westerhoff counsels, we need not "worry that the arts can lead us away from a faith that does justice." Rather, he suggests that "great art is prophetic as well as priestly, that it both brings us into contact with the holy and confronts us with a critical revelation on our common life." Moreover, the artist "teaches us that we cannot live in our own private experience, but must in some way incarnate it or bring it into being" (pp. 44-45).

One facet of art and symbolism underestimated by Western Christians is the contribution of iconography. My interest in icons, first kindled by two artist friends who restored and copied them, flared with the appearance of Henri Nouwen's lovely book *Behold the Beauty of the Lord: Praying with Icons.*[47] This volume, which contains four foldout reproductions of icons so that the reader can study them while learning about them, attracted me to worship that allows icons to be escorts into a deeper world. Nouwen explains in his Ukraine journal that icons are not illustrations or decorations but "true windows on the eternal." Though at first "these sacred images seemed somewhat forbidding" to him, he exults that "they gradually revealed their secrets to me and led me far beyond my daily preoccupations into the Kingdom of God."[48]

Icons are not only a means for worship. By the exact procedure required for painting them, by the jewels that adorn not the painting but the person represented, by the exuberance with which they are embraced, by the knowledge involved in understanding them, and by their invitation to the life of the Christian community, they also model for us the combination of discipline, imagination, emotion, intellect, and will required for worship.

Frederica Mathewes-Green describes the movement from looking at an icon to responding to all that it incarnates. She insists that viewing icons

> is not like admiring a delicate Renaissance Madonna. Something in their dignity and startling immediacy demands a more personal response. The

47. Henri J. M. Nouwen, *Behold the Beauty of the Lord: Praying with Icons* (Notre Dame: Ave Maria Press, 1987).
48. Nouwen, "Pilgrimage to the Christian East," pp. 14-15.

Orthodox refer to icons as "windows into heaven." Kissing would probably be a Western Christian's last response to these icons. But for the Orthodox it is the obvious response, the only response that conveys the tenderness, gratitude and humility that these mysteries demand.

. . . The holy invisible Lord surrounds us and we grasp for his elusive presence, kneeling down awestruck with our foreheads to the floor, tasting heaven on the eucharistic spoon, laying kisses on his image and each other. An outsider might expect Eastern Orthodoxy to be stiff, esoteric and rigidly ritualistic. But it is not superstition that requires us to give formal, ritual kisses; we feel such gratitude to God for saving us, such awe at his majesty and joy in the fellowship of the saints that we respond from the heart.[49]

The Liturgical Worship of the Christian Community

When I am writing, I don't like the isolation of my study crammed with desks and books but no other people. Yet sitting at my computer while thinking and writing about liturgy has felt like worship in the company of the Christian community. Reflecting on the "work of the people" in which we participate together with the best that worship planners, musicians, artists, and liturgists have to offer sends waves of thankfulness through my bones. It makes me yearn for worship that will demand of me the strongest discipline, the most creative imagination, the most passionate emotion, the highest intellect, and the most rigorous will — in short, genuine adoration of God.

I believe, with John Nordin, that "doing liturgy with power can prove compelling for visitors and regulars alike." I, too, have seen again and again "those contemptuous or merely weary of boring, ineffective public ritual be grateful and intrigued when they experience effective ritual. I believe that complaints about the obscurity of 'traditional' liturgy are really complaints about incompetent ritual."[50] I go beyond Nordin, however, to believe that "contemporary" liturgies can also prove compelling when they satisfy the three criteria (of God, character, and community) around which

49. Frederica Mathewes-Green, "The Kissing Part," *The Christian Century* 111, no. 12 (13 April 1994): 375.

50. John Nordin, "Can Traditional Ritual Be Evangelistic?" *dialog* 33, no. 3 (Summer 1994): 230.

this book is built, when their music passes successfully through the selection grid of Chapter 8, when the Word of God (as accentuated in Chapter 9) is proclaimed in truth and purity, and when the worship is truly the "work of the people."

Both new and old liturgies can also be equally welcoming to strangers, for hospitality depends upon vitality, which can characterize any kind of worship that genuinely carries the presence of God and the involvement of the community in a public way. Visitors will be attracted to liturgies in which the participants love what they are doing because God is in their midst.

Since worship is a time when we gain a foretaste of heaven, perhaps we can learn how to worship better from those who yearn for heaven more. Nouwen writes that, having learned the history of the Ukrainian people, he better understood "the centrality of 'long-suffering'" in their spirituality. In contrast to a large percentage of worshipers in the United States, "happiness, prosperity, physical well-being, and esteem have not been part of the experience of most Ukrainians, especially the peasants." Instead, for them, "these gifts have always belonged to the future Kingdom, of which they were able to catch only a glimpse in their splendid liturgies."[51]

Worship in the United States seems more often to be characterized by boredom than by glimpses of heaven. Is this the fault of the worship services or of the worshipers? Of course, it can be the former if the liturgy is poorly planned or clumsily enacted. Perhaps, though, boredom is more often the transgression of worshipers when we fail to do "the work of the people." Joey Earl Horstman invites us to authentic *leitourgia* in the following words:

> Boredom saps our strength, our life and potency, our excitement and capacity for wonder. . . . Sometimes we need to dance naked and with abandon before the ark of the covenant for the sheer joy and wonderment of physical movement. Sometimes we need to grieve, to weep and rend our clothing, for we live in a fallen world.
>
> Sometimes, that is, we need to immerse ourselves in life, to come off the bench and participate directly, rather than vicariously and safely. For to risk experiencing the beauty and the tragedy and the uncertainty that is our legacy is not only a cure for boredom, but may, in fact, be what worship is all about.[52]

51. Nouwen, "Pilgrimage to the Christian East," p. 14.
52. Joey Earl Horstman, "Channel Too: The Postmodern Yawn," *The Other Side* 29, no. 3 (May-June 1993): 35.

PART V

Worship *for the Sake of* the Culture

11. *Reaching Out without Dumbing Down*

> The roots of evangelism in our time lie in new understandings of worship.
>
> James F. White, *The Worldliness of Worship*

Most of the issues discussed in this book have arisen over the last few years as Christian leaders began seeking new ways to attract the nonchurched to their worship services. As we have seen, the idea that we should change our worship patterns to attract people to Christ is a mistaken notion. Furthermore, such an approach does not grapple with the extent of the issues for those who do not participate in institutional Christianity. For example, what kind of reflection is being done regarding all the backdoor losses from the Church?

The "Dark Side" of Church Growth

David Barrett reported statistics for Oxford University Press that in a twelve-month period, 2,765,100 worship attenders in Europe and North America cease to be practicing Christians — an average loss of 7,600 every

279

day. This means that every week more than 53,000 people leave churches and never come back. The percentage of active Christians in the world has fallen from 29.0 percent in 1900 to 23.3 percent of today's population. Losses in the Western and formerly Communist worlds slightly outweigh Christian growth in the Two-Thirds World.[1]

Something is seriously wrong if so many people do not find it worthwhile to continue participating in the Church! William Hendricks asserts that, though this "dark side" of church growth is neither reported nor carefully studied, it is growing. We must ask why, "despite glowing reports of surging church attendance, more and more Christians in North America are feeling *disillusioned* with the church." These are not people who "have given up on the faith. On the contrary, they may be quite articulate regarding spiritual matters. Indeed, some have remarkably vibrant spiritual lives" (p. 17). In this chapter we will bring together the main themes of all the preceding chapters in order to ask better questions about how the Church can, in its worship, reach out to the culture around it — and prevent some of the disillusionment.

Reaching Out without Dumbing Down

Christians were horrified in 1994 when an anti-abortion protester killed two people — a doctor and his escort — in his attempt to "save lives." The irony is too obvious. How can taking lives ever be consistent with the goal of preserving them? In the same way, many churches who want desperately to attract people to Christ miss the point by offering worship so shallow that not enough of Christ is proclaimed to engender lasting belief.

Some of you might protest that my analogy is too harsh, but I wonder if the practice of dumbing down worship isn't, in the long run, equally fatal to faith. If people are introduced to a Christianity composed only of happiness and good feelings, where will the staying power be when chronic illness, family instability, or long-term unemployment threaten? If worship is only fun, how will those attracted to such worship have enough commitment to work on the conflicts that inevitably develop because all of us in the Church are sinful human beings?

---

1. William D. Hendricks, *Exit Interviews* (Chicago: Moody Press, 1993), p. 252. Page references to this book throughout this chapter are given parenthetically in the text.

Hendricks heard many reasons why people leave churches from those he interviewed — but not one of them left because the worship was too deep. Some departed because of inadequate intellectual challenge, musical ineptness, insufficient attention to developing character, or little sense of community. We saw in Chapter 1 that children who watch too much television actually have smaller brains than their peers. Are our churches creating smaller faiths if our attempts at reforming worship, as Leander Keck complains, amount to "little more than a substitution of the trivial for the ossified"?[2]

Worship becomes ossified if churches lose sight of their reasons for being — love of God and neighbor. Failing to educate well so that strangers and the uninitiated are welcomed, some parishes become elitist. Deficient in fresh theologizing, many lose their motivation to love God with contagious ardor. Inadequately conscious of the world around them, many derive from worship no stimulus to work for peace and justice in the world.

On the other hand, if, in their attempts to revitalize worship, churches merely speed it up and lower its substance, then they trivialize both God and the neighbor. They don't respect their neighbors enough to offer them the solid food of God's fullness. Moreover, too small a God leads to too small a concern for the neighbor in both evangelistic care and passion for justice.

Caring for "Lost Souls"

Chapter 2 sketched several prominent descriptions of the present culture so that we will be able to plan the Church's worship with better awareness of these forces. It is odd, however, that many churches lag so far behind the times instead of addressing these cultural issues in prophetic ways. Now when many prominent sociologists recognize the dangers of television's superficiality, some churches are becoming equally trivialized as they turn their worship music into mere entertainment. While researchers are discovering that members of the boomer generation are searching for moral authority, multitudes of preachers are throwing theirs away. Even as scholars notice that one stream of postmodernists are returning to their

2. Leander E. Keck, *The Church Confident* (Nashville: Abingdon, 1993), p. 25.

roots to counteract the relativity of modernism, numerous parishes are rejecting the historic liturgy of the Church.

If we want to care for the "lost souls" of our society, the best way we can reach out to them is to offer them the richest resources of the Church. Let us give them the most faithful worship we can enact. Walter Brueggemann insists that the gospel must be both proclaimed and heard as

- intellectually credible in an unreflective society;
- politically critical and constructive in a cynical community;
- morally dense and freighted in a self-indulgent society;
- artistically satisfying in a society overwhelmed by religious kitsch; and
- pastorally attentive in a society of easy but fake answers.[3]

This list summarizes many of the needs of the boomer and buster generations explored in Chapter 2 and counteracts the idolatries listed in Chapter 3.

Neil Postman's book on technopoly discusses a variety of attributes that are necessary to be what he calls "a loving resistance fighter." By substituting the word *Church* for terms denoting the nation, we can find in his commentary sage advice for equipping Christians with the means for counteracting the adverse effects of our society. Postman elaborates the word *loving* to urge that, "in spite of the confusion, errors, and stupidities you see around you, you must always keep close to your heart the narratives and symbols that once made the [Church] the hope of the world and that may yet have enough vitality to do so again."[4] Think, for example, of the way in which the four hymns, played and sung as described in Chapter 8, nourished the people of Kazakhstan. Let us be very careful in the Church not to lose such symbols of the faith.

The first constituents on Postman's list describing those who resist technopoly are people "who pay no attention to a poll unless they know what questions were asked and why" (p. 183). This is a critical caution for the Church at a time when many practices are being changed in response to polls conducted by religious marketers who might not be

---

3. Walter Brueggemann, *Biblical Perspectives on Evangelism* (Nashville: Abingdon, 1993), p. 128.

4. Neil Postman, *Technopoly* (New York: Alfred A. Knopf, 1992), p. 182. Page references to this book in the following paragraphs are given parenthetically in the text.

asking the right questions, questions that bear in mind the importance of keeping God as the subject of worship and nurturing long-term character and community development by means of worship. Worship surveys within congregations, too, often ask the wrong questions or are answered only by those with the strongest opinions and thus should not be given the inordinate weight they often assume.

Postman suggests several other valuable traits that are applicable to those who want to resist cultural forces destructive of worship. We can reach out more effectively to persons caught in contemporary culture if we are people

- who refuse to accept efficiency as the pre-eminent goal of human relations;
- who have freed themselves from the belief in the magical powers of numbers[;] . . .
- who are, at least, suspicious of the idea of progress, and who do not confuse information with understanding;
- who do not regard the aged as irrelevant;
- who take the great narratives of religion seriously . . . ;
- who know the difference between the sacred and the profane, and who do not wink at tradition for modernity's sake. (p. 184)

Postman's educational proposal to counter the effects of technicization on culture urges schools to "make available the products of classical art forms precisely because they are not so available and because they demand a different order of sensibility and response." Since the Church's goal is to nourish deep sensibilities in worship participants in order to broaden our capabilities to love both God and the neighbor, we might join in Postman's campaign to use the arts for societal reform. He complains, "In our present circumstances, there is no excuse for schools to sponsor rock concerts when students have not heard the music of Mozart, Beethoven, Bach, or Chopin" (p. 191). We might suggest the same for churches, although we would want to widen Postman's repertoire to be more globally and ethnically inclusive.

Postman believes the artists he enumerates are relevant, "not only because they established the standards with which civilized people approach the arts," but also "because the culture tries to mute their voices and render their standards invisible." The Church should be among the social institutions that set the highest artistic standards, especially because we need excellence and greatness to worship God. Postman warns that "our youth must be shown that not all worthwhile things are instantly accessible and that there are levels of sensibility unknown to them. Above all, they must be shown humanity's artistic tools" (p. 191). In a culture of immediate gratification, the Church can, by means of its great heritage of music and art, teach habits of discipline and deeper commitment, of more thoughtful appreciation and careful reflection.

Idolatries

All that this chapter has said so far relates to the warnings given in Chapter 3 that the Church must be constantly alert to resist the culture's idolatries and reject its gods. In a country that worships money, power, efficiency, immediacy, and control, genuine worship invites us to be generous, meek (in the biblical sense), reflective, eternally minded, and obedient. In a society that idolizes famous people, the Church affirms the gifts of all the saints and offers worship as the work of all the people. In a culture where success is measured by big numbers, the Church knows its message is not popular and seeks not to swell the churches but to deepen believers' faith (a consequence of which will be that they will reach out to neighbors).

This is the ideal, but as Keck laments, in many places worship has become "thoroughly secularized." Keck recalls an occasion when the invocation was

> replaced with the rousing cheer for God: "Gimme a G; gimme an O, gimme a D." An extreme example . . . but . . . [t]here will be no renewal of mainline Protestantism until its worship of God is redeemed from such silliness and the secularization it reflects. If the Australian historian is right in asserting that "secularization is a much deadlier foe than any previous counter-religious force in human experience," then one can see immediately what is at stake in the secularization of worship — the identity and integrity of the church as church, that is, whether the church "stands faithfully in the presence of the One who is both the object and the source of faith." And the antidote to this secularization is restoring the integrity of the center of worship — the praise of God.[5]

5. Keck, *The Church Confident,* pp. 26-27.

284

The only means for keeping worship free of idolatries is to keep God the subject. God frequently loses that role if churches insist on catering to the cultural idolatry of choice. Canadian sociologist Reginald Bibby shows that "some churches today may be declining not because they offer too few choices, but *too many.*" As Bibby summarizes, "By being so graciously compliant, the groups have essentially served up religion in whatever form consumers want. They have not provided a religion based on what religion is, but a religion based on what the market will bear." The repercussion for worship is that "attendance is just another fragment to be drawn on when customers find it convenient to do so. Ironically, religious groups are losing active attenders not because they are failing, but because they are succeeding" (Hendricks, p. 113).

Success is the most dangerous idolatry the Church must resist in its worship. One of Hendricks's interviewees tried several churches after leaving one, but said, "They were all trying to beat [the church where I'd been]! . . . I felt that they were saying to themselves, 'If we did this and we did that, maybe we would have more people, too.'" Hendricks adds that among the pressures on pastors

> today perhaps the most severe is the pressure to put people in the pews on Sunday morning. So when any church appears to have discovered effective ways to do that, other churches that hear about it often wonder, "Would that work here? Maybe we should try it." Before long, countless churches are using the same strategies, with varying degrees of success. . . . The issue is not how one's congregation can be like some other "successful" (i.e., large) church, but how it can be the unique church that God intends it to be. Do we know what that church is? Do we know what particular purpose and mission God has called it to? (p. 115)

Rarely do congregations think in terms of their unique contributions as a response to an inward call from God rather than the outward statistics of marketers. Bright exceptions might include inner-city churches that shift their musical style to match neighborhood ethnic changes or small parishes that seize their role to offer hope and stability in declining rural areas.

Worship Must Be Subversive

In order to minister to persons in our television, boomer, postmodern age and yet to avoid falling into society's idolatries, the Church's worship must be subversive, as discussed in Chapter 4. It listens to the needs of those to whom it reaches out but offers them more than they think they want in the fullness of Christ's answer to their unfelt and deeper needs.

If worship is fulfilling its subversive role, it will present to church members and visitors alike what Gaddy calls *"a confrontation with reality."* When believers engage in genuine, God-focused worship, this can be for the non-Christian "like an unexpected slap in the face." As Gaddy describes it, the unbeliever first experiences "shock, then sensitivity." If the worship is authentic, the observer's personal awareness will be heightened, until the individual "suddenly sees what has been missed until the present moment, 'God *is*. God is here! God is reality, not merely a projection of optimistic ideology or an invention of noble fantasy. God is real.'" For everyone, but especially for the worship visitor who is not yet a believer, the profound discovery of God's reality will subject all one's "personal beliefs and behavior, priorities and sources of security" to serious questioning. We must ask, "What does this recognition of God say about how I have organized my life? How does it challenge my interests and the experiences, primarily professional and pleasurable, to which I have assigned the highest values?"[6]

How often does this happen? Does our worship regularly turn us upside down? If it occurred often, we would probably be much more intent on inviting everyone we know to participate in such worship, too. Even as the Samaritan woman left her water jar and ran back to the village to get her neighbors (see John 4), we would set aside our other, mundane concerns in our eagerness to share the water of life with our world.

In a surprising analogy, Martin Marty compares this subversive power of worship to the germ-killing ability of wooden cutting boards. Having read a report that 99.9 percent of existent bacteria died on the wood within 3 minutes after arrival while none died on plastic cutting boards, Marty takes the information "to promote the use of wood, as something natural and time-honored. As things of the spirit, as in acts of worship, should also be." Marty expands the analogy as follows:

6. C. Welton Gaddy, *The Gift of Worship* (Nashville: Broadman Press, 1992), p. 42.

Plastic makes a fine first impression. It is smooth, synthetic, un-memorable and thus undisturbing to our habits and routines. Translate this to worship. Take for example the widely sung if not wildly popular "praise songs." They are smooth, synthetic, unmemorable and undis-turbing. They touch the sensations but not the spirit. . . . They are not made to get into the brain cells where memories disturb or quicken us.

Then we hear the old wood stuff: shape notes, spirituals, "Southern Harmony," Genevan plain song, Gregorian chant, jazz, chorales, folk songs and, yes, even some modern songs with texture and abrasive character, and we wonder why these germkillers often get bypassed for the plastic.

One often still hears plastic, prepackaged topical sermons in which the preacher offers smooth and therefore unmemorable comment on the passing scene. Today some are rediscovering wood: natural, authentic exposition of basic biblical texts with shocking application to our time. Spiritual germs are less likely to survive.

Marty recognizes the other side of the dialectic, too, and protests worship that has become ossified by adding, "Wood, unwashed, untreated and misused, can be dangerous too."[7]

If worship only attracts and does not disturb or quicken, it will leave visitors and regular participants unchanged. For worship to be subversive, however, does not negate the possibility that it will be attractive to out-siders. As we saw in Chapters 5 through 7, worship that is planned with three essential guidelines in mind can welcome strangers with exactly what they need and most profoundly desire.

Worship That Encounters God Is a Lasting Attraction

As Chapter 5 elaborated, the key to true worship is for God to be its subject. In his *Exit Interviews,* William Hendricks discovered that many stopped participating in worship because of boredom. He summarizes, "It was not just that these gatherings were not interesting; they were not *worshipful.* They did little to help people meet God" (p. 260). As accen-tuated in Chapters 8 and 10, music style and liturgy type won't matter if

7. Martin E. Marty, "M.E.M.O.: The Cutting Edge," *The Christian Century* 110, no. 6 (24 Feb. 1993): 223.

God is not found in them, if they do not incarnate God's self-giving or enable us to respond to God's grace.

Hendricks asked a friend who was a great preacher what the preacher's objective should be. Though this friend would not have considered himself an outstanding communicator, people came back consistently to hear his messages. He responded, as this book amplified in Chapter 9, "The point of the sermon is to help people meet God, to have an encounter with God. Somewhere during that message, I want every person to have the experience of hearing God saying something to him or her personally" (p. 282). Hendricks adds,

> By now, the memo tacked up in the victorious Clinton presidential campaign headquarters is legendary: "It's the economy, stupid!" I think if I had to preach week in and week out, especially in a culture saturated with entertainment, I would tack a reminder to myself in the pulpit: "It's about God, stupid!" (p. 283)

This may seem elementary. We may think it unnecessary to reiterate. But many marketing strategies for attracting outsiders to worship do not focus enough on what is most essential. Interviews with nonbelievers indicate that parishes miss the point. George Gallop's landmark study *The Unchurched Americans* found that 41 percent of the U.S. population has no church connection, yet "six out of ten agreed that 'most churches and synagogues have lost the real spiritual part of religion.' " Though 45 percent of the "unchurched" pray every day, 64 percent say they believe that Jesus is God or the Son of God, 68 percent believe in Christ's resurrection, and 77 percent had some childhood religious training, simultaneously "about half agreed that 'most churches and synagogues today are not effective in helping people find meaning in life' " (p. 249).

If we want our worship services to reach out to the nonbelieving, we must present the real God in all his fullness and not just a thin layer of generalized spirituality. Because of his research on why people leave congregations, Hendricks instructs churches to *"Teach people theology."* As he conducted his interviews, he "was stunned by how much 'folk religion' there is on the street." By folk religion he means "popular but inaccurate ideas" about who God is and our relationship with him (p. 284).

One of the most significant ways in which God is lost in the attempt to reach out to nonbelievers is if church leaders think that we can bring people to Christ by using certain strategies or worship styles. If we think this way, we are confused about what we are doing when we worship, for, as Kurt Marquardt delineates, "The worship of God is its own end, while evangelism is a means to that end."[8]

Moreover, many other factors influence a visitor's readiness to hear God and respond to him. Gaddy reminds us, "No guarantees exist regarding a non-Christian's involvement in a worship service. The sensitivity and receptivity of each individual are crucial factors in a determination of reactions." Rather than trying to control the Spirit by their manipulations, God's people must let God be the subject, for, as Gaddy encourages, "a potential for good exists any time a non-Christian encounters a congregation devoted to the authentic worship of God." In genuine worship even a complete stranger "can sense adoration, profound conviction, honest confession, and intense joy that form a powerful witness to the reality of God."[9]

We dare not make worship too easy, for God is always beyond our grasp. Worship cannot be only cerebral or only emotional, for God is mysterious and wise. Worship must be unceasingly comforting so that through it God will address our suffering. It must be perpetually paradoxical so that we know we must worship forever. Strangers will have no need to return to our worship services if they can understand all that our worship offers of God in one Sunday gulp.

Worship That Forms Character Is a Lasting Attraction

Worship must convince us that we gain there what cannot be found anywhere else. Otherwise we could just as well visit our friendly therapist or a rock concert or whatever else uplifts our feelings. Authentic worship will teach us that we are desperate sinners, enfold us in gracious forgiveness, and empower us to go back into the world changed, eager to share God's transforming power with our neighbors and ready to do all we can to build justice and peace in the world.

Worship services exist primarily for the believers who want to wor-

8. Kurt Marquardt, "Liturgy and Evangelism," in *Lutheran Worship: History and Practice,* ed. Fred L. Precht (St. Louis: Concordia, 1993), p. 26.

9. Gaddy, *The Gift of Worship,* pp. 42-43.

ship God — though we certainly also want them to be welcoming for those who do not yet know how to worship the true God. Also, most visitors come to a congregational worship service with a friend, and most conversions occur through the influence of a friend. Because of these truths, our primary criterion for worship with regard to individuals, as discussed in Chapter 6, is not what attracts visitors but what attracts them to lasting change and what makes members strong enough in faith to reach out to nonbelievers. We must constantly ask in planning if our worship is equipping people with the kind of character that will be eager to witness to neighbors, family members, work colleagues, or strangers. Is worship forming us to yearn ardently for the privilege of worshiping and serving God?

Many churches today do not seem to be nurturing such character in worshipers. From his "exit interview" research, Hendricks concludes that many Christians suffer from a "spiritual version of chronic fatigue syndrome." This refers to people who have not left the faith and might not even have left their parish, but though they were actively involved in congregational life in the past, they seem now "to suffer from a low-grade virus of discontent." Hendricks observes that "if you hear that hacking cough of joylessness enough times from enough people, you have to start wondering what's going on." He inquires, "Why is it that so many people don't really *like* their churches — yet don't dislike them enough to leave, either? At least, not until something happens to trigger an out, such as a conflict or an alternative that looks better?"

Hendricks guesses that perhaps a majority of Protestants feel this way about their congregations. This cannot be proved, but it is perilously significant "that at least *half* of those who claim to attend church attend once a month or less — not exactly a fervent loyalty to the program" (p. 152). What form must corporate worship take so that participants share the Psalmist's longing for the "courts of the LORD"? How can it be that so many contemporary Christians feel such little need for the gifts of community worship?

As Chapter 6 underscored, nurturing believers' character depends upon keeping God as the subject and object of worship. Hendricks exclaims, *"Theology makes a difference."* With almost every person he interviewed, "teaching about God, the body of Christ, the nature of humanity, sin, salvation, spiritual growth, and other theological issues made a profound difference in people's thinking, attitudes, and behavior" (p. 262).

Wade Clark Roof's research on the boomer generation revealed significant correlations between the disciplined training of children and their retention of the Christian faith. Roof discovered that "those brought up in a permissive child-rearing environment dropped out in far greater numbers and are also less likely to return to church or synagogue." On the other hand, those who portrayed their upbringing as more strict "did not drop out as much, and if they did drop out were more likely to return to active religious participation. A disciplined approach to bringing up children appears to instill religious values and the habits of religious observance."

Roof's research statistics indicate that more rigorous nurturing of the character of children leads to longer lasting faith. Whereas 64 percent of conservative Protestants are presently practicing Christians (39 percent loyalists and 25 percent returnees), only 55 percent of mainline Protestants are (31 percent loyalists and 24 percent returnees) — and 12 percent of those currently participating have switched from mainline to conservative churches.[10] Though we cannot derive any strong claims from these statistics, they do suggest that churches might be going in the wrong direction if they dumb down the faith in order to make it more appealing to the boomer generation. Those Christian communities that have taught the faith with greater thoroughness have a higher retention rate.

Action — in this case, worship participation — springs from a combination of knowledge, feelings, and will. Parishes that nourish the believer's whole character will continue to attract visitors because of the authentic praise of God in their midst and outside their walls.

Worship That Builds the Community Is a Lasting Attraction

Though William Hendricks gathered from his interviews *"no one overriding reason why people are leaving the church today"* (p. 259), one of the common themes registered was a longing for community (p. 260). In my visits to hundreds of churches in my freelance work, I have experienced truly welcoming communities as an exception rather than the rule. I have

10. Wade Clark Roof, *A Generation of Seekers* (San Francisco: HarperCollins, 1993), pp. 178-179.

learned the importance of Patrick Keifert's call for genuinely *public* worship into which anyone can enter, instead of cozy family-type rituals that leave many out. Furthermore, during worship times congregational members often do not assist strangers so that they can participate more easily, and after worship many Christians are too busy conversing with their own friends to welcome visitors.

It is crucial that worship nourish the character of both individuals and the community, for long-term attraction to the faith depends on reinforcing follow-up. Sociologists Benton Johnson, Dean Hoge, and Donald Luidens discovered that all the programs Presbyterian churches offered "did not produce a commitment sufficiently strong to sustain itself in a milieu of family and peers in which religion was rarely mentioned." Children were most likely to continue in faith if their parents were highly committed Christians. Thus worship services cannot have as their goal simply an appeal to nonmembers. We must plan worship with substance enough to root people in faith, to establish a community of care. Johnson, Hoge, and Luidens insist that "to be effective, even the best conceived program of religious education needs the reinforcement of a rich discursive follow-up in a circle of strong believers."[11]

As Chapter 7 discussed, in order to be such a circle that welcomes and nourishes strangers, churches must be a "company of committed individuals whose lives depend upon the truth that Jesus Christ is Lord." Douglas Webster warns that we "must not obscure this truth by transforming a congregation into an audience, transforming proclamation into performance or transforming worship into entertainment." If we forget the distinction between public opinion and biblical confession in a false attempt merely to attract crowds to Jesus, genuine Christian community will vanish in the process. "If 'unchurched Harry' feels perfectly at home in our churches, then chances are that we have no longer an authentic household of faith, but a popular cultural religion."[12]

Congregations must really be the Church. This means that they won't appeal to masses of outsiders, but the attraction they do offer will be life-changing, lasting. As Stanley Hauerwas and William Willimon ad-

11. Benton Johnson, Dean R. Hoge, and Donald A. Luidens, "Mainline Churches: The Real Reasons for Decline," *First Things* 31 (March 1993): 16.

12. Douglas D. Webster, *Selling Jesus* (Downers Grove, IL: InterVarsity Press, 1992), pp. 16-17.

monish us, the Church is composed of "resident aliens" who seek to influence the world

> by being the church, that is, by being something the world is not and can never be, lacking the gift of faith and vision, which is ours in Christ. The confessing church seeks the visible church, a place, clearly visible to the world, in which people are faithful to their promises, love their enemies, tell the truth, honor the poor, suffer for righteousness, and thereby testify to the amazing community-creating power of God. The confessing church has no interest in withdrawing from the world, but it is not surprised when its witness evokes hostility from the world. . . . This church knows that its most credible form of witness (and the most "effective" thing it can do for the world) is the actual creation of a living, breathing, visible community of faith.[13]

The Church's worship ought not to be so "alien" that it does not communicate with the culture around it, but at the same time it dare not be so "resident" as to empty the gospel of its transforming power. Chapters 8 through 10 explored the balancing of this dialectic in practical terms with regard to music, sermons, and liturgy. In all of our worship planning we will ask for forms that evoke the living community of faith, that train us to be the confessing Church.

The Church Is Responsible to the World

One critical way in which the Church can reach out to the culture surrounding it is through its influence on society itself. That a multitude of churches are failing in this outreach is manifested both in the perceptions of congregational members and in those of the public.

The people Hendricks interviewed said very little about the social implications of the gospel. He found it "most disturbing" that, "for the most part, there was a deafening silence when it came to making a connection between spirituality and matters of social concern — the poor, justice, human rights, the environment, issues of public policy, and so on." Hendricks admits that he might have posed the wrong questions, but he

---

13. Stanley Hauerwas and William H. Willimon, *Resident Aliens* (Nashville: Abingdon, 1989), pp. 46-47.

also wonders if the seeming lack of concern stems from a privatistic view of religion that focuses on piety and devotional life without extending the benefits of the gospel beyond the personal (p. 259). What about the public implications of faith? In a large city, my brother searched for three years before finding a strong congregation that integrally connected faith with the world's needs for justice in its worship.

In this television age, in which many persons' "information-action" ratio is vastly reduced (as discussed in Chapter 2), the Church must find ways to nourish active, public responses to the truth it proclaims. Our worship must not only build awareness of the world's needs under God's cosmic care but also challenge and empower participants to join in God's purposes for responding to those needs as agents of his care. We do not want to attract people to worship simply for their own benefit but also to engage them in spreading the generosity of God's love throughout the world.

The privatist trajectory of contemporary churches is also perceived by public observers. In a national poll, 62 percent claimed that religious influence on their own lives was increasing while 16 percent said it was decreasing — but only 21 percent thought that the influence of religion on American life was increasing, while 65 percent suspected that it is decreasing. Jeffrey Sheler's report in *U.S. News and World Report* suggested that "the extent to which religion is marginalized and excluded from public discourse may well be related to the growing trend toward self-focused religion and a 'spirituality turned inward.' "[14] This is not to say that churches should secure a greater public role by "finding a stronger voice" in the "councils of government"; rather, as Avery Dulles notes, the Church's "proper sphere of competence" has always been "in religious and moral formation."[15]

Worship must primarily provide this formation. As God's passion for justice is proclaimed, God's people are nurtured in the same character. Unless God's global care is fully displayed in formative music, Word, and liturgy, worshipers will continue to have little influence on the public sphere.

14. Jeffrey L. Sheler, "Spiritual America," *U.S. News and World Report* 116, no. 13 (4 April 1993): 50.

15. Sheler, "Spiritual America," p. 50.

A Passion for the Gospel

In this critical time when churches are rapidly decreasing in numbers and influence, how should Christian communities respond? For many, the answer has been to change their worship style, but this is not enough, unless a congregation's entire ethos is changed in the process. In fact, the opposite is often the case, for the new worship styles of many parishes focus inward on the individual instead of outward for the world's sake. Then members and visitors only ask what worship means for them and what they can get out of it. Arthur Just asserts that this "has serious ramifications not only for our liturgiology and ecclesiology, but for our missiology as well." Outreach programs will continue to fail because, if "the vision of the worshiper is inward and the goal educational, then it is almost impossible to shape an evangelical vision for the church that is outward and transforming."[16] Our worship should cause us to ask instead, Who is God? How does God want to use me and the community to which I belong for his purposes in the world? How does worship form us to be God's people for this place and time?

Worship for the sake of the culture around us will not cater to that culture but will clearly communicate to the pluralist public the basics of the faith.[17] Leander Keck calls for a "new apologetics" — not "to dispel opposition, nor to make the Christian faith acceptable to that elusive thing called 'the modern (or postmodern) mind,'" but "to present the Christian faith and its tradition as an intelligible and plausible construal of reality" (p. 107).

Keck berates churches that are "spooked by the charge that concern for thorough and accurate knowledge, clear thinking, concise expression, and thoughtful use of the English language are the marks of an elitism that must go," as evidenced by the "shoddy thinking and incompetent use of our language" found in many worship attempts to appeal to the general public. God's people will fulfill their vocation for the culture's sake only if we can communicate effectively who we are, what we believe, and what difference that can make (p. 110).

---

16. Arthur A. Just, "Liturgical Renewal in the Parish," in Precht, ed., *Lutheran Worship*, p. 29.

17. Keck, *The Church Confident*, p. 105. Page references to this book in the following paragraphs are given parenthetically in the text.

This requires a passion for the gospel and for other people. Keck insists that we must recover the conviction "that one *ought to be Christian,*" that "the gospel is true enough that believing it makes a decisive difference at the center of one's life." Christians should be characterized by "a deep love and compassion for persons whose lives are in disarray because they do not or cannot yet rely on their Creator, are not yet rightly related to their God" (p. 116).

This double passion is nurtured by authentic worship — but statistics, interviews, and my personal experience all suggest that such worship is noticeably lacking in many churches. As a result, Christianity overall is gradually declining in numbers and influence.

Is there hope for the Church? Hendricks insists that there is. This hope is

> the very sure hope of Jesus' promises that He would build His church and nothing, not even hell itself, would overcome it. However, nothing in the promise obligates Christ to maintain "our" church. He has committed Himself only to building *a* church, *His* church.
>
> So the issue is not how to get people back into churches, but how to make our churches into His Church. (p. 253)

This book's questions and reflections are one attempt to help us be Christ's Church more faithfully in our worship. It is not important that you agree with everything that has been said in these pages. What is important is that we keep asking questions and never think that we have arrived at the answer, for that will become a new idolatry.

The Church at the turn of the century must reject many reigning idolatries by asking better questions. As Neil Postman declares in his fight against some gods of the television age, "To ask is to break the spell."[18]

18. Neil Postman, *Amusing Ourselves to Death* (New York: Viking Penguin, 1985), p. 161.

12. The Church as Its Own Worst Enemy: Is It Happening Again?

Whatever else is true, it is emphatically not true that the ideas of Jesus of Nazareth were suitable to His time, but no longer suitable to our time. Exactly how suitable they were to His time is perhaps suggested in the end of His story.

G. K. Chesterton

The Origins of Unbelief in the United States

In research for his book *Without God, Without Creed: The Origins of Unbelief,* James Turner expected to find the usual answer to the question of how modern thought "simply dispensed with God." Various pieces of the puzzle had already been studied — "Renaissance and Enlightenment skepticism, the effects of Biblical criticism, the impact of Darwinism on theology, the rise of scientific naturalism, the implications of post-Cartesian philosophy, and more." This work implanted "a vague but compelling impression that the rise of science, and the spread of critical ways of thinking associated with science, undermined belief in God." Recent historical scholarship highlights also "the effects of industrialization, urbanization, and technological change, as well as the less easily

297

defined social change labeled secularization." Above all other corrosive forces occasionally nominated, "scholars usually identify science and socioeconomic change as the sources of God's problems."[1]

Turner expected that his own attempt to track the origins of unbelief would point to these answers as the primary causes. He reports his enormously disturbing findings as follows:

> The individual elements . . . conformed to anticipated contours, but the contours together produced a surprising picture, almost a photographic negative of what I had expected to see. Though both science and social transformation loom large in the picture, neither caused unbelief. . . . Put briefly, unbelief was not something that 'happened *to*' religion.
>
> On the contrary, religion caused unbelief. In trying to adapt their religious beliefs to socioeconomic change, to new moral challenges, to novel problems of knowledge, to the tightening standards of science, the defenders of God slowly strangled Him. (p. xiii)

In his prologue, Turner begins with the Middle Ages and argues that at that time it was difficult, but not impossible, to reject Christianity. All alternative religious traditions also assumed the existence of some sort of God. Turner observes that during that era "so interwoven was God with daily life and with the workings of nature that virtual extraction from one's surroundings would have been necessary to make unbelief plausible" (p. 2).

Turner is not talking about uniformity of belief or its effectiveness, but about the "*assumed reality* of God" that was "twined inextricably" through everyone's life. Belief seemed "not so much a formal tenet as an apperception hovering around the edges of consciousness." It "almost verged on a felt sense of the structure of things, in the way that one 'believes' in the change of the seasons or the rising of the sun." That is why it was such a monumental shift that by the late nineteenth century "unbelief had become a fully available option." Consequently Turner must ask, "If God permeated the world, how could normal people cease to

---

1. James Turner, *Without God, Without Creed: The Origins of Unbelief in America* (Baltimore: The Johns Hopkins University Press, 1985), p. xii. Page references to this book in this chapter are given parenthetically in the text.

believe in Him? How could a culture dispense with one of its most deeply rooted, most essential axioms?" (p. 4)

Turner tracks the answer through forces such as the Reformation, state power, religious toleration undermining ecclesiastical sway, economic innovations, capitalism, technology, printing, trade, and other children of capitalism (pp. 9-11). Especially he notes the effects of a new secularized structure for intellectual life that was "less subject to churchly restraints, more open to conflicting ideas, less apt to stultify or freeze out questioning about God and His ways," developed just when ecclesiastical authority was tottering (p. 13).

It goes far beyond our purposes here to trace Turner's entire exposition through the flowering of seventeenth-century mysticism and the move of church leaders toward rationalization or to a pietism that denied reason's primacy. He sketches eighteenth-century responses in rationalized and moralized belief (pp. 35-72), the nineteenth-century rise of evangelicalism, and new innovations in intuition as knowledge and in religion as emotional response (pp. 73-113).

The conclusion of Turner's exposition of four centuries of changes is, however, significant for our purposes here. He summarizes, "It is hard to conceive of a religion more up-to-date, more finely tuned to changing social realities." But the price of this timeliness was that "baffling and offensive antiquities . . . had to be softened or cast away." Thus religion became "plunged more deeply into the needs and wishes of human beings — or a God sculpted more closely to the image of man" (p. 113).

Turner then describes several social changes that pushed "God's direct presence farther from everyday experience into an intangible spiritual realm" (p. 119), the status reduction of the clerical vocation (p. 121), and the change in conception of knowledge to include the need for verification by personal experience (p. 132). All the confusions that Christianity was weathering (pp. 141-67) included the rise of various heresies, especially transcendentalism, which was the largest influence because of its literary impact (p. 163).

In concluding his book's first part, "Modern Belief, 1500-1865," Turner remarks, "It was a supreme irony that the Christian churches had, by their own teachings about God and the road to Him, contributed so richly to the mess in which they now found themselves" (p. 167). They thus prepared for the period that forms the subject of the book's second part, "Modern Unbelief, 1865-1890," in which Turner explores these three aspects that engendered unbelief:

> (1) intellectual uncertainties about belief that produced the conviction that knowledge of God lay beyond human powers, if such a Being existed; (2) moral problems with belief that led to the rejection as immoral of belief in God and the erection of a nontheistic morality; and (3) the transfer of reverence from God to other ideals. (p. 172)

Turner's conclusions on each of these three topics are significant for the subject of this chapter.

In his chapter entitled "The Intellectual Crisis of Belief" (pp. 171-202), Turner demonstrates how "religious leaders had themselves to blame if some members of their flock inclined to give science a quitclaim to knowledge" (p. 192), for "it was, after all, theologians and ministers who had welcomed this secular visitor into the house of God" and "who had obscured the difference between natural and supernatural knowledge, between the tangible things of this world and the impalpable things of another" (p. 193). Thus Turner concludes that the churches

> played a major role in softening up belief. Theologians had been too unwilling to allow God to be incomprehensible, too insistent on bringing Him within the compass of mundane human knowledge, too anxious to link belief with science, too neglectful of other roads to knowledge, too insensitive to noncognitive ways of apprehending reality — *too forgetful*, in short, *of much of their own traditions as they tried to make God up-to-date.* And the leaders of the churches got away with this as long as science depended on God, as long as the new conception of knowledge that science exemplified did not reach its ultimate conclusion. But when it did, theology paid the price for ignoring the complexity of the question of God, for suppressing the transcendent mystery that was supposed to exceed human understanding. One might say that most theologians had lost faith long before any Victorian agnostics. (p. 202, emphasis added)

Turner's chapter entitled "The Immorality of Belief" (pp. 203-25) discusses questions of theodicy, authority, truth, progress, and compromises with evil. In this case, the error of the theologians and ministers ("their blasphemy") was to forget the tensions that must exist between humans' wishes and the Creator's intentions. "*They had let gather dust the ancient wisdom* that creation transcended human grasp" (p. 224, emphasis added).

In the chapter entitled "A More Excellent Way" (pp. 226-47), Turner deals with agnostics' inheritance of the churches' morality because of church leaders' enthusiasm for the idea of progress. Turner grieves that "the guardians of belief thus paved the road to unbelief" because their faith in progress

> only capped a longer and larger trend. For generations now, a growing number of ministers and theologians had understood the need to get right with modernity. The most influential *had courted modernity by playing down the antique teaching* that God transcended human grasp and human purposes, that His ways were not man's. They had talked instead of God's congruence with the business of this world. They had spoken mostly of morality rather than spirituality, of religion's uses in the palpable human world rather than its difficult and tenuous straining toward some purported other realm. . . . With this strategy *church leaders kept religion in tune with the secular world,* but sometimes at the price of allowing this world to call the tune for God. . . .
>
> More than a little irony lurked here. Leaders of the church were surely not wrong to insist that belief had to express itself in practice, that faith and morality were linked, that any God worth credence had to provide some grounding for human moral striving. But they had *neglected tensions in their own ancient traditions.* (pp. 245, 247, emphasis added)

In his final chapter, "Sanctity without Godliness" (pp. 248-61), Turner shows how agnostics found replacements to satisfy the profound spiritual hungers formerly assuaged by belief — consolation in loss and grief, security against fears and chaos, orientation in uncertainty. "Perhaps most universally, God offers a sacred center on which to release feelings of awe, dependency, exaltation, and reverence springing from the deepest wells of the mind" (p. 248). Again, "God's official agents had helped to arrange for His displacement" (p. 253) by art and nature and a religion of humanity.

Various developments external to religion generated the milieu in which unbelief grew — the rise of modern science, social and economic change, the unsettling caused by industrialization and urbanization — but, "in the final analysis, these forces only raised new questions; it was religious leaders who gave the answers." It was their reactions to the external exigencies and not the strains themselves that shaped unbelief. "In the end, the most influential church leaders *tried to protect belief by making peace with modernity, by conceiving God and His purposes in terms as nearly compatible as possible with secular understandings and aims.*" Though "a minority insisted that a transcendent God must utterly elude human grasp[,] their case, their God seemed too out of step, too remote" (p. 260, emphasis added).

Turner's epilogue (pp. 262-69) presents a powerful summary of the way in which thinking about God had moved "away from the nonhuman and transcendent, toward the human and worldly. And it is this new posture toward God, this growing worldliness of belief" that appears most often when the attempt is made to explain the possibility of unbelief. It is the "crucial ingredient . . . in the mix." To put it precisely, "unbelief resulted from the decisions that influential church leaders — lay writers, theologians, ministers — made about how to confront the modern pressures upon religious belief." Some of these responses were not the products of careful reflection, but "the choices, taken together, boiled down to a decision *to deal with modernity by embracing it — to defuse modern threats to the traditional bases of belief by bringing God into line with modernity*" (p. 266, emphasis added). Turner concludes as follows:

> They were not mistaken in believing that any resilient belief must ground itself in human thought and experience. But they frequently forgot the tension that, by definition, must exist between an incomprehensible God and the human effort to know Him. They were hardly fools to insist that any God must be lord of this world, but they did not always remember that this world could not define Him. . . .
>
> Put slightly differently, unbelief emerged because church leaders too often forgot the transcendence essential to any worthwhile God. . . . They did this because, trying to meet the challenge of modernity, they virtually surrendered to it. These ministers and theologians well understood that belief could not continue in its old tracks. They did not grasp firmly enough that it did not simply have to jump to the new, that belief could modify secular wisdom in the very process of adapting to it. (p. 267)

The lesson to be drawn from all of this, Turner suggests, is that those who believe in God dare not whittle God down to make him accessible to our human comprehension — that is, if we want belief to last over the long haul. "The universe is not tailored to our measurements. Forgetting that, many believers lost their God" (p. 269).

Is It Happening Again?

I have summarized and quoted Turner so extensively because the lesson he teaches is so often overlooked in the worship wars at this turn of the century. Turner makes it clear that faith was lost, not because churches did not adapt themselves to changes in the culture around them, but because they sacrificed the wisdom of their traditions too eagerly and too submissively in favor of capitulating to societal idolatries and demands. What might have happened if theologians and ministers had instead responded to the cultural challenges with careful reflection and dialectical balancing of old and new?

Turner shows clearly that threats from the culture in which the Church resided were not the cause of unbelief; rather, responses to these threats were. Church leaders reacted by making basic changes in the Church itself — to its own destruction. Is the same thing happening today in connection with congregational worship? Consider the following trends:

- many parishes are responding to the immediacy and superficiality of the television age with television-style music and performers that prevent worship from being "the work of the people";
- many churches react to the boomer generation's emphasis on choice by offering variety without continuity;
- many congregations are joining the postmodernist stream of root-lessness by discarding the Church's historic traditions;
- many worship leaders are falling prey to the gods of this age — to idolatries of success, numbers, money, power, fame, and popularity;
- many preachers offer therapeutic self-help instead of keeping God as the subject and object of their sermons and the congregation's praise;
- many church leaders accede to "endangered minds" by dumbing down the faith or feeding only the emotions instead of building character;
- many worship participants seek their own individual comfort instead of understanding themselves as part of an ongoing community of God's people who live out the social implications of the gospel.

All of these responses by the churches to the threats of the surrounding culture result in endangered faith. It is true that our worship must be in the vernacular so that it is accessible to members and visitors alike. However, worship that truly keeps God as the subject and object will remain subversive. As we seek to respond especially to the boomer and buster generations in a postmodern, technologized age, we can speak the language of the people without losing the subversive nature of faith in our worship.

Will we let a process similar to the one Turner describes happen again? We will if the extreme "traditionalists" or "contemporaryists" win the worship wars, for the former will prevent us from adapting to changing times, and the latter will adapt to the changes without the wisdom of the past.

There is an alternative. We could ask better questions. We could plan worship that keeps God as the subject, that nurtures the character of the believer, that forms the Christian community to be a people who reach out in God's purposes to the world.

Our worship could reach out without dumbing down the faith, but in order for this to happen we must ask better questions. This book is written with the hope and prayer that it will engender some of them.

APPENDIX

A Series of Children's Sermons on the Church's Historic Liturgy

These children's sermons on various elements of the liturgy were offered at the point in the service when the liturgical piece usually takes place. To keep this brief, I will simply list the moment when the message should be given, the subject of the sermon, the physical action for the children to make, and the lesson to be gained.

1. Time: At the usual place for the children's sermon after the Gospel reading.
   Subject: Epiphany colors and banners.
   Action: Walking around to look at symbols on altar, lectern, pulpit, and banners.
   Lesson: In different seasons of the Church year we see special colors and symbols to remind us of what Christ did for us. In the Epiphany season, gold crowns him King.

2. Time: After opening announcements.
   Subject: Acolytes bow at the altar before and after lighting the candles to signify reverence for the holy place, this house of worship.
   Action: After watching acolytes and discussing why they bowed, children go to communion rail and bow together.
   Lesson: We act differently when we are in worship to remember that this is a special time and place to meet God.

3. Time: After opening announcements.
   Subject: The organ prelude.
   Action: Listening to three different kinds of preludes — a trumpet fanfare, a Lenten meditation, and a chorale melody in the pedal.
   Lesson: Organ preludes help us prepare for worship by directing our thoughts to God, quieting our busy minds, introducing a hymn tune, leading us in prayer.

4. Time: Before confession.
   Subject: Why we need confession.
   Action: Kneeling at the altar rail.
   Lesson: Humbleness before the holiness of God and Joy in forgiveness.

5. Time: The usual place for the children's sermon.
   Subject: Lent colors and banner.
   Action: Counting the crosses.
   Lesson: The value of Lent for repentance and for meditating on all that Christ did for us.

6. Time: Before the prayer of the day.
   Subject: Responses, "The Lord be with you" and "And also with you."
   Action: Extending hands to the pastor when we speak or sing to him just as he extends his hands to us.
   Lesson: Enfolding the pastor in God's love and ours.

7. Time: Before the First Lesson.
   Subject: Location of Bible passages.
   Action: Turning in the Bible to the places for the First Lesson, Epistle, and Gospel.
   Lesson: Why we have three lessons each Sunday and the relationship between the parts of the Bible.

8. Time: After the opening Palm procession.
   Subject: Palm/Passion Sunday.
   Action: Waving the palms as we walk in, clapping hands perhaps as the modern version, falling on our face on the floor.

Lesson: How would we respond if Jesus came in here to be with us today? How do we honor Jesus, the King of all?

9. Time: Before the Gospel Lesson.
Subject: Responses, "Glory to you, O Lord" before the Gospel and "Praise to you, O Christ" after.
Action: Singing the responses and jumping to our feet.
Lesson: Eagerness to hear and gratitude for hearing the Gospel; preparing for the first high point of the worship service.

10. Time: Before the offertory.
Subject: Offerings.
Action: Passing the baskets, wondering if we could put ourselves in.
Lesson: God owns all of us, and we give him a part of our money to remember that.

11. Time: Before Communion.
Subject: Responses and the Words of Institution.
Action: Getting ready for the Eucharist — bringing in the bread and wine.
Lesson: Preparing for the second high point of the service.

12. Time: In the middle of the choir festival.
Subject: Music in various styles.
Action: Children learn an easy descant to a hymn and sing it accompanied by several adults and children playing flutes.
Lesson: Using our gifts to praise God.

(This message could be divided into two — one to emphasize styles of music and one to emphasize offering our gifts like the young flute players.)

Works Cited

Achtemeier, Elizabeth. "An Excellent Woman." *The Christian Century* 110, no. 24 (22 Aug.-1 Sept. 1993): 808-9.

Alexander, John. "Bleeding Hearts: How Church Communities Can Flourish." *The Other Side* 29, no. 3 (May-June 1993): 61-63.

———. "Bleeding Hearts: Jobs against the Church." *The Other Side* 29, no. 4 (July-Aug. 1993): 52-54.

Asimakoupoulos, Greg. "Please Take Out Your Hymnal." *Discipleship Journal* 82 (July/Aug. 1994): 24-27.

Aune, Michael. "*Lutheran Book of Worship:* Relic or Resource?" *dialog* 33, no. 3 (Summer 1994): 174-82.

Barna, George. *The Frog in the Kettle: What Christians Need to Know about Life in the Year 2000*. Ventura, CA: Regal Books, 1990.

———. *Marketing the Church: What They Never Taught You About Church Growth*. Colorado Springs, CO: NavPress, 1988.

———. *User Friendly Churches: What Christians Need to Know about the Churches People Love to Go to*. Ventura, CA: Regal Books, 1991.

Barna, George, and William Paul McKay. *Vital Signs: Emerging Social Trends and the Future of American Christianity*. Westchester, IL: Crossway Books, 1984.

Barna Research Group. *National and International Religion Report* (21 March 1994), as cited in *Discipleship Journal* 14, no. 4 (July/Aug. 1994): 14.

Bartlett, David L. "Texts Shaping Sermons." *Listening to the Word: Studies in Honor of Fred B. Craddock*, pp. 147-63. Edited by Gail R. O'Day and Thomas G. Long. Nashville: Abingdon Press, 1993.

Beker, J. Christiaan. *Suffering and Hope: The Biblical Vision and the Human Predicament*. Grand Rapids: William B. Eerdmans, 1994.

Bellah, Robert N., and Christopher Freeman Adams. "Strong Institutions, Good City." *The Christian Century* 111, no. 19 (15-22 June 1994): 604-7.

Bellah, Robert; Richard Madsen; William M. Sullivan; Ann Swidler; and Steven M. Tipton. *Habits of the Heart: Individualism and Commitment in American Life.* Berkeley: University of California Press, 1985.

Benne, Robert. "Cambridge Evangelicals." *The Christian Century* 110, no. 30 (27 Oct. 1993): 1036-38.

Bly, Carol. *Letters from the Country.* New York: Penguin Books, 1981.

Bobier, Michelle. "A Baptist Among the Episcopalians." *New Oxford Review* 59, no. 6 (July-Aug. 1992): 13-16.

Bounds, E. M. *Power Through Prayer.* Edited by Penelope J. Stokes. Minneapolis: World Wide Publications, 1989.

Brauer, James L. "The Church Year." *Lutheran Worship: History and Practice,* pp. 146-74. Edited by Fred L. Precht. St. Louis: Concordia, 1993.

Brueggemann, Walter. *Biblical Perspectives on Evangelism: Living in a Three-Storied Universe.* Nashville: Abingdon, 1993.

————. *Finally Comes the Poet: Daring Speech for Proclamation.* Minneapolis: Fortress, 1989.

————. *Israel's Praise: Doxology against Idolatry and Ideology.* Philadelphia: Fortress, 1988.

————. *The Message of the Psalms: A Theological Commentary.* Augsburg Old Testament Studies. Minneapolis: Augsburg, 1984.

Buttrick, David. "Who Is Listening?" *Listening to the Word: Studies in Honor of Fred B. Craddock,* pp. 189-206. Edited by Gail R. O'Day and Thomas G. Long. Nashville: Abingdon, 1993.

Caemmerer, Richard R. *Preaching for the Church.* St. Louis: Concordia, 1959.

Christensen, Bernhard. *The Inward Pilgrimage: Spiritual Classics from Augustine to Bonhoeffer.* Minneapolis: Augsburg, 1976.

"Converting Others Not a High Priority." *The Christian Century* 111, no. 19 (15-22 June 1994): 601.

Coupland, Douglas. *Generation X: Tales for an Accelerated Culture.* New York: St. Martin Press, 1991.

————. *Life after God.* New York: Pocket Books, 1994.

Dawn, Marva J. "The Concept of 'The Principalities and Powers' in the Works of Jacques Ellul." Ph.D. dissertation, University of Notre Dame, 1992.

————. *The Hilarity of Community: Romans 12 and How to Be the Church.* Grand Rapids: William B. Eerdmans, 1992.

————. *Joy in Our Weakness: A Gift of Hope from the Book of Revelation.* St. Louis: Concordia, 1994.

————. *Keeping the Sabbath Wholly: Ceasing, Resting, Embracing, Feasting.* Grand Rapids: William B. Eerdmans, 1989.

———. *Sexual Character: Beyond Technique to Intimacy.* Grand Rapids: William B. Eerdmans, 1993.

———. "What the Bible *Really* Says about War." *The Other Side* 29, no. 2 (March-April 1993): 56-59.

Dean, William. "What Nixon Knew." *The Christian Century* 111, no. 16 (11 May 1994): 484-86.

Dearmer, Percy. *The Story of the Prayer Book.* New York: Oxford University Press, 1933.

Downey, Sabine. "Out in the Open." *The Christian Century* 111, no. 13 (20 April 1994): 406-7.

Dulles, Avery. "Tradition and Creativity in Theology." *First Things* 27 (Nov. 1992): 20-27.

Dyrness, William. *How Does America Hear the Gospel?* Grand Rapids: William B. Eerdmans, 1989.

Ellul, Jacques. *The Ethics of Freedom.* Translated by Geoffrey W. Bromiley. Grand Rapids: William B. Eerdmans, 1976.

———. *The Humiliation of the Word.* Translated by Joyce Main Hanks. Grand Rapids: William B. Eerdmans, 1985.

———. *Jesus and Marx: From Gospel to Ideology.* Translated by Joyce Main Hanks. Grand Rapids: William B. Eerdmans, 1988.

———. *The Meaning of the City.* Translated by Dennis Pardee. Grand Rapids: William B. Eerdmans, 1970.

———. *The New Demons.* Translated by C. Edward Hopkin. New York: Seabury Press, 1975.

———. "Notes Innocentes Sur la 'Question Herméneutique.'" *L'Evangile, Hier et Aujourd'hui: Melanges Offerts au Professeur Franz J. Leehardt,* pp. 181-90. Genève: Editions Labor et Fides, 1968.

———. *Propaganda: The Formation of Men's Attitudes.* Translated by Konrad Kellen and Jean Lerner. New York: Alfred A. Knopf, 1965.

———. *Reason for Being: A Meditation on Ecclesiastes.* Translated by Joyce Main Hanks. Grand Rapids: William B. Eerdmans, 1990.

———. *The Subversion of Christianity.* Translated by Geoffrey W. Bromiley. Grand Rapids: William B. Eerdmans, 1986.

———. *The Technological Bluff.* Translated by Geoffrey W. Bromiley. Grand Rapids: William B. Eerdmans, 1990.

———. *The Technological Society.* Translated by John Wilkinson. New York: Vintage Books, 1964.

———. *The Technological System.* Translated by Joachim Neugroschel. New York: Continuum, 1980.

———. *Violence: Reflections from a Christian Perspective.* Translated by Cecelia Gaul Kings. New York: Seabury Press, 1969.

Frei, Hans. *The Eclipse of Biblical Narrative: A Study in Enlightenment and Nineteenth-Century Hermeneutics.* New York: Yale University Press, 1974.

Gaddy, C. Welton. *The Gift of Worship.* Nashville: Broadman Press, 1992.

Gawronski, Raymond T. "Why Orthodox Catholics Look to Zen." *New Oxford Review* 60, no. 6 (July-Aug. 1993): 13-16.

Gieschen, Thomas. "Contemporary Christian Music: Problems and Possibilities." Unpublished paper presented at "Lectures in Church Music," Concordia University, River Forest, IL, 6 Nov. 1986.

Glendon, Mary Ann. "Tradition and Creativity in Culture and Law." *First Things* 27 (Nov. 1992): 13-19.

Green, Bernard D. "Catholicism Confronts New Age Syncretism." *New Oxford Review* 61, no. 3 (April 1994): 18-22.

Grindal, Gracia. "To Translate Is to Betray: Trying to Hand the Lutheran Tradition On." *dialog* 33, no. 3 (Summer 1994): 183-90.

Guinness, Os. *Dining with the Devil: The Megachurch Movement Flirts with Modernity.* Grand Rapids: Baker Book House, 1993.

Hauerwas, Stanley, and William H. Willimon. *Resident Aliens.* Nashville: Abingdon, 1989.

Healy, Jane M. *Endangered Minds: Why Our Children Don't Think.* New York: Simon and Schuster, 1990.

Heim, David. "Sophia's Choice." *The Christian Century* 111, no. 11 (6 April 1994): 339-40.

Hendricks, William D. *Exit Interviews: Revealing Stories of Why People Are Leaving the Church.* Chicago: Moody Press, 1993.

Hendricksen, David. "Observations Regarding Worship, Carpet, and Music." Unpublished paper.

Himmelfarb, Gertrude. "Tradition and Creativity in the Writing of History." *First Things* 27 (Nov. 1992): 28-36.

Horstman, Joey Earl. "Channel Too: The Postmodern Yawn." *The Other Side* 29, no. 3 (May-June 1993): 34-35.

Hoyt, Will. "On the Difference Between a Hero and an Apostle." *New Oxford Review* 61, no. 3 (April 1994): 23-24.

Hunt, Michael J., C.S.P. *College Catholics: A New Counter-Culture.* New York: Paulist Press, 1993.

Hunter, Graeme. "Evil: Back in Bad Company." *First Things* 41 (March 1994): 36-41.

Hymnal of the Moravian Church. Bethlehem, PA: Department of Publications and Communications, Moravian Church, 1969.

Jacobs, Alan. "To Read and to Live." *First Things* 34 (June/July 1993): 24-31.

Johnson, Benton; Dean R. Hoge; and Donald A. Luidens. "Mainline Churches: The Real Reason for Decline." *First Things* 31 (March 1993): 13-18.

Just, Arthur A. "Liturgical Renewal in the Parish." *Lutheran Worship: History and Practice,* pp. 21-43. Edited by Fred L. Precht. St. Louis: Concordia, 1993.

————. "Liturgy and Culture." *Lutheran Worship Notes* 27 (Autumn 1993): 1-2.

Kavanagh, Eva. "Prayer of the Flesh." *The Other Side* 29, no. 3 (May-June 1993): 56-60.

Keck, Leander E. *The Church Confident.* Nashville: Abingdon, 1993.

————. "Romans in the Pulpit: Form and Formation in Romans 5:1-11." *Listening to the Word: Studies in Honor of Fred B. Craddock,* pp. 77-90. Edited by Gail R. O'Day and Thomas G. Long. Nashville: Abingdon, 1993.

Keifert, Patrick R. *Welcoming the Stranger: A Public Theology of Worship and Evangelism.* Minneapolis: Fortress, 1992.

Kennan, George F. "American Addictions: Bad Habits and Government Indifference." *New Oxford Review* 60, no. 5 (June 1993): 14-25.

————. *Around the Cragged Hill: A Personal and Political Philosophy.* New York: W. W. Norton, 1993.

Kolden, Marc. "Homosexual Ordination: The Real Issue?" *dialog* 33, no. 3 (Summer 1994): 163-64.

LaCugna, Catherine Mowry. "Freeing the Christian Imagination." *dialog* 33, no. 3 (Summer 1994): 191-95.

Lasch, Christopher. *The Culture of Narcissism: American Life in an Age of Diminishing Expectations.* New York: W. W. Norton, 1979.

L'Engle, Madeleine. *The Love Letters.* New York: Farrar, Straus and Giroux, 1966.

Leupold, Ulrich S. "Introduction to Volume 53." *Liturgy and Hymns,* pp. xiii-xx. Edited by Ulrich S. Leupold. Volume 53 in *Luther's Works.* Helmut T. Lehmann, general editor. Philadelphia: Fortress, 1965.

Lewis, C. S. *Letters to Malcolm: Chiefly on Prayer.* New York: Harcourt, Brace and World, 1963.

Lischer, Richard. "Preaching as the Church's Language." *Listening to the Word: Studies in Honor of Fred B. Craddock,* pp. 113-30. Edited by Gail R. O'Day and Thomas G. Long. Nashville: Abingdon, 1993.

————. *A Theology of Preaching: The Dynamics of the Gospel.* Nashville: Abingdon, 1981.

Long, Thomas G. "And How Shall They Hear? The Listener in Contemporary Preaching." *Listening to the Word: Studies in Honor of Fred B. Craddock,* pp. 167-88. Edited by Gail R. O'Day and Thomas G. Long. Nashville: Abingdon, 1993.

Luther, Martin. "Concerning the Order of Public Worship" (1523). Translated by Paul Zeller Strodach. *Liturgy and Hymns,* pp. 9-14. Edited by Ulrich S. Leupold. Volume 53 in *Luther's Works.* Helmut T. Lehmann, general editor. Philadelphia: Fortress, 1965.

————. "An Order of Mass and Communion for the Church at Wittenberg"

(1523). Translated by Paul Zeller Strodach. *Liturgy and Hymns,* pp. 17-40. Edited by Ulrich S. Leupold. Volume 53 in *Luther's Works.* Helmut T. Lehmann, general editor. Philadelphia: Fortress, 1965.

Lutz, H. Benton. "The Self-Absorbed Masquerade." *The Other Side* 29, no. 4 (July-Aug. 1993): 44-47.

MacDonald, George. *The Curate's Awakening.* Edited by Michael R. Phillips. Minneapolis: Bethany House Publishers, 1985. (Originally published as *Thomas Wingfold, Curate* in 1876.)

————. *The Prodigal Apprentice.* Edited by Dan Hamilton. Wheaton, IL: Victor Books, 1984. (Originally published as *Guild Court* in 1867.)

Mahedy, William, and Janet Bernardi. *A Generation Alone: Xers Making a Place in the World.* Downers Grove, IL: InterVarsity Press, 1994.

Mankowski, Paul V. "The Skimpole Syndrome: Childhood Unlimited." *First Things* 33 (May 1993): 26-30.

Marquardt, Kurt. "Liturgy and Evangelism." *Lutheran Worship: History and Practice,* pp. 58-76. Edited by Fred L. Precht. St. Louis: Concordia, 1993.

Marty, Martin E. "Build a Parking Lot, and the People Will Come (and Go)." *Context* 25, no. 4 (15 Feb. 1993): 3-4.

————. "Holy Ground, Sacred Sound." Public lecture at Zion Lutheran Church, Portland, OR, Nov. 14, 1993.

————. "M.E.M.O.: The Cutting Edge." *The Christian Century* 110, no. 6 (24 Feb. 1993): 223.

————. "M.E.M.O.: Instrument of Grace." *The Christian Century* 109, no. 36 (9 Dec. 1992): 1151.

Mathewes-Green, Frederica. "The Kissing Part." *The Christian Century* 111, no. 12 (13 April 1994): 375.

Meyer, Lester. "A Lack of Laments in the Church's Use of the Psalter." *Lutheran Quarterly,* Spring 1993, pp. 67-71.

Mitchell, Henry. "The Hearer's Experience of the Word." *Listening to the Word: Studies in Honor of Fred B. Craddock,* pp. 223-41. Edited by Gail R. O'Day and Thomas G. Long. Nashville: Abingdon, 1993.

Mitchell, I. N. "Liturgy and Culture." *Worship* 65, no. 4 (July 1991): 364.

Mittleman, Alan L. Review of *Renewing the Covenant: A Theology for the Postmodern Jew* by Eugene Borowitz. *First Things* 30 (Feb. 1993): 45.

Moravian Daily Texts. Bethlehem, PA: Department of Publications and Communications, Moravian Church, 1994.

Mulholland, M. Robert, Jr. *Invitation to a Journey: A Road Map for Spiritual Formation.* Downers Grove, IL: InterVarsity Press, 1993.

Mullet, Steve. "Quick Quote." *Current Thoughts and Trends* 10, no. 3 (March 1994): 20.

Myerhoff, Barbara. *Number Our Days.* New York: Simon and Schuster, 1978.

Myers, Kenneth A. *All God's Children and Blue Suede Shoes: Christians and Popular Culture.* Westchester, IL: Crossway Books, 1989.

Neuhaus, Richard John. "The Innovationist Edge." *First Things* 27 (Nov. 1992): 64-66.

Nordin, John. "Can Traditional Ritual Be Evangelistic." *dialog* 33, no. 3 (Summer 1994): 229-30.

Nouwen, Henri J. M. *Behold the Beauty of the Lord: Praying with Icons.* Notre Dame: Ave Maria Press, 1987.

———. "Finding a New Way to Get a Glimpse of God." *New Oxford Review* 60, no. 6 (July-Aug. 1993): 6-13.

———. "The Gulf Between East and West." *New Oxford Review* 61, no. 4 (May 1994): 7-16.

———. "Pilgrimage to the Christian East." *New Oxford Review* 61, no. 3 (April 1994): 11-17.

O'Day, Gail R. "Toward a Biblical Theology of Preaching." *Listening to the Word: Studies in Honor of Fred B. Craddock,* pp. 17-32. Edited by Gail R. O'Day and Thomas G. Long. Nashville: Abingdon, 1993.

Otto, Rudolf. *The Idea of the Holy.* Translated by John W. Harvey. London: Oxford University Press, 1923.

Pelikan, Jaroslav. *The Vindication of Tradition.* New Haven: Yale University Press, 1984.

Peters, Ted. "Worship Wars." *dialog* 33, no. 3 (Summer 1994): 166-73.

Pittelko, Roger D. "Worship and the Community of Faith." *Lutheran Worship: History and Practice,* pp. 44-57. Edited by Fred L. Precht. St. Louis: Concordia, 1993.

Postman, Neil. *Amusing Ourselves to Death: Public Discourse in the Age of Show Business.* New York: Viking Penguin, 1985.

———. *Technopoly: The Surrender of Culture to Technology.* New York: Alfred A. Knopf, 1992.

Rienstra, Marchiene Vroon. *Swallow's Nest: A Feminine Reading of the Psalms.* Grand Rapids: William B. Eerdmans, 1992.

Robinson, Haddon W. *Biblical Preaching: The Development and Delivery of Expository Messages.* Grand Rapids: Baker Book House, 1980.

Roof, Wade Clark. *A Generation of Seekers: The Spiritual Journeys of the Baby Boom Generation.* San Francisco: HarperCollins, 1993.

Sanneh, Lamin. *Translating the Message: The Missionary Impact on Culture.* American Society of Missiology Series, no. 13. Maryknoll, NY: Orbis Books, 1989.

Sass, Louis A. *Madness and Modernism: Insanity in the Light of Modern Art, Literature, and Thought.* New York: Basic Books, 1992.

Sayers, Dorothy L. *The Whimsical Christian.* Grand Rapids: William B. Eerdmans, 1969.

Schalk, Carl. "Music and the Liturgy: The Lutheran Tradition." *Lutheran Worship: History and Practice,* pp. 243-61. Edited by Fred L. Precht. St. Louis: Concordia, 1993.

Schmidt, Wayne E. "The Place of Worship." *Lutheran Worship: History and Practice,* pp. 175-218. Edited by Fred L. Precht. St. Louis: Concordia, 1993.

Schultze, Quentin J., et al. *Dancing in the Dark: Youth, Popular Culture, and the Electronic Media.* Grand Rapids: William B. Eerdmans, 1991.

Sennett, Richard. *The Fall of Public Man: On the Social Psychology of Capitalism.* New York: Random House, 1978.

Sheler, Jeffrey L. "Spiritual America." *U.S. News and World Report* 116, no. 13 (4 April 1993): 48-59.

Small, Joseph D., and John P. Burgess. "Evaluating 'Re-Imagining.'" *The Christian Century* 111, no. 11 (6 April 1994): 342-44.

Smith, Christine. *Preaching as Weeping, Confession, and Resistance: Radical Responses to Radical Evil.* Louisville: Westminster/John Knox Press, 1992.

Smith, Jane Stuart, and Betty Carlson. *A Gift of Music: Great Composers and Their Influence.* Westchester, IL: Cornerstone Books, 1979.

Stackhouse, John G., Jr. "God as Lord and Lover." *The Christian Century* 109, no. 33 (11 Nov. 1992): 1020-21.

Stott, John R. W. *Between Two Worlds: The Art of Preaching in the Twentieth Century.* Grand Rapids: William B. Eerdmans, 1982.

Tapia, Andrés. "Reaching the First Post-Christian Generation." *Christianity Today* 38, no. 10 (12 Sept. 1994): 18-23.

Taylor, Barbara Brown. "Preaching the Body." *Listening to the Word: Studies in Honor of Fred B. Craddock,* pp. 207-21. Edited by Gail R. O'Day and Thomas G. Long. Nashville: Abingdon, 1993.

Tucker, Gene M. "Reading and Preaching the Old Testament." *Listening to the Word: Studies in Honor of Fred B. Craddock,* pp. 33-51. Edited by Gail R. O'Day and Thomas G. Long. Nashville: Abingdon, 1993.

Turner, James. *Without God, Without Creed: The Origins of Unbelief in America.* Baltimore: Johns Hopkins University Press, 1985.

Turner, Philip. "To Students of Divinity: A Convocation Address." *First Things* 26 (Oct. 1992): 25-27.

Ugolnik, Anthony. "Living at the Borders: Eastern Orthodoxy and World Disorder." *First Things* 34 (June/July 1993): 15-23.

Van Harn, Roger E. *Pew Rights.* Grand Rapids: William B. Eerdmans, 1992.

Vitz, Paul C. *Psychology as Religion: The Cult of Self-Worship,* 2nd ed. Grand Rapids: William B. Eerdmans, 1994.

Webber, Robert. "The Divine Action in Worship." *Worship Leader* 1, no. 3 (June/July 1992): 7, 49.

Webster, Douglas D. *Selling Jesus: What's Wrong with Marketing the Church.* Downers Grove, IL: InterVarsity Press, 1992.

Wells, David F. *God in the Wasteland: The Reality of Truth in a World of Fading Dreams.* Grand Rapids: William B. Eerdmans, 1994.

———. *No Place for Truth; or, Whatever Happened to Evangelical Theology?* Grand Rapids: William B. Eerdmans, 1993.

Westerhoff, John H., III, and John D. Eusden. *The Spiritual Life: Learning East and West.* New York: Seabury Press, 1982.

Westermeyer, Paul. "Professional Concerns Forum: Chant, Bach, and Popular Culture." *The American Organist* 27, no. 11 (Nov. 1993): 34-39.

———. "Three Books of Worship: An Ecumenical Convergence," *The Christian Century* 110, no. 30 (27 Oct. 1993): 1055-57.

White, James F. *Introduction to Christian Worship,* rev. ed. Nashville: Abingdon, 1990.

Willimon, William H. "Impressions and Imprints." *The Christian Century* 110, 33 (17-24 Nov. 1993): 1149.

Woodward, Kenneth L. "Dead End for the Mainline?" *Newsweek,* 9 Aug. 1993, pp. 46-48.

Wuthnow, Robert. "Church Realities and Christian Identity in the 21st Century." *The Christian Century* 110, 16 (12 May 1993): 520-23.

Yankelovich, Daniel. *New Rules: Searching for Self-Fulfillment in a World Turned Upside Down.* New York: Random House, 1981.